Radio in Context

Radio in Context

Second Edition

Guy Starkey

First edition 2004
Second edition 2014

Published by
PALGRAVE MACMILLAN
Houndmills, Basingstoke, Hampshire RG21 6XS and
175 Fifth Avenue, New York, N.Y. 10010
Companies and representatives throughout the world

PALGRAVE MACMILLAN is the global academic imprint of the Palgrave Macmillan division of St. Martin's Press, LLC and of Palgrave Macmillan Ltd. Macmillan® is a registered trademark in the United States, United Kingdom and other countries. Palgrave is a registered trademark in the European Union and other countries.

ISBN 978–1–137–30225–0 paperback
ISBN 978–1–137–30223–6 hardback

This book is printed on paper suitable for recycling and made from fully managed and sustained forest sources.

A catalogue record for this book is available from the British Library.

To Claire, Kay and Tom, and in memory of Philip

Contents

List of figures   *x*
Preface   *xii*
Acknowledgements   *xiii*
How to use this book   *xv*

Chapter 1   **Introduction to radio**   *1*
Radio in context: milestones and motives   *1*
Institutional contexts   *4*
Capturing audio   *6*
Location work   *11*
Real-time manipulation   *14*
Recording techniques   *19*
Editing audio   *22*
Analysing radio: applying media theory to radio contexts   *25*

Chapter 2   **Speech packages**   *33*
Speech packages in context   *33*
Making packages   *36*
Finding an angle   *38*
Interviewing for packages   *40*
Planning interviews   *42*
Scriptwriting for packages   *47*
Production and post-production   *49*
Analysing packages   *51*

Chapter 3   **Live sequences and phone-ins**   *58*
Programme contexts   *58*
Producing sequences   *59*
Planning a sequence programme   *60*
Allocating roles   *62*
Presentation style   *64*
Sequence content   *66*
Presentation techniques   *69*
Links   *71*

Competitions 72
Live interviews 73
'Driving' the desk 75
Analysing sequences 78
Phone-ins 83
Analysing phone-ins 87

Chapter 4   **Music scheduling, formats and branding** 89
Programming principles 89
Scheduling software 93
Using the software 96
Automation 99
Copyright 102
Branding 103
Formats 105
Communicating the brand 109
Producing idents 111
Analysing idents 113
Measuring audiences 114

Chapter 5   **Magazine programmes** 119
Magazines in context 119
Producing magazine programmes 121
Theme tunes, menus and signposting 123
Planning the content 124
Production roles 126
Programme items 127
Linking material 129
Live interviews 131
Outside broadcasts 134
Analysing magazine programmes 136

Chapter 6   **Advertisements and trails** 143
Advertisements in context 143
Planning a campaign 146
Scripting advertisements 149
Legal and regulatory constraints 153
Producing advertisements 154
Using music and effects 156
Transmission 158
Making trails 159
Analysing advertisements and trails 161

Chapter 7   **Light entertainment**   *165*
Light entertainment in context   *165*
Producing light entertainment   *168*
Planning a quiz or a panel game   *170*
Practical issues   *172*
Analysing light entertainment   *175*

Chapter 8   **Drama**   *178*
Radio drama in context   *178*
Developing a scenario   *183*
Writing drama scripts   *187*
Time and place   *189*
Characterization   *190*
Developing a narrative   *191*
Interpreting a drama script   *196*
Production techniques   *197*
Creative approaches   *200*
Analysing radio drama   *201*

Chapter 9   **Documentaries**   *206*
Documentaries in context   *206*
Documentary forms   *207*
Structure and style   *209*
Using music   *215*
Other sounds   *218*
Ethical issues   *218*
Libel   *220*
Reporting restrictions   *222*
Other legal issues   *224*
Analysing documentaries   *226*

Appendix: Finding work in radio   *231*

Glossary   *233*
Bibliography and Further Reading   *250*
Index   *261*

Figures

1.1 A range of microphones with different pick-up patterns 8
1.2 The audio characteristics of different microphone types 9
1.3 Indoor and outdoor acoustics 12
1.4 The main mixer controls, their functions and purposes 18
1.5 Portable recording devices with integrated microphones 20
1.6 Different routes for transferring audio from portable recording equipment to separate editing environments 23
2.1 Location work 37
2.2 Idea bubbles used for mind mapping 38
2.3 Correct and incorrect positions for location interviews 45
2.4 An example of a cue sheet for a package insert in a magazine programme 51
3.1 The clock for the first hour of *Steve Wright in the Afternoon* on BBC Radio Two 61
3.2 Neil Fox 'on air' on Capital, before moving to Magic 105.4 70
3.3 The layout of a typical self-operated radio studio 76
3.4 Screenshot of the PhoneBOX telephone handling software 86
4.1 A music policy screen and part of a log in Selector XV 95
4.2 An example of the information needed in copyright declarations when using music 102
4.3 Comparison of a range of stations, according to demographic criteria of age and class 104
4.4 Logos from EMAP's Big City stations and GWR's The Mix stations in 2003 106
4.5 Audience research data 117
5.1 *Woman's Hour* presenter Jenni Murray interviewing politician, broadcaster and novelist Edwina Currie 132
6.1 UK top ten national advertisers in the year 2011 149
6.2 Sample pricing information for a radio advert made by a production house for a single local station 152
6.3 A screenshot of a simple advertisement in post-production on SADiE 157
7.1 *Just a Minute* being recorded on location at the Playhouse Theatre in London 170
8.1 *Radio Times* listings for a sitcom, a soap and a single play, all broadcast on the same day in 2003 on BBC Radio Four 182
8.2 Budget for a typical 45-minute *Afternoon Play* on BBC Radio Four 186
8.3 A short drama script, illustrating the main conventions of layout 194

8.4   A studio designed for drama recording, with separate control
room and performance areas   *198*

8.5   Using a crossed pair of unidirectional microphones to create a
stereo effect   *199*

9.1   Budget for a typical 28-minute feature documentary on BBC
Radio Four   *208*

9.2   Diagrams showing the use of music under speech at the
beginning and end of a section   *217*

9.3   Post-production work on a documentary, using Adobe
Audition   *225*

# Preface

This book is largely a result of years spent working in the radio industry, and of teaching and designing curricula based on that experience. During that time, radio has changed dramatically – in the technology it uses and in the way the industry is structured. Most of that change has been positive, enhancing the possibilities for producers and programmers, and extending the range of employment opportunities for new recruits. For listeners in most parts of the world, this has meant greater choice and the chance to be more discerning than ever.

As production methods have become less mechanical and more computer-based, many of the core concepts and approaches used to make radio have remained constant. Central to this are the relationships between words and music, between voices and sounds, between fact and fiction – and between the radio practitioner and the listener.

The intention of this book is to engage with both professional practice and a range of theoretical perspectives appropriate to academic study of the medium. In most areas of media studies, the interface between practice and theory is problematic. Practitioners do not often consciously engage with the theory developed by academics, and some academics are uncomfortable with some of the vocational aspects of practice. In fact, neither practice nor theory can exist in isolation, and each one can be enriched by the other.

It was with great pleasure that I accepted the challenge of updating the book, some eight years after its first publication. One of the biggest changes in the radio world has been the development of social media, which most stations now use extensively. This is not, though, a guide to using either Facebook or Twitter, which I have left for others to write.

Neither is this a book about mobile phone apps or digital transmission technology, but the development of new ways of accessing radio content is, I believe, a sign of a healthy medium that is here to stay.

I would, however, like to add my thanks to the many colleagues and friends in industry and in academia who have contributed thoughtful and supportive feedback on how useful they found the first edition and how it could be improved.

GUY STARKEY

Acknowledgements

The author wishes to acknowledge, with thanks, the support of the Centre for Research in Media and Cultural Studies, University of Sunderland, England. Thanks, too, to all those who have contributed illustrations or data for inclusion in the text, or helped with advice and feedback during the preparation of the book.

The author and the publishers are particularly grateful to the following individuals and organizations for permission to reproduce copyright material:

Beyer-Dynamic, pages 8, 9, 199
Katy McDonald, page 37
Capital Radio, page 70
Clyde Broadcast, page 76
Broadcast Bionics, page 86
RCS, page 95
RAB and RAJAR/IPSOS-RSL, page 104
EMAP and GWR, page 106
RAJAR/IPSOS-RSL, page 117
BBC, pages 130, 132, 170, 182
Jenni Murray and Edwina Currie, page 132
Nielsen Media Research, page 149
Studio Audio & Video, page 157
Paul Merton, Sir Clement Freud, Claire Bartlett, Nicholas Parsons, Sheila Hancock and Graham Norton, page 170
Radio Times, page 182
Beverly Eckert, The Kitchen Sisters (Nikki Silva and Davia Nelson) and Ben Shapiro, pages 213–14*
Sherina Sobers, page 225
Adobe Systems, page 225

*Sean Rooney, who is described as the 'male caller' on page 213, was Beverly Eckert's husband. He worked in risk management for Aon Corporation in Tower Two, the World Trade Center, New York until 11 September 2001. Most of the material in the BBC's *The Twin Towers: A*

Memorial in Sound was excerpted from NPR's Peabody Award winning documentary series, *Sonic Memorial Project*.

Every effort has been made to trace the copyright holders of material quoted in the text, but if any have inadvertently been missed the author and publishers will be glad to make full acknowledgement in subsequent editions of this book.

How to use this book

The book is divided by different radio genres because most practitioners – and students – work within a single genre at a time. The exception is the first chapter, which is an introduction to the most common
generic skills and concepts, to which the other chapters often refer.
The subsequent chapters may be read in any order, depending on the
reader's programme of study, although it would be unwise to tackle
documentary production, for example, before working on a much
shorter speech package. The glossary at the end of the book provides
another common reference point, and words defined in the glossary
are printed in bold the first time they appear in any chapter. The
appendix lists a number of successful strategies for gaining first-time
employment in radio.

Within each chapter, different sections cover professional practice
and theoretical perspectives on that practice, and there are references
to suggestions for further reading. Each genre is set within wider
historical and institutional contexts. To get the most out of the book,
readers should also listen to the radio extensively and critically. Over
the course of each chapter, practical exercises that are suitable for
inclusion into a programme of learning develop practical and critical
skills. Activities range from finding and listening to broadcast examples, to planning, producing and evaluating original work. When writing evaluations, readers will find ideas and guidance at the end of each
chapter, as examples from the genre are considered according to a
range of theoretical perspectives. Here, media theory is applied to
different radio contexts.

Because references to suggested listening can quickly become dated,
as can web links, these will be updated regularly at the author's web
site, at www.guystarkey.com/palgrave.

Introduction to Radio

Radio in context: milestones and motives

Listeners tuning in to radio stations hear sounds. Occasionally they may also perceive silence. It is the interplay of sounds and silence – most commonly in music and speech – that constitutes the radio broadcasts they hear today. Since a number of early pioneers, including Guglielmo Marconi, first demonstrated 'wireless' transmission and reception at the beginning of the last century (Crisell, 1997, 10–14), producers and audiences have played different, but often complementary, roles in making meanings out of radio broadcasts. This book examines both sides of a usually symbiotic relationship.

Making radio involves the production and arrangement of different sounds in an order that satisfies at least one **purpose**. Possible purposes include to inform, to entertain and to educate – three objectives that were enshrined in the British Broadcasting Corporation's Charter, under which it was incorporated on 1 January 1927. The BBC's first Director-General, John (later Lord) Reith, adopted a rather puritanical interpretation of the Corporation's mission, while in the 1930s commercial stations such as Radio Normandy and Radio Luxembourg broadcast to large audiences in the United Kingdom who preferred to tune in to them for their diet of more entertaining programming (see Chapter 7). Radio developed along very different lines in the United States, where it was seen more as a medium for commercial exploitation, rather than the public service **model** that tended to be adopted in Europe. David Sarnoff, later head of the Radio Corporation of America, is widely credited with having the idea of radio services as discrete channels of broadcasting output (Crisell, 1997, 12), and in

2011 15,587 different stations were broadcasting to a population there of more than 300 million.

In the United Kingdom, the BBC was forced to introduce its first all-day pop music network, Radio One, as late as 30 September 1967, because pirate broadcasters – such as Radio Caroline – based on ships and abandoned military forts just outside British territorial waters had demonstrated the public's appetite for the music that had inspired the rock and roll generation and kept the sixties swinging (Hill, 1996, 206–7). Licensed, landbased commercial stations, broadcasting from the mainland, were not allowed to challenge the BBC's domestic monopoly of radio until 8 October 1973, when the first **Independent Local Radio (ILR)** station, LBC, began broadcasting news and talk to London (Carter, 1998, 3). By contrast, the United States immediately favoured the commercial model, but kept stations local and regional, rather than national.

Commercial radio is used in order to persuade, to alter behaviour and to sell the products and services of advertisers (see Chapter 6), and when it is owned by private companies or individuals and run for profit, the main purpose is to make money for them. Some radio stations are run to support communities, distinguished either by geographic or socio-economic criteria, or to promote particular religious beliefs, and although the Community Radio Association began campaigning in 1983 for licensed 'access' radio, successive British governments resisted such calls until beginning a small scale experiment in 2002. However, the first hospital radio station in the United Kingdom was set up by volunteers in York in 1926, and campus radio began there too, in 1967, although initially these stations were not allowed to broadcast to the wider communities outside their premises. Special event licences, and from 1991, Restricted Service Licences ('RSLs') have enabled the running of low power, temporary stations. For example, some schools, colleges and universities have done this for educational purposes, providing training for their students, while also entertaining and informing their audiences (Gordon, 2001). Landbased pirates, some broadcasting from their own bedrooms in residential tower blocks, are often criticized for unlicensed use of the **frequency spectrum** to satisfy their own 'selfish' desire to get 'on air' by any means – but the development of terrestrial **digital platforms** for radio, such as **Digital Audio Broadcasting (DAB)** and **Digital Radio Mondiale (DRM)**, as well as satellite broadcasting and the Internet, have greatly increased the opportunities for individuals, groups and commercial interests to reach audiences both near and far.

The list of purposes above is not exhaustive, and different elements of radio programming may fulfil more than one purpose at a time. Whatever the purpose, the motive behind it may be political, commercial, altruistic or simply the need to earn a living. During the Second World War, William Joyce (known as 'Lord Haw Haw') broadcast Nazi propaganda to Britain in order to demoralize the British. His attempts at persuasion were largely unsuccessful, and he was later hanged for treason. Most politicians understand the power of radio to persuade, and in 1970 Radio Northsea International, another offshore pirate station, tried to affect the outcome of the British general election by broadcasting Conservative Party propaganda. Some commentators felt they helped the party win (Street, 2002, 112). In France, in 1980, Radio K was set up in Marseilles to influence the presidential elections in favour of the Parti Socialiste (but nicknamed 'Radio Caca' by critics who found its approach overly didactic). Most countries operate short-wave stations broadcasting around the world, which they use to put across their own perspective on world events and their own domestic situations. The editorial stance on an international crisis usually differs between the Voice of America, Radio Beijing and Radio Moscow. There are many other examples to be found, including the BBC World Service (see Chapter 9). In some dictatorships, the government tightly controls broadcasting so that alternative views don't get airtime – but as in many democracies, radio stations in the United Kingdom are obliged by the way they are regulated to be fair and impartial in the way they cover political issues (see Chapter 9).

A more widely acceptable way of persuading listeners to alter their behaviour is through **public service announcements**, or **PSAs** (see Chapter 6). Selling them products or services through radio advertising generates income for commercial radio stations from the advertisers, and in effect creates jobs in the radio station and often profits for owners or shareholders. Products and services often get talked about 'on air' without any payment being made – in interviews, **packages** and news items for example – and many individuals and organizations are keen to generate such 'free' publicity through public relations and marketing activities. Even programmes that seem intended merely to entertain can have other purposes – a music sequence might include brief speech items about healthy lifestyles or stopping smoking (Chapter 3). The BBC's long-running soap opera *The Archers* was introduced in 1951 in order to educate the farming community about issues and developments in agriculture. Most listeners who tune in today, do so for its entertainment value (Chapter 8).

Exercise 1.1

Continue the table below, filling in the two blank spaces and adding more examples of radio production activities, their purposes and the motives behind the purposes. Discuss your answers in class – for example, can the play described below really entertain?

Production activity	Purpose	Motive
▸ writing the script for a radio advert	▸ to persuade ▸ to inform ▸ to create interest	▸ selling a product or service ▸ earning money ▸ creating employment
▸ making a party political broadcast	▸	▸ getting more votes in an election
▸ recording a radio play about HIV	▸ to inform ▸ to change attitudes ▸ to entertain	▸

Institutional contexts

Ownership of a radio station allows considerable control of what it broadcasts. The lone landbased pirate is answerable to nobody – unless criminal gangs get involved – and may only be concerned that the premises may be raided, the equipment seized and criminal charges brought by the authorities. Most other radio stations are owned and controlled by someone other than the 'on air' talent. This may be a board of directors or simply a single individual who has invested the considerable sums of money required to equip proper studios, pay staff and meet the many other financial implications of running a professional radio station. Large groups of licensed commercial radio stations can achieve economies of scale, by sharing expertise and concentrating particular activities in skill centres, such as for production, music scheduling and personnel functions. For example, the largest in the UK, Global Radio, now produces programmes in London for broadcast on local and regional stations it owns all over the country (Starkey, 2011, 156–9). Where stations are owned by other media – such as newspapers or television – they can also find economies in the cost of news coverage, for example, or even exploit their increased control of the advertising market to push up the cost to advertisers of buying airtime and space.

Ownership may affect the editorial stance of a radio station, and newspaper proprietors are notorious for dictating what opinions should be expressed in their own titles. Different methods of funding public service radio, including taxation and subscription, may shield it from commercial and proprietory influence. In the United Kingdom the BBC's domestic radio services have been funded by a broadcast receiving licence fee since 1922. Although the Government decides how much this will cost the public – and therefore, how much the BBC will receive – there is wide agreement that the arrangement has preserved the Corporation's independence for much of its history (Crisell, 1994, 21, 98). The Charter imposes obligations on the Corporation, which is overseen by the BBC Trust, the members of which are chosen to broadly reflect a range of political opinion (see Chapter 9). In turn, its staff must work to its *Editorial Guidelines* (BBC, 2013), which set standards of **taste and decency** and impose rules about such issues as balance and **impartiality** (Chapter 9). All other radio broadcasters are licensed by a **regulator** – initially the Independent Broadcasting Authority (1972–91), then the Radio Authority (1991–2003), and now Ofcom, whose other roles are to maintain standards (see Chapter 9) and respond to complaints. The increasingly lighter touch of the regulators (Carter, 1998, 9), and the relaxation by the Communications Act 2003 of initially very stringent rules on ownership have created an often very lucrative environment which has proved attractive to overseas interests, such as the American group Clear Channel. Controversial mergers of large companies, which threaten to restrict choice, may attract the attention of the Competition Commission, but the localness and independence of the first wave of ILR has disappeared from all but a handful of stations, even if listeners do have a lot more choice than in 1973 (Starkey, 2011, 156–9).

Rapid growth in the radio industries has increased job opportunities in most territories. Growth and technological change both affect employment patterns, too, although short- and medium-term **freelance contracts** have long been characteristic of the commercial sector, where managers want to be able to reduce costs if advertising incomes decline. Individual presenters may become expendable if their audience **ratings** fall (Chapter 4), although success can bring handsome financial rewards. The greatest job security may lie in permanent **staff contracts**, although even large and relatively stable organizations such as the BBC can decide to make redundancies. Flexibility and **multi-skilling** are key to finding work and remaining in employment, in what can be a very exciting and satisfying environment.

Capturing audio

For sound to occupy a place in a radio broadcast, it must first be captured and then manipulated in such a way as to make it broadcastable, and to suit the purposes of the producer. Radio stations often use recordings or live **audio** that someone else has produced for them – for example, a hit song or a news report from an agency or news service. They also frequently use sounds and speech which are naturally occurring – traffic noise or bird song for instance – or which they generate themselves, such as commentaries, interviews and scripted film reviews. The initial act of capturing a sound, though, has to be done effectively, in such a way that the sound is broadcastable in terms of its technical quality and that it has an impact on the listener which is close to what is intended. (Chapter 8 explains why two coconut halves banged together are probably not intended to be interpreted literally as the banging of coconut halves.)

Capturing original sound usually involves the use of at least one **microphone**. One will suffice for an interview, the recording of a simple sound effect for use later or for a single presenter to introduce songs in a music sequence. Careful and creative use of a single microphone can capture all the audio for more elaborate productions, too. A panel debate, such as the BBC's *Any Questions* (Radio Four) could use as many as seven microphones, and a live music recording at its Maida Vale studios could use a dozen or more, with each instrument and vocalist having a dedicated **mic**, and a drum kit using several. A simple stereo recording would normally use two mics – one for the left **channel** and one for the right – although single stereo mics are sometimes used by reporters, and relatively recent advances in technology now enable even the capture of surround sound for film and television by a single microphone.

Two crucial issues in microphone use for any purpose are which one to use, and how to use it. Knowing a range of different solutions to those questions, depending on the circumstances, is essential – although a **mic** obviously needs to be working and to have a patent connection either to a recording device or through a **mixer** to a live transmission system. That means the mic needs to be connected by a lead which has no breaks in it, and preferably has robust industry-standard XLR plugs at each end, which if undamaged will provide an uninterrupted signal from the mic to the next stage in the process, even if the mic and the lead move around a bit during use. This point is so important that you should always take care of microphone leads and connections, resisting the temptation to imitate old recordings of certain performers on television, swinging the mic around by the lead for visual effect. Today, mics and recorders are often integrated units.

Exercise 1.2

Continue the table below, filling in the blanks and adding further scenarios, showing how many microphones would be needed for a range of different tasks in audio capture. Discuss your findings in class.

Task	Number of microphones	Microphone positions
Recording a panel game.	8	One each for: presenter, four contestants, scorer; two effects mics for audience reactions, left and right.
Recording an interview in the street.	1	Connected to a portable recorder, and hand-held by reporter.
Interviewing two people in the studio.	3	One each for: presenter, two interviewees.
Recording a gig performed by a local band in a small hall.		
Presenting a sports phone-in.		

Choosing the correct mic for the task depends on the nature of the task, and sometimes the available budget. Static microphones for studio use are available which have such specialized technical characteristics that they cost in excess of £1,000. Browsing through suppliers' catalogues can provide a useful insight into the range of microphones on offer: the different uses they are best suited to, and their technical characteristics. The frequency response indicates the range of audible frequencies over which they can turn sound waves into electronic signals, and the signal-to-noise ratio shows how much unwanted background hiss is generated by the microphone's circuitry alongside the sound you are actually seeking to capture.

The **microphone type** relates directly to the pick-up pattern of the mic – that is, how sensitive it is to sound, in each direction around it. Figure 1.1 shows six different microphone types, and Figure 1.2 shows how different microphone types are suited to different tasks.

On location it is most usual to hold a single mic by hand, the reporter or presenter talking into it, and in an interview moving it in

Figure 1.1

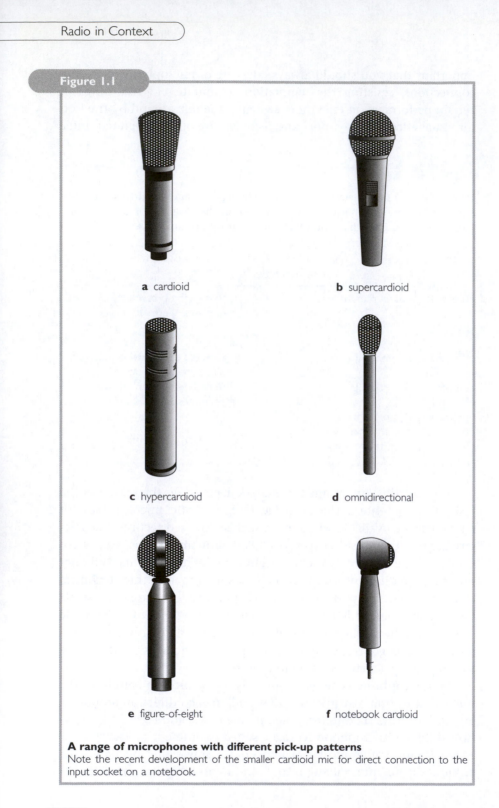

a cardioid

b supercardioid

c hypercardioid

d omnidirectional

e figure-of-eight

f notebook cardioid

A range of microphones with different pick-up patterns
Note the recent development of the smaller cardioid mic for direct connection to the input socket on a notebook.

Figure 1.2

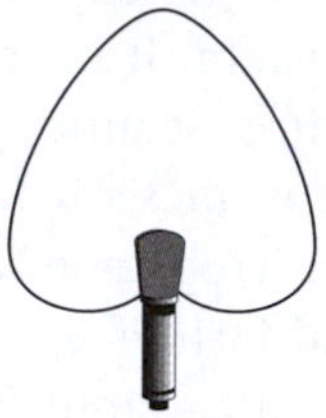

Cardioid microphones have an inverted 'heart-shaped' pick-up pattern, making them *uni*directional. They are particularly useful for reducing ambient sound from other directions, when doing location work, or for ensuring separation between a number of different mics being used simultaneously. (Supercardioid mics are more sensitive with a narrower heart shape and so more directional.)

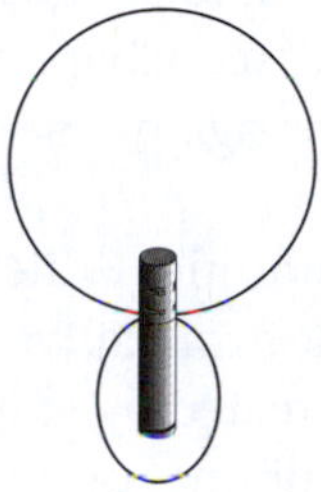

Hyper-cardioid microphones are suitable for location work, including interviewing, where some directionality is desirable. Can be particularly suited to close-mic work in studio, by presenters, actors and singers. (Mics with a 'lobe' pattern are highly directional and used to pick up patterns from some distance away. They include for example, the rifle mics used in television production.)

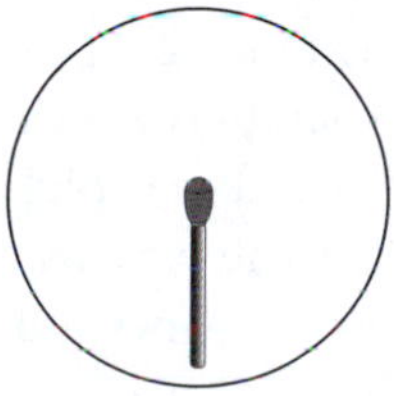

Omnidirectional microphones are equally sensitive to sound coming from all directions. They are suitable for location work, including interviewing, where ambient sound is not too distracting. Talkback systems use omnidirectional mics, but they are usually unsuitable in multi-microphone environments or in the presence of a public address system (PA).

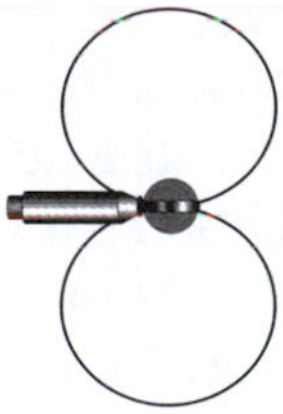

Figure-of-eight microphones can be particularly useful for multiple use, with actors standing on both sides. Often used in music recording studios with, for example, complex string instruments.

The audio characteristics of different microphone types make them suitable for different tasks and circumstances.

front of the interviewee to capture the answers. In radio studios mics are usually fixed, often on anglepoise arms that offer flexibility over positioning, or suspended from the ceiling. Stands or booms, which are placed either on the floor or on a table, for example for a **'round table'** debate, are more likely to pick up unwanted noise from people's shoes, knees or elbows if they fidget and knock the table or kick the stand.

Microphones with the characteristics shown in Figure 1.2 are available in different sizes and styles. Depending on the situation, on location the producer might decide to attach a tie-clip mic to an interviewer and one to the interviewee – but, again, it is important to avoid knocking the microphones or fidgeting around. Television makes much greater use of boom mics or rifle mics on location, in circumstances where the producer wants the microphone to be out of vision, and these are designed to be positioned farther away from the source of the audio. 'Radio' mics are clipped onto clothing or hand held and do not use wires to send their audio. They are used in radio for roadshows and **outside broadcasts** (OBs) (see Chapter 5), where the presenter needs to move about easily, but again, they are much more common in television.

As well as directionality, position also determines which sounds a microphone will pick up and reproduce electronically. Chapter 8 explains how certain dramatic effects may be created by varying microphone position, but for speech most microphone use requires the sensitive end with the grille to be approximately 10 to 15 cm (4 to 6 in) away from the mouth of the person who is talking. Speech – especially English – makes frequent use of what phoneticists term plosives, such as the 'p' sound in the tongue twister 'Peter Piper picked a peck of pickled pepper'. This sound is created in just the way the phonetic term suggests, by sending a (small) explosion of air forward from the mouth. If this rush of air hits the sensitive end of a microphone, it causes an internal disturbance, which the mic interprets electronically as a sudden booming noise called **popping**. Because it corrupts the reproduction of the speech – often very loudly, depending on the extent of the popping – this is to be avoided if the audio is to be broadcastable. A **windshield** may be fitted over the grille of some microphone types to reduce this effect (so called because outdoors any strong winds can cause a similar disturbance), but the surest way to avoid popping is to position the mic a little to the side of the mouth. It should still point towards the mouth, because that is the source of the desired sound, but if it is out of the way of the plosives, the interviewer simply won't pop the mic – and neither will the interviewees if this technique is used when capturing their answers.

Handling noise – also called **mic rattle** – can be produced in handheld microphones if the user is careless and doesn't take steps to prevent it. Depending on how well the pick-up inside the mic is insulated from the outer casing, even small movements of the user's hand while it is live can be turned into distracting clunks and clicks which will detract from the audio. If the lead is allowed to move freely at its connection with the microphone – especially if its position is changed during use – mic rattle is very likely. The best way to eliminate it is to loop the lead back under the lower side of the mic and hold it firmly between two fingers of the same hand, effectively providing a buffer between the rest of the lead and the microphone casing (see page 37).

Location work

On location, choosing where to work can be as important as your choice of mic and how you handle it. The quality of your audio will depend on both **acoustics** and the presence or absence of **ambient sound**. The wrong acoustic on your audio can make it unsuited to your purpose or even unbroadcastable. In Chapter 8, you can explore the creative use of different acoustics in radio drama, setting a play in a cave or a cathedral without even going there, but for most purposes a relatively neutral acoustic is the most desirable. In essence, acoustics relate to the nature and amount of reflected sound in a particular location. While some sound goes directly from the source to the microphone, additional, reflected sound produced by the same source may hit hard surfaces – such as walls, floors, ceilings, brick, rock and stone – and return to be picked up again by the microphone just moments later.

For example, a classroom without carpets or soft furnishings, but with a number of people in it, their bags and perhaps some curtains, has enough hard, reflective surfaces for a noticeable amount of sound to be reflected back to the microphone, very shortly after it is first created. In most public buildings, the stairways or toilets provide an even more reflective environment and the **reverb** or echo it creates will be more noticeable than that in the classroom. Because cathedrals and large caves are also highly reflective environments, they also produce echoes – but the greater distances the sound has to travel in them in order to meet a hard surface and then return in the direction of the mic makes the delay on the reverb greater, and the echo sounds more obvious. Of course, the sound doesn't travel in one simple back and forth movement, it may be bounced around many times before being picked up by the microphone again. That's why different locations, with their differing characteristics, sound acoustically different. Outdoors, unless you are standing next to a particularly reflective surface, such as a wall, for the microphone to pick up any reverb would be very unlikely: sound simply travels away from the original source and does not return.

Figure 1.3

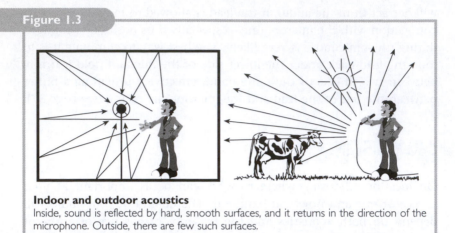

Indoor and outdoor acoustics
Inside, sound is reflected by hard, smooth surfaces, and it returns in the direction of the microphone. Outside, there are few such surfaces.

Listening for any length of time to voices with a large amount of reverb can be more tiring to the ear than listening to speech without it. The sound is not being reproduced faithfully, as it was originally spoken. Cutting without good reason from sound recorded in one type of acoustic to another can also seem odd. For this reason, radio studios are usually acoustically treated to reduce reverb to a minimum, as well as to prevent unwanted ambient sound coming in from outside. On location, unless there is a specific reason for wanting a reflective acoustic on your audio, it is best to choose somewhere with soft furnishings, carpets, curtains and even portable screening – in fact anything that will soak up sound waves rather than reflect them back around the room.

Ambient sound is, as suggested above, sound that is already present in a given location, normally without your having to create it yourself. If carrying out a location interview, having chosen to record in a room with a fairly non-reflective acoustic, you then sit next to a noisy fan or air-conditioning unit, it is unlikely that your recording will be broad-castable when you play it back. The noise added by the machinery and picked up by the microphone will be an unwanted distraction from what is being said – and it may even be loud enough to drown out your interview altogether. If, however, your interview is actually about air-conditioning systems, and if it is not too loud compared to the voices, the sound could enhance the recording.

Choosing a location, either indoors or outdoors, for audio capture involves paying close attention to the ambient sounds being produced there or which are likely to be produced. A good deal of common sense and editorial judgement on your part is needed to ensure that your item is a success. A telephone may suddenly ring, interrupting the flow of an interview – potentially a small disaster if live 'on air'. A fast train may suddenly hurtle past a railway platform, or a pneumatic drill may suddenly start up on a building site. By contrast, standing next to a river or in a field of lowing cattle could add considerably to an item about life in the countryside.

Ambient sound must be actively managed. If present, it can provide a useful background or, like the noisy fan, it could be too loud compared to the preferred sound – for example, the interview – which should be very definitely in the foreground. Depending on the proximity of the mic to the source, you can vary the ratio of foreground to background, because the sensitivity of the mic to a particular sound decreases the farther away it is from its origin. For example, it should be possible to speak loudly into a mic held very close up to the mouth in a noisy environment such as an airport or a nightclub and achieve a recording that has an intelligible (yet forced) voice in the foreground and a lively and very noticeable background behind it. This effect depends on either using an **automatic level control** (**ALC**) or manually setting the **level** so the voice peaks at the correct point on the scale (see below).

Generally, though, you will have greater control over a recorded piece if you minimize the amount of ambient sound when recording the speech and then record some extra **wild track** of just the **atmosphere** on its own, which can be mixed in later. This can be done at your leisure when you can more easily control the foreground to background ratio and adjust the **mix** if it doesn't sound correct on playback (see the section on mixing). Some types of ambient sound, if present on a recording, will make **editing** the speech very difficult without it being noticeable. For example, a ticking clock in the background, if edited, will probably lose its regular 'tick tock' rhythm in the editing **process** and sound very odd indeed. Similarly, music in the background will lose its beat if the speech in the foreground is edited, and any listeners who know the tune or the words will notice the edits very markedly, even if they don't understand immediately what has happened in the production process. Avoid music and anything with a regular beat or sequence when making a recording, if you are likely to want to edit it later.

Your experiments with microphone position may suggest a useful way of eliminating (or at least reducing) unwanted ambient sound which is coming from a particular direction – if you are using a **unidirectional** mic. Turning yourself and your interviewee, if you have one, to face the direction the sound is coming from (by standing side by side) should allow you to keep the mic pointing at you both and away from the unwanted sound.

Exercise 1.3

Select an appropriate mic for a simple hand-held recording with a portable recorder, and experiment with microphone position, talking into the mic continuously. This may also develop your ability to ad lib live 'on air' when there is some unexpected time to fill! Do this where there is plenty of ambient sound – even other people in your class carrying out the same exercise – so you can hear the foreground/background effect changing as you move the mic around. Note down your findings in the grid below. N.B. If your mic is omni-directional, repeat the exercise with a directional one and compare both sets of results.

Microphone position	Is there any popping? Yes/no	Is the ambient sound louder or quieter than your voice?
In front of mouth, 10 cm away, pointing at mouth		
In front of mouth, 15 cm away, pointing at mouth		
A little to the side of mouth, 15 cm away, pointing away from mouth		
A little to the side of mouth, 15 cm away, pointing straight at mouth		

Real-time manipulation

Sound from a microphone – or from any other **sound source**, such as a CD, a **MiniDisc (MD)** recorder/player, or a PC using audio editing or **playout software** – usually needs some form of manipulation before it can be put to air via a radio station's transmitter. Other possible sound **sources** include tape recorders and turntables (gramophones or record players), although these began to disappear from radio stations in the late 1990s (Bantock, 2002). In studios and at more complex outside broadcasts, sound is manipulated through a mixer (or **mixing desk**). The simplest operation consists of balancing the levels from the different sound sources so that there are no unwanted variations in volume from one to the next. For example, if two mics are live, each for a different presenter, usually both presenters should be at the same level, with neither sounding louder to the listener than the other. When a recording is played such as from a CD, again, it shouldn't sound noticeably louder or quieter than the presenters, and if it is a song with an introduction (or **intro**) they may want to talk over the beginning of it (a **talkover**), in which case they will want the song to start at a lower level and then reach full volume just as the vocals begin. In most radio programming, an even, consistent overall volume is preferable, without quieter or louder elements which might make listeners feel they need to turn up or turn down the volume on their own radio receivers.

All of this is fairly simply achievable using the mixer. In studios these can be quite complex, but for location work they can be relatively simple. Mixers all work on the same basic principles, and it is worth spending some time becoming familiar with the particular layout and characteristics of each one as you encounter it. Even the most experienced radio presenters who use the same mixing desk each day have to concentrate very hard to avoid mistakes if they transfer to a different studio with an unfamiliar layout.

To beginners, the array of knobs and buttons can look daunting, but each one will have been carefully placed according to a fairly logical layout. The first principle is that mixers are usually arranged with a vertical **channel** for each sound source. Try to identify similar columns of controls, each one probably having a label identifying the sound source to which it is connected. Often, a channel may have a dual purpose, being switchable between two different sources in order to increase flexibility. These should have twin labels and some way of identifying which way a switch should be set, in order to choose between the two. There are likely to be at least eight separate channels on a radio studio desk, although small four-channel mixers are often used for simple OBs and it is possible to have any reasonable number of them, depending on how much potential for complex operations might be wanted. In music recording studios, 72-channel mixers are common because of the large number of mics and instruments that could be used at any one time. The BBC, for example, uses desks with between 40 and 56 channels at its Maida Vale studios, but very advanced desks can have 96 or more. These look even more daunting to beginners, but they are rarely, if ever, used for any live radio work.

Each channel will have a **gain** control, which is used to control the level of sound passing through it. This works in conjunction with the **fader** below it, which also regulates the amount of sound, but is easier to use than a knob and allows quick fades up and down as well as fine adjustment. Many mixers also have a button to turn each channel on and off altogether, which can catch out the unwary operator who hasn't noticed if it is in the off position. Broadcast mixers often have a set of **eq** controls for **equalization** of each channel. These are usually switched in and out of the circuit by a single button so you can turn the equalization on or off easily. The effect of adjusting the eq is similar to adjusting the tone controls on a radio set, and some hi-fis have more sophisticated graphic equalizers.

In both cases, you are choosing to boost or to reduce the amount of particular frequency ranges within the sound spectrum within which the audio is located. Increasing the higher frequencies improves clarity to a point, but then makes the sound 'tinny', whereas boosting lower frequencies makes the sound more bassy. The key difference between the tone controls at home and the eq on the mixer is that on a radio or a hi-fi you are applying the changes to the whole of the audio, whereas on the mixer, you are just affecting the individual channel on which the eq is being adjusted. Mixers usually divide the audible frequency spectrum into high, middle and low frequencies, or quite frequently into high, upper middle, lower middle and low. Again, the layout and characteristics usually differ between different mixers, depending on how they are configured, but the underlying principles are normally the same.

Every broadcast mixer should have a **pre-fade listening** (PFL) facility on each channel. This allows the operator to listen to a sound source before putting the fader up, and so before putting the source to air. This is important in live work, because the listener doesn't want to hear you testing the microphones and setting the levels while a song is playing or a recorded interview is playing out. It is important to be able to line up a sound source, not just to make sure it is the correct song to be played next, or the right part of an item, and that it is ready to go, but also to make sure that when it does go to air, the source will be playing at the correct level. **Pre-fading** an item before putting up the fader should route that source via a different listening circuit that becomes audible in the operator's headphones (and on the studio speakers if they are set to take PFL as well). The level from that source should become measurable on one or two of the meters on the mixer.

Meters on mixers are usually **peak programme meters** (PPM) as opposed to the **volume unit** (v/u) **meters** more commonly used on portable recorders. Traditionally calibrated in easily readable numbers up to six, PPM meters display the peaks – literally, the highest points – in the audio. Different standards may apply in some studios, but in radio a common approach to levels is for all music to peak around 4.5 and for speech to peak around 5. This difference is because most recorded music is highly compressed in the recording stage, using a wide range of audible frequencies because it consists of several different instruments – or perhaps it was produced by a synthesiser or a computer set to produce an overall sound with plenty of impact. In the 1960s the American music producer Phil Spector created a number of records for such bands as the Ronettes, which used several overlays of different instruments and voices to create an effect that became known as his 'Wall of Sound'. By contrast, a single piano playing a gentle solo would not normally have been recorded with much compression, and it might need a boost to higher than 4.5 in order to sound comparable in volume to the rest of the programme, especially to the listener driving on a noisy road.

Setting the level in advance for each individual source is as simple as selecting the PFL on each channel in turn, listening to the audio on the headphones, and adjusting the channel's gain control until the peaks are reaching the correct level on the meter. Then you must remember to re-**cue** the audio if it is a recording and switch the channel back out of PFL and resume monitoring the output of the desk when each level has been lined up. On some mixers, the meters may be LED displays, rather than a scale and a pointer, and on digital mixers there are likely to be several different metering options selectable via menus on the display.

Often there will be **pan** controls for each channel, which can be used to position the audio for that channel either to the left or the right of the **stereo image** – for instance, in a studio interview the two mics could each be panned a little to either side of the centre. Normally pan 'pots' will be left in the centre position, but in Chapter 8 we explore some more creative uses of stereo in a variety of different **contexts**. The other controls on the mixer may include switching of channels to different outputs, for example, for sending **clean feed** to a different location when doing an interview 'down the line', when the remote person needs to hear the studio output without also hearing a return send of what he or she is saying. There may be a **ducking** control on some channels, which can automatically lower the level of music, for instance, when a presenter speaks to do a talkover.

In addition to the column of knobs, switches and faders relating to

Figure 1.4

Control	Function	Effect	Purpose
Talkback (eight buttons)	Communication off-air	Allows people in studio to communicate with other areas	Talking to and hearing people in control room, newsroom, remote contributors
Monitor selection (five buttons)	Selecting which output to monitor	Sends selected output to headphones and speakers	Choosing to hear desk output, clean feed, another studio, alternative sources, or via a radio receiver
Headphone and speaker levels	Setting overall levels of speakers and headphones	Raising and lowering monitoring levels	Allowing monitoring of output and PFL at comfortable levels – improper use may cause permanent damage to hearing
eq	Equalization (shown with high, mid and low frequency controls)	Boosts or lowers selected audio frequencies	Changing the tone of output from the audio source
Aux	Routing channels to different outputs	Sends audio from the channel to outputs selected	Sending clean feed to outside contributors, recording one source while another plays on air
Pan	Panning a channel to the left or right	Sound from the channel appears farther to left or right of stereo image	Creating drama in which voices and other sounds are given different positions on a virtual stage; setting apart multiple presenters or interviewees
Gain	Setting level on a channel	Increases or decreases the level of audio from that channel	Consistent levels, avoiding the need for listeners to make adjustments to their volume controls
PFL	Pre-fade listening	Allows operator and others to hear sources before fader is raised	Checking material, setting levels and lining-up material without affecting the programme output
Fader	Fading channel in and out; fine adjustment to the level of a channel (shown faded out altogether)	Bringing the sound source routed through this audio channel in and out of the programme	Lowering levels for talkovers and mixes, quick and slow fades in and out, maintaining consistent levels

The main mixer controls, their functions and purposes. Above are some of the general controls, which apply across the mixer. Below them are the different controls that apply separately to each individual channel.

each channel, there are others that relate to the overall operation of the mixer. Usually these will be grouped logically, with, for example, **talk-back** controls arranged together, allowing communication between the studio and other locations such as the newsroom and voice booths.

The best way to become familiar with the working of any studio and its mixing desk is to practise using it while it is off-air. Record a range of different mixes and fades, as well as mic work and talkovers, then play them back to hear what effect your actions have had. This is the most effective way to learn, so be critical!

Recording techniques

Recording, either in the studio or on location, is one of the most common activities in radio production. In the studio, traditional analogue reel-to-reel tape recorders have mostly disappeared, as have MiniDisc and **Digital Audio Tape** (**DAT**) recorders, in favour of PC-based systems. For location work, the most common portable tape recorder was made by Uher, and some radio journalists cherish fond memories of this robust battery-powered machine, which made broadcast-quality recordings in often very difficult circumstances. They may also remember its great weight, their coat pockets bulging with spare reels of tape and the longer times taken to edit with **razor blades** (see page 22), compared with those offered by the relatively new digital technologies. DAT, launched in 1987, uses digital encoding to record long **durations** of audio signals and indexing information onto small cassettes. Their operation was constrained by the need to rewind and fast forward for recording and playback and they are already dying out. MiniDisc recorders, **solid-state recorders** and PC-based systems benefit from much quicker access to specific points on the recording media – and the storage capacity of PCs has continued to increase with developments in internal technology and access to servers via local area networks. MiniDiscs themselves are small, so spare discs may be easily carried around in a pocket – but they are also disappearing from the industry. Removable PC cards and ordinary memory sticks, although much more expensive than MDs, are now firmly established as the recording media of choice for most location recording for radio.

Recording into any recording device involves making sure that the levels do not exceed those tolerances with which it can efficiently cope. When in record mode, a meter will show how much signal is being fed into the machine, whether it is from a studio mixer or, on location, from one or more microphones connected directly to it. You should make sure the levels are not peaking too high – or too low, either, or the recording may not be of a satisfactory quality. Some mixers and recorders will have a **limiter** built into them, which will prevent levels exceeding the maximum tolerances, but it is good industry practice not to rely on the limiter, if there is one.

Before setting off with a portable recorder, it is important to make a test recording, speaking into the microphone and – unless using ALC if available – adjusting the level control so the meter shows the voice peaking just before the 'danger' zone on the scale. Play the recording back to ensure the microphone, leads, removable medium and recorder are all working properly, but then turn off the loudspeaker or it will cause **feedback** or **howlround** when you next begin to record.

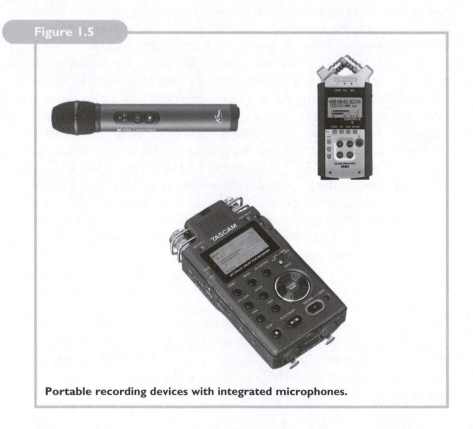

Figure 1.5

Portable recording devices with integrated microphones.

It is also advisable to check the battery power will be sufficient for the task ahead, perhaps taking spare batteries or a battery charger as a back-up for recharging between different tasks. There are a number of common-sense safety precautions involved in even the simplest of location recording activities. Health and safety must be uppermost in the minds of anyone working in radio, in the planning stages and when putting plans into action. A very complex outside broadcast could involve the use of crash barriers to hold back large numbers of the general public and liaison with the police over the closing of roads and crowd management (see Chapter 5).

When recording on location with a single recorder, perhaps with a separate lead and microphone, the main safety consideration should be for yourself – and you should also ensure you don't, by your own actions, put other people in danger. Planning should take very careful account of the location and any particular dangers presented by traffic, industrial equipment, steep drops, escaping gases and so on. The law requires you to seek permission before working on somebody else's private property (which may include shopping centres), and it is good practice to ask about any potential hazards at the time of being granted permission. Standing for any length of time on a public right of way, such as a pavement, could legally constitute an obstruction, but the most important consideration is that in doing so you do not place others in danger by causing them to step into the road in order to pass round you. Other people can also represent a threat to your own, and your equipment's, safety and there are bound to be locations where personal safety will require you to avoid certain times (such as after dark), to take someone else along with you or even to abandon the idea and make alternative plans.

Once you have made a recording, it is important to secure it, by taking it out of the recorder if it is on a removable medium such as a card, and putting it somewhere safe, such as a pocket. If you lose the recorder on the way back, at least you'll still have the recording! Both MiniDiscs and DATs have write-protect tabs on them, and these are useful to prevent accidental over-recordings which could lose your valuable programme material even before you have heard it yourself. Some removable media can be labelled clearly on the outer casing to prevent accidental loss. You may wish to electronically label cards or sticks and individual tracks on them for quick recognition, and this may be done using the display on the recorder and its various controls, depending on the type, make and model. A particular problem with some MD recorders was that they would automatically begin recording at the start of the disc, overwriting your previous recordings, unless you manually moved them on – perhaps by using an 'end search' button if there was one. Audio cassettes are seldom used now in the radio industry, as the superior technical quality and relative affordability of digital media make them increasingly attractive. Cassettes also had to be protected and labelled, though, just like open spools of tape before them.

Editing audio

Editing recorded audio material used to be done by physically cutting that magnetic tape with a one-sided razor blade, removing the unwanted sections of tape, and then joining the tape back together again with sticky splicing tape laid carefully across the join. In the early 1990s the first computer-based production software began to slowly revolutionize radio production, as **non-linear** editing and mixing became available on PCs and dedicated, custom-built hardware, such as the Short-cut by 360 Systems. While experienced editors of magnetic tape could identify edit points, mark them with a soft **chinagraph pencil** and perform each cut and **splice** in a **splicing block** very quickly and efficiently, the much-increased speeds offered by non-linear systems made them very difficult to resist. Some software, such as DAVE 2000, mimicked the possibilities of tape, allowing only deletion of material and its rearrangement. More sophisticated systems, such as Fast Edit, soon offered the ability to mix and to **process** the audio as well. Others, such as Cool Edit Pro (renamed Adobe Audition in 2003), were distributed via the Internet and offered serious competition to more expensive, but highly regarded professional systems such as Pro-Tools and SADiE, which initially required the purchase of bespoke hardware with particular sound cards and hard drives for audio storage.

With all PC-based systems, as the capacity of hard drives has developed rapidly from a typical 2 Gigabytes in 1998 to a thousand times that in 2013, the amount of memory (or RAM) and the processor speeds have increased, so initial reservations about the PC's ability to cope simultaneously with large amounts of audio have melted away. It was usually inappropriate to **dub** very long pieces of audio into a PC from cassette or MiniDisc. If producing a two-minute package, it was usually better to pre-select which parts of a 20-minute long interview you were going to actually use, and pause the new recording while fast-forwarding through the unwanted material. (See the sections on package and documentary production in Chapters 2 and 9.)

In order to edit, though, audio recorded on a portable device usually had to be transferred into an editing environment through a **dubbing** process. Today, if the removable medium in the recorder is a PC card, which allows immediate transfer to any other hardware with a compatible card reader, no dubbing is necessary, because the audio files can be copied almost instantly by a modern PC. Some integrated microphone and recorder solutions (such as the iXm and before it the Flashmic, or the Zoom with its built-in microphones) plug straight into an ordinary USB socket for fast file transfer. Dubbing was normally done through the mixer in a studio, at a specialized workstation equipped with playback facilities and a small mixer already connected to a PC, or at another PC simply by making a new connection between the original recorder and the sound card via the PC's audio input socket. This is rarely done now.

Any audio may be edited – speech, music, sound effects – but usually the aim is to make the edits as 'invisible' as possible. That is, they should not be obvious to the human ear, so edited music should not skip a beat and the lyric or tune should not be disrupted so as to easily seem altered. Human speech also has its own normal patterns of light and shade, intonating up and down, and being organized in

Figure 1.6

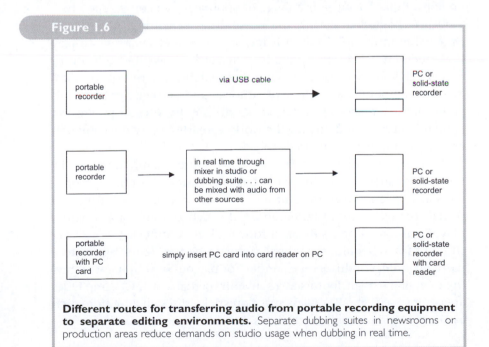

Different routes for transferring audio from portable recording equipment to separate editing environments. Separate dubbing suites in newsrooms or production areas reduce demands on studio usage when dubbing in real time.

Table 1.1 Approaches to editing speech

Reason to edit	Possible action
Neaten an interview and remove unwanted material such as digressions	Identify and delete any gaps, repetitions, interruptions and digressions
Make acceptable for broadcast on grounds of taste and decency	Identify and remove any language deemed inappropriate for the time and context of broadcast
Remove unwanted ambient or malfunction noise, e.g. interruption by phone, occasional mic rattle	Identify offending audio and delete it, making join as imperceptible as possible
Improve own or another's contribution to a speech recording	Remove 'ums' and 'ers', long pauses or stumbles over words – provided result still sounds natural

Different editing actions required for different purposes. Note the importance of reviewing any edit objectively, and being prepared to re-do it if necessary.

identifiable phrases which are punctuated by laughter, grunts, and pauses for breath. Clumsy or over-ambitious editing which ignores the need to make the speech sound natural makes the edits sound very obvious. Table 1.1 suggests a range of approaches to editing speech.

Other chapters deal with the possibilities of editing, mixing and **processing** in greater detail. It is important, as a general rule, to play back audio as it is being edited, in order to hear whether the edit or mix which you have just done sounds acceptable in terms of technical quality, audibility and a range of editorial and aesthetic criteria. It is good industry practice to listen back critically to work in progress at regular intervals – and to save the work regularly in case the computer crashes or the software freezes.

It is very common for PCs or if you use them, Macs, to be networked, and so, once the audio has been loaded into the appropriate software, and saved in a **format** such as .wav or .mp3, it may be stored, copied and transferred about the network and subsequently played out 'on air' in its finished form – all from different PCs. Other situations may require the edited audio to be transferred again, to a particular folder or drive, for example, for playout or simply for archiving or giving to contributors as a souvenir, perhaps on a CD. .mp3 files are compressed, so take up less space on sticks, discs, in a filestore such as Dropbox or as email attachments.

Analysing radio: applying media theory to radio contexts

Academic study of the media has traditionally centred on a number of different aspects of the processes of production and reception. Radio broadcasting began experimentally in 1906, just 11 years after the Lumière brothers opened the first cinema in Paris, and 30 years before the BBC began the world's first regular television service, but academics were slow to apply to radio the developing principles and practices of mass media analysis. The pioneers of media studies in the United Kingdom, Leavis and Thompson (1933), sought to protect children from malign influences in the cinema, by teaching them to discriminate between putative elements of 'good' and 'bad' in their viewing, but – probably because the BBC then reflected the 'Reithian' values of its first Director General – radio was not perceived as a threat to their moral values. Film appreciation soon became accepted as a discipline in schools, and in 1950 the British Film Institute appointed its first Film Appreciation Officer. The Royal Television Society was founded in 1927, yet it was not until 1983 that the Radio Academy was formed to promote the discussion and appreciation of radio, and as an interface between professionals and between the industry and academia. The print media fared much better, and the development of the media studies curriculum was initially concentrated on film, television and the press. A small but growing number of academic books, such as Crisell's seminal first edition of *Understanding Radio* (1986), and the creation of the Radio Studies Network in 1996, have combined with the increasing popularity of radio in vocational courses to belatedly raise its profile in further and higher education, as explained more fully in Starkey (2012).

Most of the traditional approaches to media studies can be applied to radio. Whereas much of the existing literature is contextualized within different media, few of the concepts developed within it present real difficulties when translating them to the 'newer' context of radio – which is startlingly absent from even the most authoritative texts. In the *Dictionary of Media and Communication Studies* the definition of **voice-over** referred only to film and television (Watson and Hill, 2000, 329). However, relatively recent work by academics has begun to develop a body of literature that focuses on the peculiarities of radio; but as well as consensus, theorizing such a diverse and versatile medium can produce its own controversies. For instance, because listeners must create their own images, based on the information they hear, Crisell compared the medium with blindness, acknowledging that one of the main benefits of listening to radio derived from its reliance on the imagination (1994, 6–11). The notion that radio is blind has persisted with a durability that defies the often pejorative connotations of blindness – which is not a physical state to which many would aspire.

Radio, however, is not itself blind. It is the experience of *listening* to radio that is akin to blindness (McWhinnie, 1959, 21–8). From the perspective of a listener, radio is my sighted friend who sees things I cannot and describes them to me as best it can – as unable to provide me with complete, given pictures as in turn I am to pass instant pictures on to my other friends when I tell them what I have seen. Radio's problem, if problem it is, lies not in its powers of perception but in its ability to articulate, because other media can enhance their **discourse** with images that explain more fully and less controvertibly what they choose to portray. Yet radio can articulate more clearly than human beings, because its voice can produce a far wider range of sounds – including music – than our own mouths can. Furthermore, radio has developed strategies to partially overcome its disability, by arranging sounds according to a number of informal rules that are understood in similar ways by producers and listeners alike. Producers need to understand the limits on their powers of articulation, and to use the restricted syntax and lexicon available to them – the language of radio – in ways in which the momentarily blind listener can interpret.

When studying radio, writing **evaluations** of production processes and finished **products** can be richly enhanced by including informed and objectively critical discussion of how they relate to the theory that underpins deeper understandings of the media generally, and radio in particular. Media practitioners who reflect in informed ways on their work are likely to find that they have a greater understanding of the contexts in which they operate, and that they are better able to achieve outcomes that satisfy their objectives. For example, the study of **institutions** relates to the way the industry is organized. It concerns such aspects of ownership, regulation and employment as are discussed in the introduction to this chapter, each of which can have a significant impact on what is actually transmitted. Detailed historical perspectives, such as those written about the UK by Briggs (1995), Crisell (2002), Street (2002), Hendy (2007) and Stoller (2010), can add further context, and a greater understanding of current tensions and trends. A more international outlook may be gained by comparative study across territories – perhaps including such works as Neer (2001) and Duval (1979).

Textual analysis considers each element of a radio broadcast as a separate text, be it a whole programme, a news **bulletin** or a single advertisement – just as in film studies students may **deconstruct** a whole western or a trailer for a Hollywood blockbuster. It involves systematic examination of a range of different aspects, each of which is as intrinsic to radio products as to those in any other medium. Often textual analysis can seem preoccupied with minute detail, but it is intended to develop understanding of particular phenomena in single texts and to draw conclusions where possible of a more general nature. **Intertextuality** involves making comparisons between different texts, be they similar in nature or different. Textual analysis is normally organized under the six headings of **genre**, **codes** and **conventions**, **semiotics**, **representation**, **ideology**, and **audience response**, all of which are interrelated. There are several examples of these approaches in the other chapters of this book.

Studying genre involves identifying the common characteristics of a number of texts that are generically associated with each other, and that would normally require similar production techniques in order to create them. The term itself is disarmingly transparent, being derived from the French word for 'type'. Examples of different genres include the documentary, the **trail** and the **phone-in** programme, and as the content in this book is itself divided by genres, the discussion of genre in future chapters is relatively straightforward, being presented by way of contextualization in the opening paragraphs. Of interest in a particular text is the manner in which it relates to the accepted norms of the genre: which common characteristics it displays, and to what extent they are in evidence. That text can then be compared with other examples of the same genre, either current or historical, in order to discover how it relates to them. For example, how do music sequences (see Chapter 3) differ in **style**, approach and content between stations playing chart music and those playing classical music? The widest range of different genres is often to be found in the speech output of public service radio stations, such as BBC Radio Four and NPR in the United States. This can present cultural difficulties to younger students of the media, who may be unfamiliar with their output, but academic study can and should include dealing with the previously unknown.

There are often comparisons to be made between the **narrative structures** that are common to different genres, and how they are used in different texts within genres and **sub-genres**. These may be **open**, **closed**, **multi-strand** and even **investigative**, depending on the arrangement of the discourse within the text. For example, an open structure leaves matters unresolved at the end of the text, with more important information to follow, such as in the next episode of a series, or the second half of a football commentary. A closed structure is one in which the key issues are resolved at the end – when, for example, the final whistle has been blown and the commentary ends with the final score. Multi-strand **narratives** are explored in Chapter 8, in the context of soap opera, and other sub-genres in radio drama occasionally depart from the more conventional approach of beginning/middle/ending, to present a more challenging discourse which can be described as alternative. An Internet radio station which, through on-screen interactivity, permits listeners some flexibility over the sequencing of what they hear – often called 'listen again' – can reasonably be described as investigative, in the same way as the term is applied to encyclopaedias, web sites and dictionaries, none of which is usually read continuously from start to finish.

Codes in the very academic context of textual analysis are not to be confused with the published **codes of practice** issued by regulators and professional bodies such as, in the United Kingdom, Ofcom and the National Union of Journalists. They do, however, also govern the behaviour of producers and consumers of radio in that production involves a process of systematically **encoding** meanings, while listening involves audiences in **decoding** them according to jointly held perceptions of what is meant by various techniques and arrangements of sounds. For example, a drama producer may wish to indicate a change of scene, and many listeners to radio drama recognize a fade out, followed by two seconds of silence and then another fade in, as meaning just that: a change of time or place (see Chapter 8). Using this common understanding the producer communicates information to listeners who in turn understand what is meant as effectively as users of semaphore or Morse code – except in radio the transmission of messages is normally one way. All of these codes are in essence systems into which signs are organized, but like languages, media codes have evolved from practice, rather than being devised by any single individual. They may be verbal as well as technical – sounding sad to tell bad news, for instance. They may also be structural, and Roland Barthes (1990) identified five different codes as appropriate to the study of any narrative.

Conventions are norms of accepted behaviour, and in radio production they relate to established procedures and ways of performing common tasks. For example, it is a conventional use of the traffic and travel **jingle** that it precedes the detail of the report to which it refers, rather than following it. Ending a news bulletin with a light, possibly funny story is another convention, and it would significantly break with convention to lead the bulletin with the 'funny', rather than with the outbreak of a killer virus in the town. Radio is rich in conventions, and producers' reasons for breaking them in order to innovate or be groundbreaking must be clear and compelling, or their efforts are likely to be read as merely 'unprofessional'. Textual analysis can include detailed discussion of conventions and how they are applied, adapted or broken, as well as suggesting reasons why. It may be useful to consider, for example, to what extent using different codes and conventions acts as a useful form of shorthand in which large amounts of meaning are compacted into a relatively limited time span. The traffic jingle may consist of just four beeps of a musical car horn, but even to relatively new listeners, it clearly announces the start of the traffic and travel bulletin. They may, of course, respond differently: those making or planning a journey may pay increased attention, those who are not may be more inclined to retune to a station which plays more music.

Semiotics (or **semiology**) is the study of signs and how they construct meaning. Dating back to the work of Ferdinand de Saussure (1916), it recognizes the influence of both linguistics and culture in determining how audiences 'read' the various elements of sign systems such as the arrangement of sounds and silence in radio. C. S. Peirce (1960, vol. I, 196; vol. II, 143, 161, 165, 168–9) categorized signs as the **icon**, the **index** and the **symbol**, depending on how literally they represented the meanings they were intended to convey: the icon most closely resembling the subject, and the symbol tending towards the abstract.

Although de Saussure died in 1913, and Peirce in 1914, their work is as relevant to the study of radio now as it was to become to television – even though it had not even been invented. The barking of a dog is an aural icon of dog barking, just as a photograph is iconic of the object it portrays. The barking is also indexical of the presence of a dog, even though the characteristics of a dog are greater than just the sound of its bark: hearing the barking suggests to audiences who have a more sophisticated understanding of the sign that also present are a tail, a nose, four legs and a head, even though they are not literally represented in sound. Finally, the barking may be symbolic of something external to the dog – the arrival of the postman, the presence of a burglar or its owner throwing a stick for it to catch – and audiences will make these more abstract **readings** according to a range of other factors. Among them will be the presence of other sounds, such as the rattle of the garden gate, the breaking of a window, or the owner shouting 'Go fetch, Fido', and it is the arrangement of multiple signs which creates the codes that contribute to a discourse. Cultural influences affect each listener's reading of a text, too, in that the symbolism of the dog barking representing the arrival of the postman may not be understood in countries where postal services do not deliver to individual addresses.

Issues of representation may be raised by radio texts, too, because choices have often been made over what may be said, and by whom. The main issues relate to questions of gender, ethnicity, class, and age, because these are the principal categories into which human beings are divided by birth, rather than by choice. People's location within any category can determine the range of opportunities realistically open to them. Being working class may limit access to certain professions, clubs and social gatherings, as can being female, black or old, depending on how enlightened the society happens to be. Profiling of workers in particular professions has indicated that artificial barriers based on prejudice may have skewed the representation of certain **demographic** groups in the better positions, while other groups of people have been **stereotyped** as more likely to commit crime, to be dishonest or to be stupid. On radio, a textual analysis may consider the choice of presenter and of interviewees, in order to determine the validity and fairness of the representation being made – particularly as the media play an important role in **naturalization**, or making something seem correct because it is commonplace. In a drama, the **characterization** may be controversial (see Chapter 8), and on a music station there may be an acute predominance of young, white male presenters – some of whom may use language about women which denies them equal status or equates their worth to their appeal to young white men. The language used in any script may raise issues of representation, which deserve to be critically analysed – Fleming (2002, 154–63) considers age, ethnicity and gender in greater detail.

Ideology permeates media representations in that certain systems of ideas and beliefs are often favoured over others, as discussed in the context of radio drama (see Chapter 8) by Blue (2002). This can be done either overtly or subtly. One might have to listen to archive recordings of Radio Moscow from before the 1990s to hear much evidence of a Marxist-Leninist view of the world, because capitalism is now the dominant ideology in most western countries. There are societies where broadcasting is more influenced by Islam than by any other belief system, and the discourse presented on their radio stations will usually reflect positions that condemn aspects of capitalism as sinful. Ideology affects audience readings of broadcasts, because listeners' own perspectives affect how they view the opinions and representations of others. Some men will be ideologically opposed to equal opportunities for women, for instance, and a political discussion programme involving representatives of all a country's political parties would probably appear outrageously unbalanced to an anarchist. In the United Kingdom, it is usually presented as quite natural that there should be a monarchy, and republican views are often presented as maverick or deviant. Reversing this trend in, for example, a current affairs programme or a drama, might be considered a challenge to the dominant ideology.

The ways audiences react to the media have been explained according to a number of different models or theories. Early assumptions about audiences considered them to be lumpen, unthinking and undiscerning masses, who would consume media only passively – each listener assimilating broadcast messages in exactly the same way, as simple receivers of ideas and information. The **hypodermic needle** model claimed that listeners responded to what they received in the crude manner of **stimulus-response**, just as the same muscle injected with the same stimulant would flex instinctively in the same way in anybody. Conversely, the **uses and gratifications** model (McQuail, 1972) contended that audiences are in fact active, discerning individuals, who each use the media to satisfy their own differing needs, taking from any individual item that which provides some form of gratification. Thus, among other things, listening to a traffic and travel bulletin satisfies a need for information, laughing along with a **sitcom** provides some enjoyment of life, and following a soap opera serves to provide material for use in later conversations.

Considered analyses of radio audiences now acknowledge the diversity of active, individual responses, often making 'reading' rather than 'receiving' a more appropriate description of listeners' interactions with radio texts. Producers normally intend their audiences to make a particular, **preferred reading** when they make radio programmes, but it is difficult to close off every conceivable **alternative reading** because of the multiplicity of nuance and the **polysemy** of words and sounds (see Chapter 8). It is, however, important to recognize the distinction drawn by Crisell (1994, 14–15) between listening to the radio and merely hearing it in the background, as well as that between academic study of audiences and the regular audience **research** which radio stations carry out to find out which programmes are popular and which are not (see Chapter 4).

Finally, it is worth noting here, that although this book explains the contexts and techniques of radio production, most radio output is now accompanied by at least some parallel content which is distributed via relatively new digital platforms, including the Internet, mobile phones and the apps which run on them, and terrestrial, cable and satellite television. While our main focus is on radio genres, much of this parallel web content extends and positions the main audio content, in the way that once only printed publications or television could show listeners what radio presenters really do look like. These additional dimensions to today's radio can prove highly interesting, as long as they are also considered critically, as suggested is appropriate by Curran, Fenton and Freedman (2012).

Of course, the suggestions above of ways in which to consider radio in its various contexts are not exhaustive. Later in this book we will apply them to the different genres studied, but despite the relative newness of radio studies, there are a number of other books which offer a wide range of different perspectives from highly respected academics. They include Chignell (2009), Crisell (2004), Crisell (2012), Crook (2011) and Rudin (2011). Two journals deserve particular attention, *The Radio Journal: International Studies in Broadcast and Audio Media* and the *Journal of Radio & Audio Media* (formerly the *Journal of Radio Studies*). For a more extensive and relatively recent literature review, see Starkey (2012).

The following chapters are about making radio within specific genres, that audiences actually want to listen to in sufficient numbers to provide paid employment for radio professionals – both new and experienced. Each chapter considers how theory can inform practice, and how practice may usefully be reflected upon according to a number of theoretical perspectives.

2 Speech Packages

In this chapter you will:

▸ learn how speech packages are made and used in radio
▸ research, plan and produce your own speech package
▸ consider ways of analysing packages you hear and make yourself.

Speech packages in context

The most common role of the pre-recorded speech **package** is to inform listeners about a subject which the radio station considers they will find interesting. Packages are used in news **bulletins** of shorter **durations** – such as two, three or four minutes which are typical on music radio stations – and in longer news programmes which may last 15, 30 or even 60 minutes. The longer the news bulletin or programme, the more easily it can accommodate longer packages, and there are no rules about how long a package should itself last, other than those set by individual stations or programmes which determine the typical length of the packages they wish to include in their output (Rudin and Ibbotson, 2002). Music programming often includes speech packages, too, when a mixture of music and speech is intended, and the added variety of a package can considerably enhance a radio station's output. Magazine programmes often use packages between other, apparently live studio-based items. (See Chapters 3 and 5 about live sequences and magazines.)

The term 'package' is sometimes replaced by **'feature'**, depending on the culture of the radio station or network in which it is used. 'Feature' can also refer to the kind of whole programme described by Kaye and Popperwell (1992, 75), as a 'stew' containing 'every ingredient in the medium'. Drawing comparisons between the feature programme and the documentary inevitably suggests 'featurette' and 'mini-doc' as other synonyms for the package. Yet another is **'wrap'** – usually used in a news **context** to mean a short, simple package which may consist simply of a reporter delivering a two- or three-part script to wrap around one or two short clips of interview. In the 1970s the original **ILR** news provider, Independent Radio News, began using the American term **'billboard'** to refer to an extended news wrap, for use in longer news bulletins and music and speech programming.

Depending on the context, a package may also be intended to entertain and/or to educate. Speech on radio can be amusing, and it is a common misconception that all packages have to be about serious issues, such as euthanasia or healthy lifestyles. Other ideas for lighter packages could focus on how people pick their lottery numbers, or what millionaire winners do with their winnings. In essence, a package tells a story – probably true, rather than fictional – which deals with an issue in greater depth and with greater detail than could be achieved in a live script read by the newsreader or the programme presenter. An important ingredient in many packages is **actuality** – recorded sounds which add greater variety and hence colour to what would otherwise be a comparatively dry **narrative** delivered by a reporter. This usually includes spoken comments from interviewees (who may be experts on the subject of the package), and further description added through the creative use of non-verbal sound effects. Other comments may take the form of **vox pops**, which consist of a range of opinions on a single topic, **edited** together in a juxtaposition which invites listeners to compare the different responses, and which purports to be representative of the views of a particular cross-section of society (see pages 54–5).

It is vital that the content and style of a package suit the main **purposes** for which it is intended. The package must also be appropriate to the context and the **target audience**. There is a role for music, too, depending on the subject and the nature of the radio station. BBC Radio One is targeted at young people between the ages of 15 and 24, and while speech on that station often moves at a faster pace than on Radio Four (which characterizes its output as 'intelligent speech'), it is also likely to have a musical background or **bed** under it. This style is a result of producers' assumptions, however correct, about the interests and short attention spans of their listeners. Radio Four producers, by contrast, do not generally feel that in order to keep listeners' attention there has to be a musical accompaniment to the verbal **discourse** they create in their packages by putting different elements of speech and actuality together. A package for Radio Four would only include music if it significantly contributed to the meaning of the piece, by depicting, for example, a scene at the annual Notting Hill Carnival. It is unlikely that the music for that package would be found on CD in the record library. The reporter is much more likely to use the actual sounds from the event: in short, actuality.

Exercise 2.1

Continue the table below, filling in the blank spaces and adding more examples of speech packages on a range of different radio stations. Discuss your answers in class – for example, you should reconcile the duration, the style, and the content of each package with its context and target audience.

Context and target audience	Duration	Content	Style
BBC Radio One: during *Newsbeat* (the lunchtime news magazine) – 15–24 year olds			Upbeat, fast-paced presentation; constant 'dance' music bed; interview clips very short
BBC Radio Four: during *Six o'Clock News* (half-hour long news programme) – listeners wanting 'intelligent speech'			
Your local commercial radio station, during news bulletins (audience varies according to station)			
An international broadcaster, such as Voice of America or the BBC World Service, during an extended news bulletin – listeners in other countries			

Typically, a package briefly tells a story: a word that can suggest fact, as well as fiction. Except in an intentionally **spoof** context, such as a comedy programme or – if care is taken – on April Fools' day, audiences tend to recognize the package as a piece of journalism, either hard or soft. Harder items are more news-oriented, while softer ones include lighter items and pieces that, although serious, aren't particularly related to the day's news and might have more in common with the feature pages of newspapers and printed magazines. Packages use various **codes** and **conventions**, which include the spoken **cue** that precedes the item, the reporter linking the various elements of the package together, the tone used – whether serious or light-hearted – and the evidential nature of the interview clips and the actuality. Consequently, the listener is most likely to construe the package as something genuine and truthful, and to knowingly or carelessly include false information or interviewees who aren't genuinely who you say they are would be an abuse of the listener's trust.

This concept of truthfulness – situated as it is within the **realist paradigm** (see pages 52–3) – becomes more problematic when sound effects are used to add variety and interest to a package. For example, the reporter turning round a short piece on the Notting Hill Carnival to a short deadline may be tempted to use some actuality from last year's event in order to cut corners. The **ethical** question here is whether it matters if the actuality is from a previous year, when industrial practice means the reporter is unlikely to state in the package that the sounds are actually old ones and not from the event being described at all. In television, an honest solution would be to add a small caption stating they are 'library pictures', but in radio there is no easy solution that doesn't take up time in the report. The ethics become more problematic when the **audio** isn't even from the same event, but from a similar one elsewhere (Starkey, 2007, 1–5).

Making packages

The first decisions to be made relate to the context and the target audience, as well as the subject matter. There probably is no single subject that couldn't be made into an interesting package – provided the approach is correct and the producer or reporter has thought through how to make the piece interesting and accessible. Accessibility in radio terms is about dealing with a subject in a way in which most fairly intelligent members of the target audience can understand what is being said, without feeling excluded because there are words and concepts used which are too specialized or unfamiliar. Some radio stations and some programmes deliberately target minority audiences who do have specialist knowledge of a certain field – for example, the medical profession. It would be time-wasting and patronizing to explain to that audience the use of a catheter because they use them often in their profession. Care should also be taken over the language used, as explained in the later section on scriptwriting (pages 47–9).

Finding an appropriate idea for a package can be the result of **brainstorming** or **mind mapping**. This **process** can be done individually or in a group, and it often involves writing down a topic or a subject

Figure 2.1

Location work can be both time-consuming and enjoyable, as well as adding interesting atmosphere that can 'paint pictures' in the listener's mind. Note the looped microphone cable, as well as the wearing of hard hats in response to a risk assessment.

heading in an idea 'bubble', then surrounding it with sub-topics, each in its own bubble. Each of these new bubbles may itself suggest a number of other ideas to explore in the same way – or you may by now have already found what you are looking for. This process often happens, either formally or informally, in the regular editorial meetings held in newsrooms and programme teams. Sometimes ideas for packages come about with very little effort, and sometimes a good deal of brainstorming is needed before inspiration strikes. The idea should suit the duration, being able to be dealt with in just a few minutes. Some ideas may require different contexts to be explored convincingly, and might be more suited to a documentary (see Chapter 9).

A survey in the publishing industry of magazine editors suggested that many of their ideas for feature items came from looking at rival publications, so it would be naive to suggest that all packages which get produced in radio are entirely original and owe nothing to the work of others, whether printed or broadcast. However, there are ethical and legal reasons why trying to be original is better than lazily copying other packages you may hear, and practically, listeners would soon get bored with the same material being endlessly recycled. The biggest audiences, and the best professional reputations, will be built on new ideas and approaches, which tell listeners interesting (and true) stories they don't already know!

Finding an angle

The terms of reference of a package must be understood clearly from the earliest stages of the production process. This is because a subject as vast as, for example, 'crime', could fill whole series of documentaries several times over (see Chapter 9). To create a five-minute package about crime, which deals with the subject in any meaningful way, it has to be narrowed down considerably to an aspect within a sub-topic of a topic connected with it. So, while the issues of crime and all related aspects are far too broad, detailed and complicated to be reduced faithfully to a five-minute piece to be produced in a short time, a package about a recent reduction in crime in the station's own listening area would be more easily achievable. This is where the brain-storming process can really help.

Figure 2.2

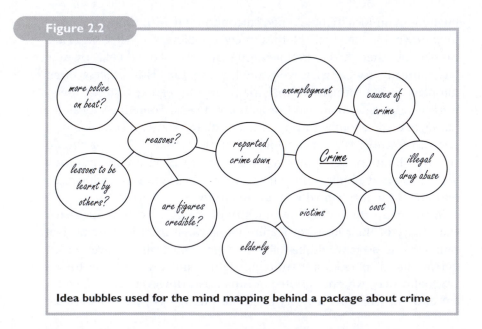

more police on beat?

unemployment

causes of crime

reasons?

reported crime down

Crime

illegal drug abuse

lessons to be learnt by others?

are figures credible?

victims

cost

elderly

Idea bubbles used for the mind mapping behind a package about crime

Part of deciding the terms of reference is deciding on the particular **angle** from which to approach the sub-topic, and it is the angle that most closely defines the content. The following are all different angles to the story about crime figures:

▸ Is the downward trend a result of falling unemployment or because of increased numbers of police officers on the streets?
▸ What lessons can be learnt from policing in the area, that others could adopt?
▸ Can we believe the official figures, or have they been manipulated?

The choice of angle will influence the type of interviewees to be included. In the first package, it will be necessary to consider how much the unemployed can be blamed for crime – and it may be a sociologist or some other expert in the field who can offer the best-informed perspective on that aspect of the question. It is unlikely that the same expert sociologist will have much relevance to the other two packages, and in such a short piece as this, there is no room for any time-wasting through digression.

Common to all three package ideas, though, might be the Chief Constable of the local police force. His or her perspective on why the figures have gone down is clearly going to be both relevant and authoritative, for this is the person whose policies may provide the answer. The key considerations when identifying potential interviewees are their relevance to the package and whether or not they are the right source of authoritative comment. A person's opinion only constitutes worthwhile evidence for inclusion in a package in this way if he or she has some form of credentials that are appropriate to the role. For instance, the Chief Constable can speak about crime in the whole area from the general, informed perspective gained from the experience of running that police force. An individual police officer, though, while unable to speak from such a broad perspective, should certainly be able to offer a different kind of evidence: that of personal experience patrolling the streets, arresting suspects and dealing with the victims of crime, for example.

Each perspective might have an important role to play in the package, but it is also important not to use either interviewee in the wrong way. For instance, the constable may have experience of only certain neighbourhoods in the area, or of certain types of crime, and the Chief Constable may not have actually hustled anybody into a police van on a Saturday night for quite some time. Similarly, a package about a medical condition would probably be best informed by an interview with a specialist in that particular field of medicine, than with a general practitioner who perhaps only infrequently encounters patients with that condition. Finding the right person will probably take a considerable amount of **research** (see page 42). Occasionally, someone who seems well qualified to speak on a subject, and who is willing to do so, will not be the correct choice. Some people just don't sound very appealing in front of a **microphone** – perhaps because their voices are not **radiogenic**, or more usually because their speech patterns are inconsistent (stuttering) or dull (they drone in a flat monotone, with little light and shade to their speech). Some stuttering could be reduced in the editing stage, but unless a droner is prepared to submit to some coaching from you, it may be better to find an alternative – without, of course, causing offence. Often it can be useful to ask if he or she knows someone equally qualified, but of the opposite sex, on the pretext of wanting to produce a more balanced package from the perspective of gender.

Interviewing for packages

Arranging interviews can sometimes be very frustrating, especially for students working on a package for their coursework. Generally, celebrities and the busier politicians can be almost impossible to interview, simply because they receive so many such requests that they have difficulty satisfying all the broadcasters and newspaper journalists who contact them. In the United Kingdom, the Royal Family rarely give interviews to broadcasters, and when they do, they have usually been arranged weeks in advance. That doesn't mean beginners shouldn't try to interview celebrities, just that they need to be realistic about their chances and plan alternatives to follow up very soon, if they don't seem to be making early progress with their first choices.

Celebrities who have given generously of their time to student broadcasters include radio personalities, television film critics and pop stars. One 16-year-old 'doorstepped' a Premier League footballer when the tabloid press considered him very hot property. He was rewarded with an exclusive radio interview for which many newspaper journalists would have paid handsomely. The student agreed to only use the material in his coursework, though, before the interview – and he wisely kept to his agreement. Remember that there are penalties for harassment, as well as for trespass, and you should think carefully about both the legal and the ethical issues involved in being over-persistent in your approach.

Before agreeing to be interviewed, most people will want to know what the package is about, and what the questions will be. Most professional broadcasters try to resist allowing their interviewees any form of editorial control, and often the **codes of practice** to which radio stations must adhere insist that they do not – or at least, that they 'consider carefully whether it is appropriate to proceed at all' (BBC, 2013, 6.4.13). One good reason for not providing the questions in advance is that inexperienced interviewees are sometimes so lacking in confidence that, if they know what the questions are, they prepare written answers and try to read them out verbatim into the microphone. This normally results in a very stilted delivery that just sounds like they are reading, and not like normal speech at all. It is often a useful compromise to just indicate to interviewees what *areas* of their specialist knowledge you are going to ask about, and you might suggest that if they are concerned about remembering details, that they make simple lists and note down any important figures or key dates, rather than writing a script.

Ethical standards of behaviour include keeping to any promises made when agreeing on the interview, so it's best to make as few as possible. When a journalist agrees comments are 'off the record', that means the comments won't ever be attributable to the person who made them. Hiding someone's identity in a newspaper is easier than in the broadcast media, and it is rarely worth using an interview clip that has been electronically processed to disguise the voice, particularly if the statements made are unremarkable and unlikely to get the interviewee into trouble. Making up false names to disguise a person's identity is also ethically dubious in all but the most extreme of cases – and this should not be done routinely, because it detracts from the evidential quality of the material. The first package above could make good use of an unemployed person who has been repeatedly moved on by the police, but if a reasonable research effort doesn't unearth one, an alternative interviewee should be found, rather than deceiving the audience.

Occasionally, in order to secure the best interview, broadcasters have to compromise, even so far as agreeing to the interviewee having a veto over all or part of the content. The police Chief Constable mentioned above might have a keen interest in influencing the content and conclusions drawn in the third package, especially as the angle suggests the questioning might be more cynical – or at least, challenging – than in the first two. An important professional decision is whether to accept the conditions being laid down, or to politely decline the interview and identify an alternative.

Planning interviews

The questions to be asked will depend on what you want from the interview – and it certainly is a waste of time and effort to record long interviews which have only little relevance to the subject and the angle, and most of which will never be used. It is far better to be both relevant and focused, and so the earliest stages of research should usually be spent wisely, in finding out about the subject matter. Only when the reporter has a deep enough understanding of the issue to explain it to a more general audience, can the production work begin in earnest – and the quality of the research is likely to show in the quality of the finished piece.

Research can be from a range of different **sources**, often categorized as either 'primary' or 'secondary'. Broadly, **primary sources** are those which provide information first-hand, the most obvious being face-to-face interviews or talking with someone over the telephone. Written responses to your letters or e-mails are also primary sources, whereas **secondary sources** are all those where information has been recorded in some way, and made accessible to others. Examples include books, web pages, radio and television programmes, directories and listings, encyclopaedias, videos, newspapers and magazines. Most importantly, any research should include checking the reliability of the source. Most books undergo quite thorough quality procedures before publication, whereas anybody can post material to the web without taking much care over its accuracy. Some newspaper reporting pays less attention to issues of truthfulness and **representation** than is required for it to be a reliable source, and even someone you speak to in person may not be giving you a full or accurate account. As a reporter or producer, you have to make an informed judgement about the likely reliability of any research source, and it is good industrial practice to check details by cross-referencing them with other sources. Research findings should be kept in an orderly manner, so they can be used for scriptwriting, as well as in **pre-production**.

Questions are intended to draw out the interviewee into providing the detail, the concepts or the real-life experiences and observations that can be more interestingly articulated by this 'expert' contributor than by the presenter. Planning an interview in advance can help to keep it focused. Having a series of questions written down – or at least a bullet-point list of areas to cover – provides a **structure** for the interview. It is not a sign of weakness. It is important to *listen* to the answers, though, at the time, in case the interviewee says something remarkable that listeners would like to hear more about, or in case the answers are complicated or confused by jargon which needs further explanation. There is little use in wondering what the interviewee meant, when editing the material later, when a simple follow-up question at the time of the interview (such as, 'What do you mean by that?') could have produced some much more usable material.

Generally, **open questions** are more likely to draw out detailed responses from less talkative interviewees – that is, questions which ask who, what, when, where and why. **Closed questions** have a role too, for checking information, or even for pressing interviewees who are not being as focused on a particular point as you would like them to be (see Chapter 5). For example, 'Have you ever committed euthanasia?' is 'closed' in that it is seeking (or demanding if put firmly) either a confirmation or a denial. The impact of a positive reply could provide some very compelling radio, because of the moral and legal implications of having assisted someone else's death – even for a doctor. However, in most circumstances, a string of 'yes' and 'no' answers to a series of closed questions such as 'Did you always want to be a doctor?' would produce a very boring interview, with little interest, description or even usable material.

Open questions that ask for impressions, feelings and sequences of events tend to produce the best, most fruitful material. When constructing questions, there is usually a way of restructuring a closed one that springs more easily to mind, to make it open and so more likely to prompt the interviewee to give a fuller account. Some examples of how to do this are given in Exercise 2.2 on page 44.

It's worth remembering that not everyone will understand a question in the same way. At Radio City, one presenter habitually asked regional managers of big organizations who had begun their careers in other parts of the country 'How did you get to Liverpool?' until one of them replied, 'I took the train to Lime Street Station.' Asking double or multiple questions – two or more questions in one – allows an interviewee to be less focused, either because part of the question gets forgotten, or because he or she doesn't want to answer it. 'How did you get here and why?' should simply be two questions, each asked separately.

Continue the table below, filling in the blank space and adding more examples of closed questions that could more interestingly be rephrased as open ones. Discuss your answers in class.

Closed questions . . .	. . . which can be rewritten as:
Are you a committed Christian?	What made you become a committed Christian?
Were you pleased to be promoted to this very important job?	How did you feel about being promoted to this very important job?
Did the launch take a long time to prepare?	What stages did you go through in order to prepare for the launch?
Have you got a big part in the film?	

When going to record, all the issues about location work that were discussed in Chapter 1 apply. Interviewing in the studio, either face-to-face or using a telephone line connected to the **mixing desk** (through a **telephone balancing unit**), requires little planning other than booking the studio and practising with its operation. The poorer audio quality of most telephone lines and mobile phone calls means radio stations use either studio-quality **landlines** or **ISDN** technology to achieve better-sounding results if available. Studio work has the added advantage of all the travelling being done by the interviewee, but a clear disadvantage is the absence of relevant **ambient sound**, if it is wanted (see Chapter 1). Skype and other web interfaces can also be of poor quality.

Microphone work for interviews requires skill and careful attention to position, and it may be necessary on location to move a single hand-held **mic** back and forth between yourself and the interviewee. This of course increases the risk of **handling noise**, and care has to be taken, otherwise the mic might not be in the right place at the right time, to catch the beginning of the interviewee's answers. The later section on scriptwriting for packages suggests that the interviewer's questions might not actually be used in more sophisticated productions, and so it is likely that capturing your own voice will be a secondary consideration to securing clearly recorded responses, and allowing your questions to be backgrounded by leaving the mic close to the interviewee's mouth throughout.

Holding a microphone at arm's length for even a short time can be a physical strain, and so it is important to set up a location interview carefully, with the two parties close enough to each other to reduce arm strain. Sitting on adjacent chairs, with the mic in one hand and the recorder on a nearby table, may not be enough, and some interviewers manage the environment even more closely by putting two chairs next to each other, but facing in opposite directions, as shown in Figure 2.3.

Recording vox pops can considerably enhance a package. As a vox pop is a short sequence of different people's responses to the same question or set of questions, it is practical to standardize certain features of the recordings in order to simplify **post-production**. Cutting from one voice to another, then another and so on becomes more distracting if at each cut the background or the **acoustics** change abruptly. Recording in a single location has the advantage of keeping the acoustics and ambient sound constant, rather than changing with each new voice – *if* the ambience doesn't alter during the recording session. If it is interrupted, it modulates in tone or changes in any other way, the edits may sound like **jump cuts** anyway. Returning to a location at a different time may also cause such a problem.

The structure of a package is a defining element in any assessment of its quality. Packages of any length can be very simple productions, in the manner of a short news feature or a billboard. However, the longer they are, the more important it is to use the creative possibilities of

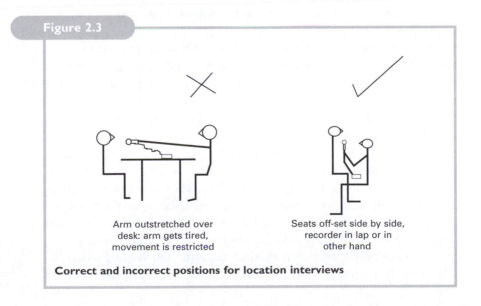

Figure 2.3

Arm outstretched over desk: arm gets tired, movement is restricted

Seats off-set side by side, recorder in lap or in other hand

Correct and incorrect positions for location interviews

radio to make them more interesting, and therefore more likely to retain the interest of the listener. Using a long interview clip without interruption is not the most imaginative way of using what may be very strong material, but which in isolation is not strong enough to prevent the 'switch off' factor. Analyses of packages intended for younger audiences (such as that in Exercise 2.1) usually suggest that where attention spans are a factor, each element in a package is shorter than average. Similarly, scripting very long reporter monologues is another way to lose listeners. Of course, sometimes material is so remarkable in its content that it can command listeners' attention for longer – if it is particularly hard-hitting, amusing or harrowing, for example – but those instances are rare, and producers should not assume their own piece is automatically so compelling that it will hold listeners for longer than anyone else's.

Structures that use shorter reporter **links** and interview clips, while being more sophisticated, are inherently more complicated to produce. Most clips will need some sort of introduction in a preceding link, and so there will need to be more links. Links need not be long, however, and they can perform the valuable additional functions of conveying to the listener both the direction and the purpose of the package. The opening link should set the scene, quickly establish some parameters as to what the package is about, and **cue** the first interview clip. Each subsequent link should move the narrative forward, **signposting** where necessary any change of direction, and cueing (either explicitly or implicitly) the next event. The final link may briefly reach a reasonable conclusion based on the previous content, providing an element of **closure**.

There may be music or relevant actuality before the first link, and the package may end on music or actuality – in fact, the most creative of packages may use music and sound to punctuate the narrative at a number of appropriate points – but these should not be used indiscriminately. The gratuitous use of music, for instance, except where a station's style demands it (such as on Radio One) can detract from a package. Where it is relevant to the narrative, and contributes positively to it, though, it can be a considerable asset, adding to the variety and, hence, interest in the production. The integration of music and effects should be done smoothly, fading under speech once it has become established, and fading out altogether when it is no longer needed. At other times, it may be appropriate for music or effects to fade in, under the speech at first, then reaching full volume when the clip ends. At a sense junction in the narrative, the music or effect can provide a punctuation mark – denoting an aural full stop, or a change of paragraph. If used effectively (see page 217) this technique can make fairly ordinary material more interesting. In every case, care must be taken over the **levels** of each element – that speech isn't drowned by music or effects, and that the overall level is constant. **Mixing** may be done live through a **mixer**, or more usually by adding extra audio in a multitrack software environment, such as Adobe Audition or SADiE. The use of music and other sounds that are someone else's **copyright** is subject to certain rules (see Chapter 4).

Scriptwriting for packages

Scripting may begin before all the audio has been collected, but it is only by reviewing interview material carefully that you can be sure to select the most appropriate clips for each moment of the package. Often, reporters and producers find they have too much material recorded, and that only a fraction of their audio gets used. Being ruthless in deciding what to use in order not to exceed the intended total duration is a professional discipline that should actually ensure only the best material gets used – and having to make such hard decisions can be disappointing. Rather than dumping recordings indiscriminately onto hard disk for editing, making an **edit decision list** on paper, and only **dubbing** across what is actually needed, are themselves important parts of the process.

Links should be written in a crisp, journalistic style to suit the sound and style of the station and the programme concerned. Care should be taken not to **libel** anyone, or to infringe any other legal restrictions on reporting (see Chapter 9). Links should be written to be spoken, rather than in the more formal style of written prose or newspaper text. Contracted forms of words, such as 'can't', 'won't' and 'couldn't' make it sound more like the reporter is speaking *to* the listener, rather than *at* the listener. The personal nature of radio is one of the medium's strengths, and this is an opportunity to exploit it to the full. Sentences should not be too complicated for the target listener to follow, because – unless they are listening to a recording – listeners can't rewind something they didn't catch first time, and listen to it again to try to decipher its meaning. Similarly, they can't look back over the script, as they might re-examine an awkward piece of prose in a book or a newspaper. Where necessary, links should *explain*, to make the package accessible to the target audience. The way the script is laid out on the page should make reading it out easier, achieving clarity by the correct use of tabs, line breaks between different items and clear headings, as in the examples below.

Links that cue into interview clips should normally identify the interviewee. After appropriate people have been found, with impeccable credentials to be speaking on the subject, it is important that the listener knows who they are in order to determine their relevance to the subject, *and* is able to interpret their contributions in terms of their positioning and perspectives on the subject. Scripts which repeat 'I asked' are less interesting than the more imaginative, and more conventional, approach demonstrated in the second of two examples below:

Example 1

Link: I wanted to know how doctors feel, when treating someone who is terminally ill and in pain. So I asked Dr Jo Smith, who is a GP from Merrytown.

Smith: I feel terrible. The patient obviously wants me to help, but there's little I can do.

Example 2

Link: So how do doctors feel, when treating someone who is terminally ill and in pain? Dr Jo Smith, a GP from Merrytown, feels terrible.

Smith: The patient obviously wants me to help, but there's little I can do.

The second approach avoids stating the obvious fact that the reporter asked a question, leads more coherently into the interview clip by accurately paraphrasing the doctor's first comment, and uses only 37 words instead of 45. Apart from being a more efficient use of airtime, if this economy of words is repeated several times over the total duration of the package, there will more time to include more interesting material.

An elaborately structured package will use several links and often return to an interviewee who has been heard earlier on. With multiple interviewees, it is important to re-identify them, so listeners don't lose track of who is speaking. On television, this is less important, as there are visual clues to **anchor** the identity of individual contributors more robustly and more enduringly than on radio. For example, the speaker in the Stetson, mounted on a horse, is undoubtedly the cowboy who was introduced to the viewers sometime earlier. Similarly, the woman pictured in front of the bookcase has been memorably positioned as the academic who has researched the Wild West. On radio, unless the voices are very distinctive and the positioning asserted very strongly, listeners will forget which voice belongs to who. The cowboy/academic combination could work on radio, *if* he has a Texan accent and she doesn't – but what if he hasn't got the accent and she has? Add the voices of the local sheriff and a tourist and it will all become very confusing, without regular reinforcement of their individual identities.

Each time an interviewee is reintroduced, the link should vary in approach from the previous one, to avoid repetition. Dr Jo Smith, a GP from Merrytown can become 'Merrytown GP Dr Jo Smith', 'Jo Smith, the Merrytown GP' and 'Merrytown's GP, Dr Jo Smith'. The simplest of links can suffice, as demonstrated here:

Link: Are doctors sometimes tempted to bring their patients'
        lives to an end? Dr Jo Smith again.

Production and post-production

Recording links for a package should be done carefully, and there is rarely any excuse for there to be a mistake – even a fluff or a stumble in part of a word. As packages are recorded, there should always be time to re-record any part that isn't of a high quality. The script should not be rushed – the writing probably deserves to be heard properly, at a pace that listeners can follow. The delivery of the script should be in the style of the station it is intended for, though, and the best way to get this right is to listen critically to other packages it broadcasts, and to rehearse and record your first few attempts to adopt that style.

Links should sound authoritative but friendly, usually bright but solemn where necessary, informed but willing to explain. Remember that the links pull the package together, take the listener through the other material and give the package both direction and purpose. So the reporter should be telling listeners the story, in a way they can follow, perhaps sounding surprised at times, and definitely using highs and lows, like light and shade, to vary intonation without going to extremes and becoming 'singsong'.

Once the links have been recorded, they can be combined with the interview material, any sound effects, music and actuality, and the whole package should be edited to smooth any awkward transitions between its various elements. Mixing should ensure music or other sounds do not drown important foreground words, and abrupt cuts out of effects will almost always sound better if replaced by quick fades under the speech. Long pauses or slow fades slacken the pace and should usually be avoided, although a longer fade at the end can be useful for the presenter of a magazine or a music programme to talk over – reading a **back announcement** if you have supplied one.

Back annos, like cues before them, can considerably improve the way the package is incorporated into the larger programme of which it is probably just a small part. A news package will normally need just a cue to precede it, so the newsreader can introduce the story, briefly set the scene, and then allow the package to do the rest. Similarly, a programme presenter can sound knowledgeable about the item, and lead the listener into it, by reading a cue as an introduction and adding a comment or some extra information at the end. The package producer should do this additional scripting, creating at the same time a paper or electronic **cue sheet** which also includes such basic information as the duration of the package (*not* including the time it will take the presenter to read the cue and the back anno), how it begins and ends (the **in-** and **out-cues**), the date of intended transmission and a title (or **catchline**) which will quickly identify the item and distinguish it from any other in the programme. An example is shown in Figure 2.4.

Although the term 'catchline' suggests a line of text, a single word will often suffice to identify the package. A programme with a number of packages on the same subject might distinguish between them by using 'Euthanasia 1', 'Euthanasia 2' and so on – or 'Euthanasia Doctor', 'Euthanasia Legal' – as catchlines. The cue sheet must be accurate in its detail, to avoid confusion. Durations and cues must be exact, to avoid confusion in the live studio or even under-runs or over-runs. The punctuation on the cue sheet must also be used carefully. In the example opposite, the inverted commas ("and") specifically **denote** the beginning and ending of speech on the package itself – and the dots indicate that the speech continues between them, but has been left off the cue sheet to keep its size manageable.

Figure 2.4

```
RADIO XYZ     THE LUNCHTIME MAGAZINE

CATCHLINE:    EUTHANASIA

TX DATE:      16/1/04

INTRO:        Sometimes doctors have to face up to being
              unable to help patients in terrible pain,
              dying a slow and debilitating death. Sometimes
              those patients ask them to break the law, and
              help them die. And occasionally, some doctors
              are tempted to carry out their patients'
              wishes, as Simon Partner has been finding out.

IN:           (fx: HEART MONITOR BLEEPS 4") "ALICE IS A VERY
              SICK LADY...

OUT:          ...MIGHT MEAN DR SMITH ENDS UP DOING TIME."
              (fx: MONITOR CHANGES TO A CONTINUOUS TONE AND
              FADES 3")

DUR:          4'57"

BACK ANNO:    Simon Partner reporting. If you have been
              affected by the issues raised in Simon's
              report, you might want to call a helpline
              number. I'll give you that number after the
              next item, which is also about euthanasia.

              NB: EUTHANASIA HELPLINE NUMBER IS 020 7XX XXXX
```

An example of a cue sheet for a package insert in a magazine programme.
In a speech and music sequence, the package might be followed by a song, and then the helpline number.

Exercise 2.3

Plan and produce a speech package for 'broadcasting' on a particular radio station and at an appropriate time. Make sure the subject and the angle are appropriate to your chosen context and the target audience likely to be listening at that time. Include actuality to add interest.

Analysing packages

Although radio's appeal to the imagination can be one of its strengths (Crisell, 1994, 7–11), and it can be very effective in fiction, there are circumstances when the imagination must be constrained. For instance, it is undesirable for a vulnerable listener to imagine on hearing a news report that the likelihood of being attacked in her sleep is much greater than in reality. The news report is not concerned with fantastic and barely believable phenomena such as vampires and monsters, and because it seeks to construct a picture of what is really happening in the world, responsible journalists feel obliged to make it as 'realistic' as possible. Responsibility in factual radio is not only to the listener, but also to those involved in the story. So, the **polysemy** which might be considered a virtue in a fictional drama is not welcome in journalism because encouraging **alternative readings** of a news report conflicts with journalistic notions of 'telling it like it is' (Dahlgren, 1995, 31–7). Words and sounds should be used in ways that recognize possible ambiguities in their meaning, and make every reasonable attempt to eliminate them. When analysing packages, it is reasonable to consider whether this has been done – and how.

Because of their journalistic nature, and that of the contexts in which they are normally used, most speech packages are situated firmly in the realist paradigm. They attempt to present a reality that would be recognizable to listeners if they were also witnessing the events or involved in the controversies described. In this way journalism seeks to be widely credible by appearing true to the objects of its representations. An exception might be the package which is overtly presented as **advocacy journalism**, where the material is reported from a single, contested perspective with which only some of those involved could agree (Fink, 1988, 18). Even here, though, the essentially partial advocate usually seeks to legitimize the account by presenting facts that are demonstrably true. Some broadcasters, such as in the United Kingdom, are constrained by rules on **impartiality** (see Chapter 9), and if an individual package is not itself 'balanced', they are expected to transmit a 'balancing' item in a similar timeslot soon afterwards (Chantler and Harris, 1992, 39).

However, just as the word '**realism**' is chronically unstable (Grant, 1970, 1), so journalistic observations of – and commentaries on – reality are epistemologically controversial. That is, on hearing a package on radio, it would be reasonable for listeners to question the validity of the reality it appears to present. How does the reporter 'know' the representation in the package is wholly truthful, balanced (see Chapter 9), and comprehensive? This question is especially pertinent when time constraints may have limited the depth and the breadth of research that has informed the piece, and the amount of material that has been included. Where one side of an argument has been represented by a single interviewee, how suitable a representative of it was that person, and might a different interviewee not have put the case more convincingly? Of two conflicting viewpoints, which had the final word – and does that matter? Which viewpoint, if either, seemed to be most effectively reinforced by accompanying material that appeared to support it, in the form of other contributions, of actuality and of the material presented as 'fact' in the reporter's own script? The package as a whole (and positioning statements in the cue material which surrounds it) constitutes a discourse, authored as well as articulated by the reporter. Its veracity, or truthfulness, deserves comparison with certain norms or understandings of what truly constitutes the reality involved.

Such comparisons can, of course, involve judgements based on **ideology**. Academic study of **myth** considers the degree to which an individual discourse contributes to someone's preferred view of the world and the way in which people perceive issues such as the nature of right and wrong. For example, few (if any) packages in BBC Radio Four's consumer affairs programme *You and Yours* consider listeners' purchases from the anarchist perspective articulated by, among others, Nietzsche (1887) that people are free to determine their own moral values, and by Proudhon (1840) that owning 'property is theft'. It is unusual to hear a financial report that questions the very existence of the stock market or people's right to make money from buying and selling shares – one of the key principles of capitalism, but one with which most communists would disagree. On *Farming Today* (Radio Four) few packages promote animal rights or accept as given the notion that ramblers should be allowed unrestricted access to the countryside, and a religious magazine programme that gave equal airtime to atheists would seem very unconventional. In each of these different contexts, there are sets of assumptions that are constantly being reinforced through **naturalization**, according to dominant ideologies that transcend most routine attempts to achieve 'balance'. For instance, a package considering the acceptability of gay people becoming priests may reflect both sides of that argument without ever considering whether there is any point to religious belief. Many practicalities of the nature of broadcasting, journalism and the relatively brief speech package made for radio all make such an approach seem entirely reasonable – yet it is also reasonable for us to question the way this package might contribute to the reinforcement of a dominant ideology. There are synergies here with the groundbreaking and at the time controversial work published by the Glasgow University Media Group (1976, 1980, 1982, 1985) about ideology in television news.

Furthermore, issues of **ownership** may surround which ideologies are acceptable for reinforcement on a particular station (see Chapter 9).

Pertinent questions arise when considering vox pops in particular. One production motive behind including them in a package or a documentary (see Chapter 9) is to make it more interesting, adding variety, controversy and even humour to the discourse. Another is usually to reinforce that discourse, by adding 'evidence' of either consensus or controversy around an issue, or by including some first-hand experience of an event or a phenomenon. However the nature of that evidence, the manner in which it was collected and the way in which it is used also deserve close scrutiny, just as it is appropriate to question the use of more formal interview material. The sample of opinion heard in the vox pop has undergone at least two processes of selection, each of which involves decision making about validity and appropriateness – according to the reporter's own values and assumptions about the subject. The second, in post-production, involves making choices based on issue 'balance', audibility, intelligibility, entertainment value and whether each statement actually contributes to the discourse by providing some useful illustration. However, the first may be the more problematic: it involves the initial choice of a **population** to sample, and how representative of that population the sample actually is.

For example, on the issue of corporal punishment, views may broadly differ across generations – older people having fainter memories of their own childhood, and their own experience of child rearing. They may also feel more vulnerable to unruly children and teenagers in public places such as shopping centres. Generally, their opinions on the issue may differ significantly from those of today's children and young parents – two other **demographic** groups. Similarly, adults of child rearing age may be sub-divided according to experience – for instance, separating parents from the childless, and the intentionally childless from those who medically have no choice in the matter. Given that there is unlikely to be a consensus across all these different groups on the issue, this being one of the great controversies of our time, the way a vox pop is represented 'on air' should fairly describe the population actually surveyed. That is, it would be misleading to intentionally or accidentally describe the views of just the pensioners as representative of a cross-section of society ('What do the people think?'), or if the reporter just interviewed a number of adults who happened to be leaving a social club for the intentionally childless, they could not reasonably be presented as expressing the views of their whole generation.

The distribution of any consensus over different populations and the appropriateness of sample sets to represent them may alter if the issue is changed to controversial infertility treatments – and they may alter again if it is changed to gender selection in pregnancy. Consequently, any notion of randomness in the choice of different people to construct a sample set of **respondents** is controvertible: where was the reporter standing, what time of day was it and were there any other relevant influences, such as the weather? Sick people may have different perceptions of the health service from those who are well enough to go out shopping on a wet afternoon – and how well qualified are most people to comment on the provision of *mental* health services, anyway?

Issues concerning representation frequently arise in reporting. Each contributor, and even the reporter, is a member of several demographic groups, relating to age, gender, class, regional origin, religion and sexuality (Boyd, 2000, 200–1). Responsible reporters attempt to recognize any values and preconceptions they may have as a result of their own positioning, and to allow for that in the production and presentation of their discourse – but how successful are they in avoiding cultural differences in their own perspectives, which may distort the representations they construct? The choice of interviewees, and even which voices to use in a vox pop, can present real difficulties for the reporter, and controversies worth exploring for the academic. For example, does all the informed medical opinion appear to come from men? Are all the burglars from a particular ethnic group, and do all the crooked plumbers seem to originate from one place? If so, these texts are probably unrepresentative of demonstrably different realities that they are actually managing to conceal. In this way, the choice of contributors can be harmful to disadvantaged groups, and so unwelcome in a liberal, 'enlightened' society. Over-reaction to such issues can, however, also distort the truth, and representations that deny any positive roles to white, middle-class, heterosexual males can be just as culpable, however much they may reinforce a particular ideology.

Reporting necessarily involves entering a community, to which the reporter does not wholly belong – except in rare instances where the subject involves only immediate colleagues, friends or family. The presence of a reporter is normally overt – this person has a microphone and a recording device, and has entered the community with the purpose of constructing a report on some aspect of it. Even if the other cultural differences are not great, it is reasonable to question the legitimacy of what the reporter is told. Only undercover reporting, carried out successfully, may be considered less affected by the process it entails (**reflexivity**), just as it would be reasonable to ask if a particular example of graffiti would even exist, if a television camera hadn't been present to 'record' the work of the graffiti artist who produced it. The dichotomy presented by so-called 'reality' television lies in its claim to show how 'real' people behave, but puts them in unreal situations in which they are acutely aware of the presence of the camera. A package that claims to portray a typical day in someone's life should also be treated with suspicion by those who seek to discuss its effects.

The codes and conventions used in speech packages provide fertile ground for **textual analysis**. The conventional **mode of address** adopted by most reporters is one of an informed, impartial commentator, confidently presenting a reasoned and reasonable discourse directly to the listener. The reporter's ownership of the discourse is signified by his or her positioning in the centre of an unfolding story – factual of course, and therefore 'true' – which uses various sounds and the testimony of others to reinforce and illustrate it. Producing a package where the reporter seems unsure of the material, or to doubt its validity, would subvert this convention enough to destroy listeners' confidence in it as a serious piece of journalism, principally because the reporter's tone and language both **connote** realism, balance and 'truthfulness'. The use of the cue material, any punctuation with music and actuality and the usually **closed narrative structure** of a package also commonly conform to well-established conventions. Intrinsic to the way these are arranged are notions of professionalism and technical ability, which correspond to the expectations of both listeners and the reporter's colleagues.

Using actuality and music may also add further layers of meaning to the package. Beginning with an establishing sound, especially after some contextualization in the cue that precedes it, can connote either time or place, and contribute effectively to the discourse because of the images it can create – taking the listener to the location of the story. It is worth considering the **semiotic** value of each of these, and how they operate. For example, the package that begins with three seconds of a police siren could appear to be about crime, noise, punishment, fear, speed, road safety or even police sirens, if the context hadn't already been specified in the preceding cue. Further **anchorage** of the intended meanings in the package takes place in the scripted links, which introduce people and concepts, present fact and interpretation, and organize the discourse in the manner of the reporter's own choosing. The reporter's own delivery, and that of other contributors, may connote further meanings, too. Injecting surprise, scepticism, bore-dom, excitement, awe or any other human emotion into the tone of the delivery can qualify a statement or something to which it refers, by placing intended or unintended values on it.

Sometimes, even in ordinary conversation, the sarcasm **encoded** into a statement is missed by the other person who might be expected to **decode** it. The readings made of speech packages by individual listeners within audiences may be considered according to the various **models** of **audience theory**. When they have no prior knowledge of the subject matter, they may simply listen out of interest, and be rela-tively uncritical of the discourse presented. Where they already have preconceptions, especially over a controversial issue, they are likely to read the text very differently from those who are already positioned by their own experience and prior knowledge on the other side of the debate (see Chapter 9).

Live Sequences and Phone-ins

3

Programme contexts

Live sequences are radio programmes that are created and put to air in real time, as opposed to programmes that are entirely pre-recorded. Sequences may, however, include pre-recorded material, and as music radio is the most common **context** for live sequences, most exploit commercially recorded songs and instrumentals to fill the majority of the airtime they occupy (see Chapter 4). Notable exceptions are those that use news, news/talk and phone-in **formats**, although a range of different combinations of music and speech can be found. The greater the recorded music content, the more sequences lend themselves to either full or partial **automation** by computer (Chapter 4). Sequences are most commonly several hours in **duration**, and they can be presented by some of the best paid of radio broadcasters, as well as some of the lowest paid. Sequence programming dates back to the 1930s, when Martin Block launched the *Make Believe Ballroom* on New York's WNEW-AM by playing recordings of 'dance' music in place of the usual more costly live studio performances by resident bands, or even **outside broadcasts** of popular performers (Neer, 2001, 27).

Sequence programmes normally position one or more presenters at their centre, and everything else is organized around them. The exceptions to this rule tend to include non-stop music sequences, where the presenter has been supplanted by brief, often repetitive **idents**, which may firmly position the programmes as offering the listener more music per hour. The development of music radio as a **genre** has produced many more examples of the presenter-led sequence than the less discursive alternative, and although radio stations can often identify non-stop music sequences which sustain and even build audience figures at certain times of the day, it is difficult to deny that listeners like to hear human beings on the radio.

The personality of the presenter can be more or less overt. Some stations have restricted presenters to reading liners, which consist of key phrases intended to form the basis of short, repetitive **links** such as those used extensively in the United Kingdom by the GWR network in the mid-1990s (for example, "The all-new 2-TEN FM, your better music mix") (Starkey, 2003a). Using liners 'on air' paradoxically casts the human presenter in the role of automaton, especially when in conjunction with automation, and the practice has been widely criticized by those who value the element of personality which people can bring to music sequences. Former BBC Radio One presenter Adrian Juste called them 'mind-numbing mantras, cold and glassy-eyed as haddock on a fishmonger's slab' (2002). The programmes – and the radio stations – which get talked about, both by listeners and in the other media, are, of course, those with the big identifiable personalities. The intimacy of radio encourages the development of a bond between the listener and the presenter – the friend 'dropping in' – and it is this recognition factor which can develop listener loyalty and the sense of belonging to the radio station's 'family' which can be one of radio's greatest strengths. As much listening is done alone, the voice on the radio can be a companion on whom listeners come to depend.

In the specific case of 'rolling' news sequences (Starkey, 2004, 25), there is usually much less emphasis on personality, although news anchors need not be entirely inhuman – but news-based and other types of phone-ins are often hosted by opinionated and even brash presenters whose tendency to extreme or antagonistic views on controversial issues may be calculated to provoke large numbers of interesting responses from listeners. In the United States, 'shock jock' Howard Stern created enough interest in his confrontational presentation **style** to spawn the 'biographical' feature film *Private Parts* in which he starred (1997: B. Thomas).

Producing sequences

Creating a new sequence, either as part of a series or as a one-off special, involves considerable thought and planning as to how it should be constructed. Depending on how much the programme is to conform to a pre-determined house style which embraces a range of such programming, the concept will be more or less original in its design. The programme may have to go through formal **proposal** and **treatment** stages, involving the production of detailed paperwork, or it may be that nothing more formal than a conversation takes place between the producer or presenter and the programme controller or the senior producer of the radio station or network concerned. At such a meeting, the basic **structure** of the programme would be agreed, the timing of regular **feature** items would be decided and typical ideas for content discussed.

Where independent producers propose sequences to commissioning editors, there is likely to be a bidding element to the **process**, and the more impressive the ideas, the paperwork and the budget, the more likely an individual proposal is to succeed. In 2013, depending on the station and the timeslot, the BBC was offering independent producers budgets in the region of £5,000 per hour for music sequences on its main national networks – to cover everything from staff to studios and administrative support, but excluding music copyright payments. However, on most local or regional stations the budget will be considerably less, and as the studios will be in-house it may not be specified in any greater detail than the presenter fees and any competition prizes. The most successful radio presenters can command huge fees (Cecil, 2009), because programme controllers perceive them to be valuable assets in attracting and retaining large audiences.

Planning a sequence programme

Planning a sequence is often easier with a **programming wheel** or **clock**, which represents an hour in an easily understandable form that quickly allows any bunching of items or unwanted gaps to be identified and remedied. The clock shows the position of each feature item in the hour, how many songs will be played in a typical programme, and where links, advertisement breaks and other fixed items such as traffic and travel **bulletins** will be placed. Of course, some music sequences don't have any speech features at all, and some stations don't broadcast adverts – but those that do, and those that carry more speech than can be found in presenter links, will find it useful to be able to balance the amount of speech and music around the hour, so as to avoid unevenness and inconsistency in their sound. If an hour

Figure 3.1

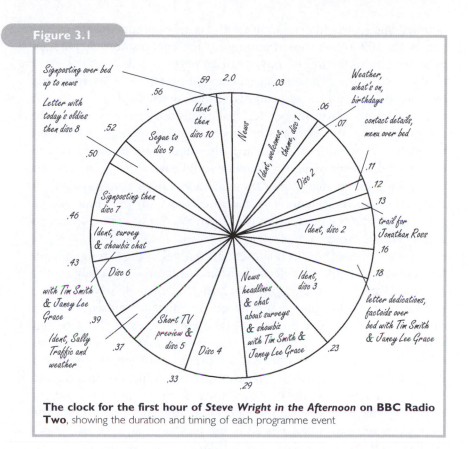

Signposting over bed up to news

Letter with today's oldies then disc 8 .52

Ident then disc 10 .59 2.0 .03

Segue to disc 9 .56

.50

Signposting then disc 7

.46

Ident, survey & showbiz chat

.43

Disc 6

with Tim Smith & Janey Lee Grace .39

Ident, Sally Traffic and weather .37

Ident, welcomes, theme, disc 1

News

Disc 2

.06

.07

.11

.12

.13

.16

.18

Weather, what's on, birthdays

contact details, menu over bed

trail for Jonathan Ross

Ident, disc 2

letter dedications, factoids over bed with Tim Smith & Janey Lee Grace

News headlines & chat about surveys & showbiz with Tim Smith & Janey Lee Grace

Ident, disc 3

.23

Short TV preview & disc 5

Disc 4

.33 .29

The clock for the first hour of *Steve Wright in the Afternoon* on BBC Radio Two, showing the duration and timing of each programme event

contains three speech **packages**, it would be unusual to want them to be concentrated near the beginning, leaving virtually continuous music for the rest of the duration. Another balance to be struck is between serious and light-hearted items, and some producers will want to consider where to place the hard-hitting investigative package, and where to position the light relief of the horoscopes or the competition.

A treatment may include clocks for each hour or just one for a sample hour, and if it is to be detailed in its approach, it should include descriptions of feature items and how they will be constructed. It should be clear who the presenter is, or if there is to be more than one, how they are to complement and contrast with each other. Any other regular contributors should be identified, and if there is a separate producer and/or other programme staff, they should also be named. There may be bespoke **jingles** or idents for the whole programme and for individual items, and music **beds** may be planned, too. A very detailed budget would even indicate the costs of producing the idents (see pages 109–14), and – depending on the circumstances – possibly even the cost of the music copyright (see pages 102–3).

While the clock is a pictorial representation of the different events in a broadcast hour, the same material may alternatively be expressed in linear form as a **running order**. Essentially a list of each element in the programme, this can be a more practical production tool in that the detail of item start times and durations can be more clearly expressed on the page. Further detail can take the form of indications of the source of the item (for example, whether live or pre-recorded) or instructions to the presenter or technical operator, but imaginative approaches to clock production (for example, colour coding of items) could achieve similar results.

Once a sequence has been launched, changes to the timing of regular items should not be made without good reason – especially on the breakfast show, when large numbers of listeners will be relying on the radio to get up and out of the house on time. A horoscope which normally begins at 0824, broadcast just a few minutes early or late, can throw listeners out of their routine and perhaps make them miss a bus or the start of school – or at least cause them to worry that they might be falling behind their own early morning schedule. For this reason, regular time checks on the breakfast show are vital, and some presenters have developed skills in giving double time checks which say the time twice while avoiding sounding too repetitive. By contrast, popular recollections of the late Jack de Manio – one of the BBC's first presenters of the news and current affairs sequence, *Today* – are usually restricted to his amiable on-air gaffes and his apparent inability to announce the time correctly (Luckhurst, 2001, 9–13). Of course, in other **dayparts**, the time is probably of less importance to listeners, and in the evening it would be pointless to place the same emphasis on time checks as at breakfast. Generally, though, moving regular items without clear, strong reasons (such as when BBC Radio Five Live might react to breaking news, or want to accommodate a budget speech or an important race meeting (Starkey, 2004, 23)), is disorienting to listeners and to be discouraged.

Allocating roles

The issue of personnel is one of both economics and personal preference. The most common **model** is that of the producer/presenter who works mostly alone with a minimum of additional support, arranging all the feature items and competitions, fixing up interviews and in some cases pre-recording more complicated parts of the programme, such as the Top Ten countdown in a chart show. Most live radio studios have, since the 1960s, been designed in such a way as to recognize the centrality of the single presenter, with all the studio equipment needed for a relatively complicated sequence programme arranged for easy operation by the one person. When the BBC launched its popular music network, Radio One, in 1967 they copied such a layout from the ship-based pirate radio stations which had popularized the longer sequence programme in the UK, and whose success they hoped to recreate. Their main competitor in the early years of Radio One, Radio Luxembourg, persisted however with the more traditional separate presenter and technical operator model – and in Luxembourg's case the two were separated not just by the window between the presentation booth and the control room, but also by their speaking different languages, the technical operator often being a native Luxembourger (Rosko, 1976, 125).

Usually one person costs less than two – and so the presenter who can present, drive the desk and produce the programme alone saves the station considerable amounts of money. Unlike in the 1960s, now that computers play a significant role in the playout of audio on most radio stations, and much of it can be automated or semi-automated, it is even easier for one individual to work alone. However, on BBC stations, especially where the speech content of sequences is particularly high, programme budgets are usually generous enough to afford at least a separate producer, and quite often a dedicated production assistant or a researcher, too.

The 'zoo format' adopted on Radio One in the 1980s by Steve Wright and developed in the 1990s on the same station by Chris Evans and in the 2000s by Chris Moyles positioned a variety of people in the studio as regular contributors, speaking 'on air' and responding to the presenter with laughter or applause when required. Since 1996, Wright – by now a regular on the more mature-sounding BBC Radio Two – has used a scaled-down 'posse' of regular studio guests. Their roles included reading out 'factoids' of interesting and occasionally topical trivia, as well as co-interviewing celebrity guests. It is generally recognized, though, that some of the most original, amusing and stimulating sequences ever produced in the UK were created alone by Kenny Everett, who would work for long hours in his home production studio to create comedy inserts to later play in between records at the radio station. The role of Everett's BBC producers was usually confined to simple **logistical** matters such as studio bookings and music copyright, as well as damage limitation with the BBC management over his more controversial material (Rosko, 1976, 34–6, 97).

Where students are working on a live sequence as a group production, it is, however, reasonable to allocate roles to one or two presenters, a separate technical operator who will drive the desk, and a producer. There is often scope for a production assistant, too, who can monitor the timings of items, bring interviewees in and out of the studio, and perhaps assist the technical operator by helping to **cue** up items on the playout system if there is one. Such a labour-intensive programme really ought to include a number of feature items, though, some of which could display relatively high **production values**, having been pre-recorded, **mixed** and **edited** with some sophistication in advance of the on-air date.

Presentation style

An important consideration in planning any sequence is the style of the programme, which will in part be determined by a combination of the station format, the day and time of transmission and the choice of presenter/s. Garfield documented the discussions at Radio One about who should succeed the controversial and arguably successful Chris Evans when he left in a blaze of publicity (1998, 180–2). Evans himself had represented a departure from the 'happy sound' of the original Radio One, which earlier became the target of satirical lampooning by comedians Harry Enfield and Paul Whitehouse, appearing on BBC 1 television as Smashie and Nicey (Garfield, 1998, 32–3). The 'permanent' replacements chosen by Controller Matthew Bannister were Mark and Lard – two men with overtly Northern English accents and rather laddish interests. The programme lasted only a few months before it was replaced by another partnership, that of Kevin Greening and Zoë Ball. Mark and Lard clearly failed to sustain Evans's audience **ratings**, and much of this can be attributed to their introverted style, which involved rather more talking to each other than talking to the audience. Before Moyles arrived, Bannister's struggles to manage change at Radio One in the face of huge audience losses and extensive adverse newspaper coverage were, in essence, due to a gross mismatch between his presenters' 'on air' work and his audience's expectations.

For this reason, it is common for programme controllers and

producers to choose presenters from **demos**, either of specially-recorded links between songs, or compiled from **airchecks** of existing programmes (see Appendix). A relatively sophisticated bid by an independent producer for the contract to provide a live sequence would probably include at least a brief demo, or a pilot of the programme, demonstrating the style of the presenter, and the manner in which the various regular items would be introduced and presented.

There is a delicate balance to be struck in dual presentation between the presenters relating to each other 'on air' – perhaps amusingly – and acknowledging the presence of the listener. By contrast, the success of Wright, Evans and Moyles demonstrated that conversation in the studio can be inclusive, while being entertaining and attracting large audiences, but some of the BBC's other experiments resulted not only in falling ratings, but at times some pretty depressing listening (Garfield, 1998, 163–8). Despite the high-profile disasters, though, multiple presentation has become more common in the United Kingdom over the last decade – partly because of Wright, Evans and Moyles – and in the early 2000s for example, the GWR network of **ILR** stations exploited what it perceived to be a successful formula by featuring different 'Breakfast Crews' on each of its stations.

Except when dealing with a particularly moving item or news story, during a period of national mourning or for some other special reason, presentation should be bright and lively. Few people turn on the radio to be depressed, and for many people it will be a form of escapism – for example, to lighten a repetitive work routine, to keep them alert when driving, or to provide a stimulating background for customers in a shop or a hairdressing salon. Because audience ratings are the principal measure of success of all but the most self-indulgent of broadcasting, making listeners want to listen and to keep listening should be the prime objective of anyone producing or presenting a lengthy sequence 'on air' (see Chapter 4). For the duration of the three, four or even five-hour-long programme, the fortunes of the whole radio station are in the hands of the presenter and the producer of the live sequence.

Of course, if handled well, there are times when, paradoxically, being downbeat can have great listener appeal. The huge ratings success of Simon Bates's *Our Tune* feature on the pre-Bannister Radio One was largely due to the emotional value of the sad listener stories he read out over an instrumental track from Zeffirelli's *Romeo and Juliet* (Montgomery, 1991, 138). His distinctive 'golden brown' voice and the pace and manner of his delivery made *Our Tune* compulsive listening, and the requested 'tune' was always a recognizable hit record, but Bates was always quick to reassert his more usual friendly joviality immediately after the item. Kenny Everett was irrepressibly effervescent 'on air' (positioning himself as 'Kuddly' Ken), and Frank Skinner's style on Absolute Radio is also light and approachable. Some stations will programme gentler music in the late evening, and presentation styles should reflect the material around their links, but there are few examples of music presenters who achieve ratings success through seeking to alienate their audiences. Some interesting biographical material exists in published form, including Rusling (2001).

Exercise 3.1

Continue the table below, filling in the blank spaces and adding more examples of presenter styles on a range of different radio stations. Discuss your answers in class – for example, you should reconcile the styles with their time slots and target audiences.

Context and target audience	Average link duration	Typical link content	Description of presentation style
Nick Grimshaw, BBC Radio One: breakfast show – 15–24 year olds		Chats about music, topical and showbiz items	Familiar, often amused and sometimes quite excitable
Your local commercial station: breakfast show – (audience varies according to station)			
Simon Bates, Smooth Radio morning show – mature females			
Steve Wright, BBC Radio Two: *Steve Wright In The Afternoon* – 25–55 year olds			

Sequence content

Until the 1960s, it was common for most genres of radio programme – including live sequences – to have **theme** or **signature tunes** at the beginning and the end (see Chapter 5), but since then the trend has been for sequences on music stations to launch straight into the first song. Certain programmes and presenters resisted the trend and remained associated with particularly recognizable theme tunes for many years. A good example was Jimmy Young, who used *Town Talk*, recorded in 1966 by Ken Woodman and his Piccadilly Brass, until it was eventually reworked and incorporated into a Radio Two jingle just for him. Famously, Alan 'Fluff' Freeman presented his *Pick of the Pops* – from 1961 on the BBC's Light Programme, then from 1967 on the new Radio One, and later on Radio Two – to a 1960 recording of *Sign of the Swingin' Cymbal* by Brian Fahey.

Sequences need **signposting**, just as the road network would be unnavigable if drivers couldn't depend on regular and clear indications as to where they are going. The similarities between signposting in sequences and that on the roads end there, because the primary aim of the live sequence is to hold the listeners' attention and encourage them to continue to listen – returning again as soon as possible. At regular intervals, the programme should indicate what is to come and – subtly – why listeners should want to hear it. This can be overdone, and producers should take care to ensure that the signposting itself doesn't become a reason to turn off the radio, or worse still to tune to another station. Only where a station is part of a range of services, such as those provided by the BBC, and where producers are confident that listeners retuning their radios won't happen across something more appealing, should they even contemplate suggesting they should do so. Much more common in presenter links, certainly before it became a cliché, was the phrase 'don't touch that dial'!

Promoting forward needs to be credible, to avoid being counter-productive. That is, the future programme events being promised should be significant enough to deserve the attention. Strong examples are a competition coming up later, a traffic and travel bulletin just 'one song away' or an interview with a celebrity 'after the news at three o'clock'. Station policy towards signposting before commercial breaks varies widely. Especially where breaks are lengthy, there is a lot of sense in promising the listener something to continue listening for, and the prospect of an uninterrupted **music sweep** of 20 minutes of classic oldies may be enough to keep large numbers of them through a barrage of advertising. Another view is that drawing listeners' attention to the break may in itself be a reason for them to tune out. A common phrase on ILR before the lighter-touch regulation of the Radio Authority and then Ofcom was 'When we come back' – as was 'I'll be back after the break' – because the previous **regulator**, the Independent Broadcasting Authority, insisted on advertising being clearly differentiated from programming. Today, many programmers feel it is unwise to suggest the presenter is going away for the duration of the ad break, in case parting company becomes too easy for the listener, who then might feel more inclined to retune or switch off.

Signposting may be more sophisticated than the simple verbal promises discussed above. Playing audio – an extract from an interview, yesterday's competition winner sounding pleased or a quick **segue** of the **hook** of each of the next four or five songs – can add interest and excitement to the programme and enhance its production values. In a chart show, as it counts down to the number one slot, playing brief clips of the main contenders can add to the intrigue, and these are probably, after all, among the audience's current favourites. **Stings** or idents (see pages 109–14) to top and tail the audio signpost, or even between different elements within it, can be used to make it more interesting. In every case, the pace of the signpost should be considered when planning what precedes it and what comes next.

Idents have an important role to play in sequences generally. They commonly identify the station, the programme, the presenter and specific features, such as regular competitions, but they also play an important role in controlling pace and providing continuity. Careful consideration needs to be given as to which ident is placed where. Again, indiscriminate use can prove alienating, but used skilfully, they can provide cohesion – holding the **product** (the programme) together and reinforcing the complementary **branding** of the programme, the presenter and the station (see Chapter 4). Just as written **discourse** is, by **convention**, punctuated with **symbols** that organize the language into sense groups, control pace and provide an element of segregation between related but intrinsically separate content, so too does the ident. There is also a recognition factor that shouldn't be underestimated – a regular feature that unfailingly begins with the same **opener** can be more effective in retaining listener loyalty because it is familiar.

Pace should only change abruptly when it will not disrupt the programme's flow or continuity. Punchy, fast items can lose impact if followed by a very soft introduction to a song which builds slowly with, for example, a light piano solo, in much the same way as thought must be given to the order of musical items when planning musical content (see Chapter 4). An ident can provide a smoother transition, especially where it is itself transitional in pace, perhaps beginning fast and hard, then shifting down to a softer ending. Similarly, a transitional ident which *gathers* pace can assist with progression from a more reflective interview (for instance, after discussing a recent death) into a brighter song intended to lift the mood of the programme and return it to a more upbeat equilibrium.

Presenters talking before or after an ident should avoid double continuity, or the repetition of what the ident itself makes clear. This can sound as though the presenter is unaware of the ident, or is ill prepared, and most unnecessary repetition can be irritating, particularly if it becomes habitual. More creative use of an ident can improve its integration into the sequence and a subtler reinforcement of its core message. Strong examples often involve the presenter referring to it obliquely, or referring to the content it precedes: before the traffic and travel **sting**, the presenter could '**tease**' news of a long delays on a major route, or simply say 'if you're on the road, this is for you'.

Presentation techniques

When addressing the audience, presenters and others should always use the singular. While it is hoped listeners are numerous, to address them as if speaking to a crowd is to fail to fully exploit one of the key strengths of the medium of radio (Crisell, 1994, 10). The relative intimacy of radio – which is often listened to by individuals working, travelling or otherwise occupied on their own – allows the broadcaster to communicate with each one as if addressing them personally. This suggests a deeper relationship than might be achieved with someone who is more obviously talking to a large number of people at once. Asking 'how are you today?', although broadcast, is more commonly read as a direct question to a single listener, who may through repeated exposure have already become a 'friend'. The ratings imperative which drives most broadcasting renders it a more sensible approach than 'how are you *all* today?' which, since it is addressed to a collective, may place less of an obligation on each listener to stay tuned.

Presenters' different modes of address were parodied by Robin Williams in *Good Morning Vietnam* (1987: B. Levinson), where his own character made considerably more impact on listeners to a fictitious forces station because of his relative informality. Others who habitually spoke 'at' their audience, rather than 'to' them, failed to connect with them as effectively, because they only addressed them indirectly – with such phrases as: 'Greetings and salutations to any and all service personnel in the area' and 'Those men who lost equipment in last

Figure 3.2

Neil Fox 'on air' on Capital, before moving to Magic 105.4. Note that he has chosen to stand at the microphone, rather than the more usual sitting position.

week's rains are asked to contact. . .'. More unusual approaches in real life include that of Wolfman Jack, whose daily sequences were broadcast across the United States from Mexico on a very high-powered transmitter, between 1962 and 1995 – also reaching appreciative audiences in Europe and elsewhere via syndication to the American Forces Network (AFN). Jack's links were punctuated by his own regular wolf-like 'barking', seen in the film *American Graffiti* (1973: G. Lucas), and he was one of Emperor Rosko's early influences before his debut on Radio One (Rosko, 1976, 153).

Beginners may rely more on scripted links than those who have many years' experience of presenting sequences. If writing links, it is important to remember that this is the discourse of the approachable but authoritative friend. Scripting should not be apparent to the listener, though, and it may be easier to sound natural if you write down key bullet points or phrases, and then practise *ad libbing* around them. Relying on a precise script makes it harder to adapt to changing situations, such as running over or under time, whereas being able to expand or contract the length of the link can be a useful skill when talking over song **intros** (see page 77). Whichever the approach used, links should use the grammar and the language of the spoken word, while recognizing that different audiences will expect different balances between familiarity and formality. An obvious comparison is between the brash, streetwise style often heard on Radio One, and the measured, respectful delivery of the BBC's cultural network, Radio Three. Being oneself, rather than a second rate imitation of someone else's on-air persona, is generally considered to be more successful.

Links

Links should have a clear direction and **purpose**, and even the most successful presenters with the longest experience will organize their thoughts before opening the **microphone fader** and beginning to speak. Although presenter chat may *sound* spontaneous, usually even the most informal of broadcasters will have planned quite carefully what they intend to say in any given link. They know in advance how the links will begin and end, and what they intend to achieve in them – be it to signpost future items, read out text messages or e-mails received, announce a competition winner or simply to commiserate with the listener over the defeat of the local football team. The best links don't confuse or overload the listeners with too much detail or complication. The link must somehow pick up off the back of the previous item, and if it is a song, a simple **back announcement** of the artist and title may be welcomed by many in the audience, particularly if the song is a long-forgotten favourite. Some stations have presentation house styles which prevent any mention of the music, although they are likely to get more than their fair share of telephone queries from listeners who want to know what a song they heard was, but couldn't quite identify from memory. A survey carried out in 2002 by

Paragon Media Strategies found 89 per cent of responses favoured more back announcing *on their own* stations.

House styles often prescribe how key ideas should be expressed, such as the station name and frequency and any positioning statement (such as 'More music variety'). Links may have to always begin or end with such information, and the rationale behind that is to enhance **brand** awareness (see Chapter 4). More recently, in the United Kingdom the practice of restricting presenters to reading out a range of simple liners has lost ground to once again encouraging them to express their personalities 'on air'. Either way, there are likely to be scripts scheduled to be read out at specific times and these may be **public service announcements**, live **trails** for forthcoming programming or promotional events, or even advertising and sponsorship messages. These may be programmed by computer and displayed at the appropriate time on a monitor, or in the case of **PSAs** written on paper or a whiteboard displayed on the studio wall (Chapter 4).

Competitions

Competitions can add both interest and excitement to sequences. The television quiz format, *Who Wants to be a Millionaire*, which is syndicated around the world, began as a phone-in segment of Chris Tarrant's top-rated breakfast programme on the original 95.8 Capital FM. Audience participation in a programme, if handled well, gives the presenter the opportunity to interact positively with listener proxies, who are often represented as 'typical' listeners. Careful screening of which listeners are put to air won't guarantee that the conversation is lively, interesting and amusing, but it makes it more likely. Local radio stations can benefit from the recognition factor when listeners hear people on the radio from their own neighbourhood, and this can enhance the appearance of localness, which the station may be attempting to exploit. The mechanics of the competition, the prize, and the answer to any question asked may even be coincidental to the interaction between the presenter and the listener – or the prize may be very valuable and represent considerable investment by the radio station in the competition as a means of drawing in new listeners and increasing audience ratings. Often such a big prize competition will be promoted well beyond the confines of the station's own output, on billboards, in the press or on television.

Recent examples of successful competitions include identifying a mystery voice or a popular song played backwards, answering trivia questions, working out a lateral-thinking problem and sorting famous names into the currently living and the deceased. More complicated approaches can include sending a **radio car** with an FM link to the studio, round to the competitor's home or workplace, perhaps with another presenter on board who will handle the remote end of the event. Relying on an FM link or even a mobile phone or wireless connection without previously testing the location for reception is, though, to tempt fate – and it would be unfortunate to give the item a hard sell, only for it to be abandoned. An unsuccessful outcome to a competition on Virgin Radio in 2002 was a £75,000 fine and the sacking of the presenter, because it involved a nine-year-old girl caller in language that breached the regulator's standards of taste and decency, even late at night (*Guardian*, 2002). Another station, BRMB, was fined £15,000 after encouraging three listeners to sit on blocks of dry ice in an endurance contest (Wilson, 2003).

Live interviews

Interviews in live sequences can enhance them considerably – or, without careful preparation, and if luck is against you, they can have an adverse effect. Beaman traced the history of the live interview, from uncertain origins at a time when nobody at the BBC felt the broadcasting of the first one ever was important enough to place on record (2000, 1–5). In the 1930s, both questions and answers would be scripted beforehand, with the interviewees reading back their own words in what was, inevitably, a comparatively stilted performance. Of course, then – as now – if interviews are broadcast live, there is more scope for disaster than when pre-recording or making a package, perhaps because the wrong word gets broadcast, the guest fails to turn up on time or – worse still – there is a potential **libel** (see Chapter 9). One of the attractions of live radio, though, is unpredictability, although sadly, some interviewees cannot be trusted to respect common and regulatory standards of **taste and decency** in their language, even 'on air'. A professional judgement by Radio One to prerecord Oasis members Liam and Noel Gallagher, rather than broadcast them live, could have avoided the negative publicity that followed their 'on air' bad language and endorsement of illegal drugs (Garfield, 1998, 247–53) on an early evening programme. Many apparently live interviews are in fact pre-recorded, affording the producer some scope for editing out unwanted material, but it is not a good use of anyone's time to pre-record a greater duration than will be broadcast and then to carry out extensive post-production on it. Pre-records risk completely losing the impetus of live work if they are approached too casually.

Before the interview, the presenter must have a clear interview plan (see Chapter 2) and a high degree of confidence that the interviewee will both sound acceptable 'on air' and also be able to perform to expectations when the microphones are turned on. Depending on the station, and how much time may be allowed between songs before programmers fear listener tune-out will become an issue, it may be necessary to break the interview into two – or more – separate parts. Four or five minutes of solid speech may be as much as the audience can take, before playing music and then returning to the guest. Generally, the interview needs to be of a high quality in order to merit more than two parts. The song in the middle may, if scheduling allows, be related to the topic (a pop star's latest release, perhaps). Care should be taken on resuming the interview, to recap on the guest's identity and any very key point made previously, so new listeners who have tuned in during the music may quickly feel involved in the conversation, as opposed to feeling disorientated and confused. Interviews need particular attention to be paid to the set-up and the exit, particularly when the guest's identity alone is insufficient to set the interview in an understandable context for the listener. Only celebrities – and those who have by accident or action achieved some notoriety – may already be well known enough to require little introduction (see Chapter 5).

Dealing with a live guest includes the meet and greet upon arrival at the station – meaning that the reception staff need to be expecting the guest. You will have a preferred point during the programme when you would like the guest to be brought in, and it should be clear to whoever is responsible for this when you want it to happen. A reasonable amount of time is needed for the guest to get settled in front of the microphone and to take in what may seem very unusual surroundings. If the guest is there for too long before the interview, he or she may just be a distraction for the presenter, and possibly have an adverse effect on the links preceding the interview. Similarly, once the interview is over there is usually a good case for getting rid of the guest as quickly – and politely – as possible. This may again be the responsibility of the receptionist, or in larger programme teams, the producer or a production assistant.

In setting up the guest microphone, it is important to recognize that the guest may move about during the interview, particularly if nervous, and setting the position and **level** of the **mic** before beginning the item (see Chapter 1) will be ineffectual if he or she suddenly sits back from it to answer the questions. Part of the preparation is to make sure the guest is comfortable and feels confident about what is going to happen when the interview begins. Explaining the importance of not moving farther away from or closer to the microphone, and even asking the guest to sit with elbows on the table, can help to discourage shifting around. When the guest is comfortable, that is the moment to position the microphone and test the level. All this must be done while a song is playing, of course, and the microphones are turned off. An all-speech programme with few recorded items to provide breaks from live microphone work presents particular problems in getting inexperienced contributors in and out of the studio.

Interviewers each have their own styles. Jimmy Young popularized the political interview on his otherwise music and consumer affairs-oriented sequence on Radio Two between 1973 and 2002. Politicians such as Margaret Thatcher and Tony Blair are supposed to have enjoyed the gentler style of the *JY Show*, when compared to that of John Humphrys on Radio Four's *Today*. Young was certainly less inclined to interrupt, and it is matters such as the balance between courtesy and insistence, between friendliness and formality and between gravitas and levity, that have to be decided by each interviewer for each particular interview in turn. An interview with the Prime Minister may share some aspects with one with a chef, but the dissimilarities are likely to be greater.

'Driving' the desk

Operating the desk for a live sequence requires precision and the ability to think ahead. Depending on the level of automation in the studio (see Chapter 4) a number of different programme items will need to be set up in advance of their being needed, and it is unusual for all but the most skilled and experienced of operators to be able to do this while performing to the microphone. Setting up microphones before they are needed, and adjusting the levels where necessary, is but one task which may need to be repeated several times during a programme. If music is to be played off CD or other separate **sources**, such as a web site, there may be some adjustment needed to their respective **channels** on the mixing desk, if consistent levels are to be achieved. Pre-recorded speech items may also need some adjustment before being put to air, as may idents (see Chapter 4), which are today most likely to be accessed via the station's playout software.

Lining up items and setting levels cannot be done with the faders open for those sources, or they will be heard 'on air' before they are wanted. Broadcast mixing desks are equipped with at least one separate circuit, which is designed for this purpose. **Pre-fade listening** (PFL) is, as its name suggests, a way of hearing (and measuring on a meter on the desk) any individual source without it being broadcast. Different desks are configured in different ways, and it is important to learn how to select PFL – and to deselect it again – on the desk you are to use, well before beginning your first programme. Using PFL becomes second nature to most desk operators as they become more experienced, but at first it may seem complicated and awkward. Some broadcasters even ignore levels, believing that the station's **compressor** will even out inconsistencies. They may have some levels set so high they make the meter readings exceed the end of the scale, expecting that the **limiter** will prevent any **over-modulation** from distorting the output. This is not good practice, and it is often disparaged by engineering staff, who may be correct in pointing out that processors cannot always cope with the excesses of some of the more casual desk operators.

Figure 3.3

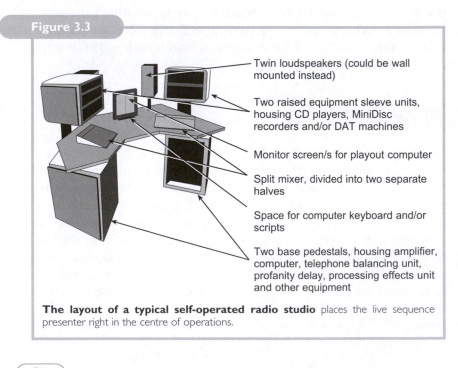

Twin loudspeakers (could be wall mounted instead)

Two raised equipment sleeve units, housing CD players, MiniDisc recorders and/or DAT machines

Monitor screen/s for playout computer

Split mixer, divided into two separate halves

Space for computer keyboard and/or scripts

Two base pedestals, housing amplifier, computer, telephone balancing unit, profanity delay, processing effects unit and other equipment

The layout of a typical self-operated radio studio places the live sequence presenter right in the centre of operations.

Levels are particularly important when doing **talkovers**. Links may be done 'dry', where the presenter's voice is the only sound broadcast, or they may more interestingly be performed over the introduction or the end of a song. Listeners sometimes object because presenters talk over their favourite songs, but unless a song is drastically cut short, they normally neither complain nor even notice this broadcasting convention. Talkovers integrate the presenter's discourse with the musical **narrative** of a sequence, allowing for a smoother transition from link to song to link. Presenters who do slick talkovers right up to the beginning of the vocals on a song often derive great satisfaction from it, too. This takes practice, attention to the duration of the intro and a certain amount of skill. If the talkover under-runs the duration of the intro it is much less of a problem than an over-run. When the presenter 'crashes' the vocal of the beginning song, it is much more likely to annoy listeners, as well as sounding much less professional and competent than the smooth, 'tight' link which would have resulted had it worked better.

The pre-recorded elements of a sequence – including music, features and advertisements – provide regular opportunities for setting up subsequent items. They are occasional stepping-stones across the often-turbulent waters of the open microphone. Where presentation and technical operation are being done from the same studio space, the operator should think ahead and line up everything that will be needed up to and including the next substantial pre-record, for only then will the next opportunity arise to line up the next few items. Studio discipline requires that the next programme team arrive in the studio in time to set up before the preceding programme ends, but *without* disrupting its last few links. Similarly, when the programme ends, they should be able to get out swiftly, after handing over to the next with a minimum of fuss. Some stations are well resourced enough to alternate between twin studios, which allows each programme team the luxury of setting up and packing away without being disturbed. It is common for presenters to establish an on-air dialogue between studios around changeover time, as has long been the practice at Radio Two.

Communication between studios, and between the studio and other contributing locations, such as the news-reading booth, a sports ground, a remote studio from where a guest is to be interviewed and so on, is normally established via the **talkback** system. In essence an intercom, talkback is used to advise the studio if there is a problem, to request being put 'on air' because a goal has been scored or to ask the remote contributor to provide some level.

Plan and produce a music-based sequence programme, either in a small team or individually. Aim to enhance the programme with speech items that are appropriate to your chosen context, target audience and daypart. Chapter 4 includes useful advice on scheduling the music for your programme.

Analysing sequences

There are similarities between analysing shorter items such as speech packages (see Chapter 2) and analysing longer live sequences, which can be of several hours' duration. Most of the concepts discussed in other chapters are relevant here, particularly because sequences often include other generic forms, such as packages, advertisements (see Chapter 6), and phone-in elements, such as competitions or discussions (pages 87–8). An interesting example is Montgomery's detailed **textual analysis** of Simon Bates's *Our Tune* (Radio One), although it now seems rather dated by its belonging to the network's pre-Bannister era (1991, 138–77). However, the practicalities of studying very long texts may mean some different approaches are needed. It may be reasonable to sample a five-hour long sequence, **deconstructing** a single hour of it in the hope that it is representative of the whole, but this must be done self-critically, recognizing the limitations of the analysis and testing conclusions against further samples of the other, 'missing' hours.

The unifying feature of most sequences is the presentation: the centrality of the presenter being reflected not just in the physical design of most studios used in the genre (see page 63), but also in the **representation** being constructed 'on air'. Presenters who operate the studio equipment themselves enjoy uncommon levels of control over those around them. For instance other contributors such as traffic and travel reporters speak only on **cue**, and studio guests are introduced and interviewed by the presenter, normally responding only to the agenda set by the questions. The zoo format (see page 63) generally positions an individual presenter in the middle of a group of sycophants, all eager to please, laughing, applauding and providing only supportive interjections to order, in feigned spontaneity – but it is not their 'show' and they are only there by invitation.

Double-headed or multiple presentation usually casts all but the 'main' presenter in the role of the sidekick, again performing to order, until the music begins again or an ident heralds the arrival of a different item. Even the music appears to collude in this – when things are going well in the studio presenter talkovers run tightly up to the vocals, so effectively the artists sing only when the presenters fall silent, and the songs are faded when the often erratic presenter discourse begins again. When presenters abuse this ability to control, and they silence or interrupt others, cut off phone-in callers or talk extensively over the end of discs they have part-faded too early, audience reactions can turn to protest and the more sinister potential of this power play becomes more apparent. On Radio One, the attitude of Chris Evans to his assistant Holly Samos (Boshoff, 1997) and Chris Moyles's encouragement of a 'sexy slapper' of a listener to strip for him in the studio can reasonably be read as legitimizing an abuse of women by men that many would consider unacceptable (Garfield, 1998, 222–6).

The gender issue in sequence presentation is an important one. Neer's account of early FM radio in the United States explains that until WNEW in New York launched an 'all-girl' line-up in 1964, such a concept was 'alien'. Exclusively male stations had been the norm, because female voices were considered 'unsuitable' for the technical characteristics of the AM broadcast band, 'medium wave' (Neer, 2001, 62–3). Forty years on, the odds may still favour male presenters. Women have made progress, but men continue to dominate in this role. Of course, there have been notable exceptions, including Alison Steele, a 'giant' of WNEW who survived the three-year 'all-girl' initiative by 12 years and whose distinguished career continued until her death in 1995. In the United Kingdom, Annie Nightingale joined Radio One in 1970 as the 'token woman', but found the culture of the station problematic (Garfield, 1998, 15).

As it is mainly men who wield the power bestowed on sequence presenters, this might reinforce notions of women as being suitable only for lesser roles. In male/female partnerships, although superficially 'balanced', the woman is the most likely to sit on the 'wrong' side of the mixing desk – and so she is positioned as the sidekick (Mitchell, 2001, 273). Various studies have examined the gender imbalance in different territories, including that by Michaels and Mitchell (2000, 240) who found that in the United Kingdom most female presenters were actually working as *co*-presenters on breakfast. It follows, therefore, that only a minority of women presenters are given their 'own' programmes. Michaels and Mitchell also asked managers why so few women succeeded in gaining such high-profile jobs in radio, and confirmed widely held impressions that fewer women actually apply.

Relatively recent 'girlification' of BBC Radio One, including the scheduling of high-profile presenters Zoë Ball and then Sara Cox on breakfast, has begun to alter perceptions about the suitability of women in a male-dominated environment (ibid, 2000, 246), but initial tabloid press labelling of them as 'ladettes' could easily confuse this message (Wells, 2002a). Women are much better represented 'on air' in news than in programmes, and as unfavourable comparisons are easy to make between the levels of intellect required to be a reporter and to be a 'DJ', the situation may not be so bleak. Perhaps more women seek what they perceive to be a more challenging role than one that is often misinterpreted as merely 'chatting up' a grateful and unquestioning audience of housewives. More considered analyses of common relationships between sequence presenters and female listeners are to be found in Barnard (1989, 141–50), although both contexts and attitudes have changed considerably since then.

Fewer presenters originate from ethnic minorities. There are obvious cultural and linguistic obstacles to complete mobility of presenters between radio stations that serve widely differing communities, just as only Welsh speakers are able to achieve high-profile roles on the BBC's Welsh-language service, Radio Cymru, and Catalonians on Catalan-speaking stations in Spain. In most markets in the United States, several stations target Hispanic communities, and presentation on them is, quite reasonably, almost exclusively by Hispanics. There are of course exceptions, and for example between 1973 and 1993 crews of mainly white English men broadcast with measurable success to Hebrew and Arabic speakers in Israel and beyond on the offshore pirate, the Voice of Peace – by restricting their links to seven seconds (Starkey, 2002). Where communities and their radio stations are not divided linguistically, though, belonging to the majority ethnic group shouldn't be a *sine qua non*. Interestingly, when white presenters such as John Ravenscroft, Nicholas Henty-Dodd and Maurice Cole adopt more **radiogenic** pseudonyms for their on-air identities (John Peel, Simon Dee and Kenny Everett respectively), it is unusual for them to choose names that are more closely associated with different ethnic or religious groups, for example Mohammed or Shlomo – although to do so could be interpreted as deceptive, and therefore ethically problematic.

There is far greater mobility across regions. In such territories as the United Kingdom, which are large enough to include a wide variety of different and discernible regional accents of the same language within their boundaries, it is much more common – indeed almost inevitable, given the instability of short-term, temporary contracts – that presentation talent will move away from its birthplace and forge a career elsewhere. This is particularly desirable in the case of national radio stations based in a capital, which can at times seem very distant from much of their audiences, and until Chris Evans recreated his on-air personality on taking over the breakfast show in 2010 BBC Radio Two's two main morning presenters were the Irishman, Terry Wogan and the Scot, Ken Bruce.

In local radio non-indigenous presenters can sound more incongruous, because often stations will exploit their localness in order to connect with their more geographically defined audience, and the presence of a northern accent in the southern county of Dorset, for example, will easily confuse this message. Although there might seem to be compelling reasons to programme only Scousers in Liverpool, Brummies in the Midlands and Cockneys in London, this is demonstrably not common practice in the United Kingdom, where acquired local knowledge of the area is often enough to inspire empathy. In Liverpool, for example (a city with an extraordinarily strong local identity), among the voices that have made the greatest impact on listeners to local radio have been not only the strongly scouse-accented Billy Butler (BBC Radio Merseyside, Radio City) and Johnny Kennedy (Radio City), but also the very Irish-sounding Arthur Murphy (Radio City), Tony McKenzie from Kent (Radio City) and Dave Lincoln (Radio City) – whose radio career began at Staffordshire Hospital Radio (Rusling, 2001, 298). It is reasonable to consider what listeners might construe, either consciously or sub-consciously, from a radio station in the Midlands – another area with strong regional accents – that only featured local voices in roles that were subordinate to presenters who sounded as though they had been brought in from elsewhere.

Just as voice can **connote** origin – and, perhaps, allegiance – in regional, class, ethnic and other terms, sequences contain many other elements that can be studied for their **semiotic** value. Tony Blackburn's early programmes on BBC Radio One featured the bark of his 'pet' dog Arnold. Although in the studio Arnold was just a sound effect, only a minority of listeners would have realized this and most imagined he was actually there – exactly the meaning Blackburn wanted the effect to connote. Peirce's categorization of smoke as indexical of fire (1960) compares with the bark as an **index** of dog – or, because of previous and further contextualization by Blackburn, of

Arnold himself. This is just one of many media constructs which are, in essence, a deception. Personality presenters who use humour extensively in their sequences may use many effects in this way (see Chapter 8). Other **codes** operate in sequences, such as the demarcation of feature items by recognizable idents that precede and succeed them, and beds that, by their repeated use, become associated with particular regular features such as horoscopes.

In addition to the obvious, structural conventions of the genre, as described in the practical section of this chapter (such as the normally **closed narrative structure**), other conventions relate to content and style. For example, the conventional **mode of address** used by sequence presenters is one that seeks to exploit and reinforce the personal relationship between the voice on the radio and the listener (Crisell, 1986, 10), who is often listening alone. How individuals approach this does of course vary. Alan Freeman's cheery but essentially glib 'Greetings Pop Pickers' contrasts with the more common 'How are you today?' formula. In fact, the former example, although a catchphrase which served Freeman well over a career spanning 40 years on the BBC's Light programme and then on Radios One and Two, ignored one of the first 'rules' of radio: that you address the listener only in the singular, as if talking to one person alone.

Presenter discourse, although apparently switching between such disparate subjects as the weather, music, interviewees, and sponsor credits, may reveal tendencies to favour a single **ideology** over competing ones. Strict guidelines operate in some territories over 'balance' in coverage of political or controversial issues (see phone-ins, right), and of course in others the role of the presenter may be to propagandize on behalf of a ruling elite or to represent a revolutionary opposition. However, even the most superficially benign chitchat over, for instance, the entertainment news in the tabloid press can be read as adding an ideological slant to the discourse. Repeated references to celebrity gossip reinforce notions of the primacy of the rich and famous and the appropriateness of fame and wealth bestowing privilege on those who are lucky enough to benefit from them. Deference to a monarchy and reverence to those born into it often underpin even amusing, gossipy tales of their infidelities and indiscretions, and these knowing insights to which listeners are regularly treated contribute to an unrelenting cross-media **naturalization** of hereditary privilege which demotes alternative perspectives such as meritocracy and republicanism to the status of either dangerous or irrelevant deviance. Brand and Scannell's analysis of Tony Blackburn's presenter discourse is rich in examples (1991, 201–26). Other examples of ideological influences permeating presenter discourse – especially in the case of **newstalk** and phone-ins – include disdain for strikers, support for strikers, disrespect for teachers and others in authority, the reinforcement of class distinctions, sexism, ageism, religious conformism and atheism (see below).

Presenters may also encourage lifestyles that some listeners will consider harmful, such as smoking, promiscuity, drug taking and drinking. **Audience response** to such issues will, not however, be uniform, and active models of audience behaviour suggest that reactions to such issues will vary. Committed smokers, for example, may resent any anti-smoking 'propaganda', of which non-smokers might approve. Campaigners against alcohol abuse will respond differently from most people on hearing talk of a heavy night's clubbing, or even of drinking a glass of wine over a meal. While marriage and dual parenthood may be among the ideals of many people, there are others who have found themselves more suited to alternatives. Ethnic minorities may have little in common with majority lifestyles, too, and so it is likely that there will be a wide range of reactions to what presenters themselves may consider to be an innocent *ad lib*.

Phone-ins

Phone-in programmes are a particular type of sequence, and the newstalk phone-in is one of the most popular programme formats in the United States. Typically all speech, the phone-in can be amusing, serious, controversial and harrowing in quick succession, depending on the nature of the calls it includes. The content may be subject-specific, such as BBC Radio Four's *Any Questions* or *Check Up*, which concern themselves with politics and health respectively. Others appear to allow the callers to set the agenda for the discussion ('Hello, what do you want to talk about?'), and can range widely within individual programmes from, for example, current affairs to patent hangover cures. Proposing a new phone-in sequence involves specifying what kind of subject it hopes to cover, even if over time expectations prove to have been misguided.

The centrality of the presenter in the phone-in sequence is not negotiable. Unlike the music sequence, which may include a minimum of speech, the phone-in requires a high level of presentation because this is essentially a dialogue between the presenter and a number of callers. The presenter plays an overt role in setting the

Exercise 3.3

Continue the table below, filling in the blank spaces and adding more examples of phone-in programmes on a range of different radio stations. Discuss your answers in class – for example, you should reconcile the content with their time slots and target audiences.

Context, title, presenter and target audience	Type of phone-in sequence	Typical length of calls used 'on air'	Description of presentation style
Radio Four: Saturday 2.02 pm, *Any Answers*, Anita Anand, average age 53	News and current affairs: listeners' responses to *Any Questions* broadcast before it		Quite formal, allows listeners to put their point, then often politely plays devil's advocate
Radio Five Live: Saturday 6.06 pm, *Six-O-Six*, Jason Roberts, football fans	Football, on Saturday evenings after matches have finished		Sometimes matey, sometimes antagonistic about callers' teams
talkSPORT: weekdays 6–10 am, *Sport Breakfast*, Alan Brazil, sports fans, mainly male			

agenda – perhaps introducing a list of acceptable topics for debate, beginning and curtailing each conversation, signposting before advertisement breaks and the news, and so on. While many phone-in hosts maintain an atmosphere of cordiality towards callers, some are more antagonistic, and this is one area in which personality is an important variable in controlling the style and nature of the sequence. In the United Kingdom in the late 1970s, James Stannage was promoted by Manchester's ILR station, Piccadilly Radio as 'the rudest man on radio' and the popularity of Stannage's late-night programme was attributed to listeners' desire to be verbally abused by him 'on air'. Television comedian Jasper Carrott (BBC1) considered Stannage's style to be so funny that he famously parodied on stage his earlier programmes on Signal Radio in Stoke-on-Trent. Similar approaches by Allan Beswick (on, for example, Red Rose Radio), James Whale (Radio Aire) and the Scottie McClue character created by Archibald Colin Lamont (Red Rose) also proved popular. In the United States the phenomenon of the 'shock jock' demonstrated the success of the format there, and

Howard Stern's career was dramatized for the cinema in *Private Parts* (1997: B. Thomas). Eric Bogosian's fictional character Barry Champlain met with critical acclaim, but his antagonistic attitude to his callers had unfortunate consequences in the film *Talk Radio* (1988: O. Stone).

Phone-ins are likely to require more personnel than a single producer-presenter, especially if the callers are to be screened before they are put to air. When the format was first introduced to the United Kingdom by London's news and information station, LBC, in 1973, genuine callers were scarce at times, particularly in the very early mornings. Failing to discriminate between callers, and to select only those which meet certain criteria is, however, tempting fate, although it may satisfy certain notions of public access radio. Ideally, every caller who is allowed to speak on the programme will have been spoken to beforehand, either by the producer or by a researcher, who should attempt to identify those who will sound most interesting, have something relevant to say and not be too much of a liability in terms of potential issues of libel and taste and decency (see Chapter 9). The call screener should quickly determine the value of the caller in terms of his or her likely contribution to the programme and the level of risk that the callers may misbehave 'on air'. There are polite ways of declining the callers' offer to take part *without* losing a listener for ever, but it is better to lose a single listener than lose hundreds of thousands of others who switch off through boredom, or to have to pay damages to someone who successfully pursues a libel action in court.

It is usual to attempt to reduce the risk of **defamation** and of swearing by callers, though the use of a **profanity delay**. This equipment delays the transmission of the programme as it leaves the studio, storing it digitally for a short time – usually ten seconds – which should be long enough for the desk operator to cut off the caller and begin something else playing out from the studio. It is important to pay attention to the callers as they speak 'on air', in case a libel or language considered unsuitable for the station gets on the air by mistake. A single, momentary lapse can cost even experienced and highly respected broadcasters their jobs, as in the case of Tommy Boyd at talkSPORT – when a failure to dump an abusive caller's remarks about the Royal Family provoked complaints (Hodgson, 2002). A convention of phone-ins is to identify callers only by their first names and locations. Apart from reinforcing radio's 'friendliness' and a station's geographical relevance to the listener, this can reduce the chance of accidental libel because of the relative anonymity of the callers (see Chapter 9).

Call screening should be done away from the live microphones of the studio, and preferably in an adjacent control room or cubicle that allows both eye contact between presenter and screener *and* communication by talkback into the presenter's headphones. The decisions as to who is put to air might be taken by a producer (if there is one) or the presenter, who should at least have some input into this – after all, it is the presenter who has to deal with the caller live 'on air'. Modern computer software, such as PhoneBox by Broadcast Bionics, allows those on both sides of the studio window to see which callers are lined up ready, a brief summary of what they *claim* they are going to say, and even a range of useful statistics, such as how frequently individual callers have been on the programme, whether they have been barred from appearing and so on. Until the arrival of such software, the physical act of putting callers live depended on raising and lowering the appropriate fader/s on the mixing desk and manually operating a **telephone balancing unit** (TBU), connecting the desk to the phone lines.

Figure 3.4

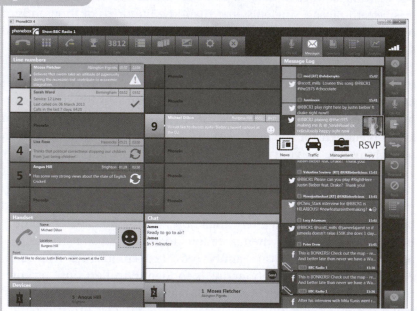

Screenshot of the PhoneBOX telephone handling software, which displays information about the callers and their contribution history.

Analysing phone-ins

All-speech phone-ins tend to be punctuated only by recorded idents repeating the telephone number and exhorting listeners to call, station and programme identification, and advertisements, if any. Others pause for music – perhaps as light relief, or perhaps because the presenter is working alone, and needs to break from the otherwise constant on-air dialogue to talk to the next batch of callers 'off air'. Of great interest is the actual discourse that is constructed during the course of the programme, by the sequence of callers, by what they say, and by the ways in which the presenter and any studio guests respond to them. Crisell identified three categories of phone-ins: expressive, exhibitionist and confessional (1994, 189–99), and there are useful comparisons to be made between examples within and across all three, especially when bearing in mind the various characteristics of the genre discussed on pages 83–6.

Where the topics are predetermined by the presenter, who asks for calls on a particular subject or a combination of subjects – or where callers are cut off rudely – audiences may have a more acute sense of the editorial control being exercised. Where callers seem to enjoy the freedom to talk to their own agenda, editorial control may be much less apparent, and it simply won't occur to many listeners how much selection lies behind the discourse presented to them. They don't perceive the role chance plays in allowing some callers, but not others, through to a busy switchboard, or that of the call screening by which someone – presenter, producer or assistant – decides which callers are then put to air and which are not. In a democracy, there are important issues of balance and bias here, especially but not only when the topics are controversial in terms of party politics (see Chapter 9). Even where issues transcend party divisions, such as over abortion or gay rights, real influence can be brought to bear on listeners, which may well alter their attitudes and future actions. However discerning listeners may be, as suggested by active models of audience response, the attention political parties pay to 'spin' and putting across their own **preferred readings** of events does suggest that they believe the media can influence voting intentions (Gibson, 2003b).

Achieving balance in a controversial phone-in can be difficult, especially where nobody seems to want to admit to unpopular views. In Liverpool, for example, left-wing callers to the city's local radio stations seem to far outweigh those on the political right, and so in

2002, immediately after the Queen Mother's death, there were far more callers put to air demanding an end to the monarchy than could have been contemplated in most other English cities. Where the presenter plays the devil's advocate, balancing some comments with opposing remarks or questioning, a succession of similar calls can seem to position the presenter on one side of the argument. Some callers will be poor advocates, too, of the position they represent in the discourse, and it is reasonable to question whether one caller actually does balance another if unable to articulate a point as clearly, if allowed less time than the other, or if subjected to harder questioning by the presenter (Starkey, 2007, 110–14).

4 Music Scheduling, Formats and Branding

In this chapter you will:

▶ learn how radio stations are formatted and branded, and music is scheduled
▶ work on scheduling music, station branding and making idents
▶ learn about and carry out audience research into listening patterns.

Programming principles

Until the late 1980s, the traditional **model** for scheduling music was permissive, in that individual programme producers (or, in the absence of a separate producer, the presenters) chose the music for their own programmes within the broad parameters laid down in a station's **music policy**. This practice served the radio industry well, from the early beginnings of the live sequence (see Chapter 3), through some of the most influential of eras, in which radio played a significant part in promoting musical **genres** from rock and roll, rhythm and blues and glam rock to disco, punk, new wave and the beginnings of house and garage. One of the most enduring **formats** through the ages has been the Top Forty, dating from 1949, when American radio stations first exploited the correlation between record sales charts and listener taste (Crisell, 1997, 136–9). As fashions for different musical genres changed, so did the nature of the music that received radio airplay, and of course airplay quickly began to influence the sales charts.

Crucial to the development of popular music was the airplay given by presenter Alan Freed in the early 1950s, to black music known as 'rhythm and blues'. He was the first to programme such acts as Bo Diddley, Chuck Berry and Frankie Lymon and the Teenagers on 'white' radio stations previously playing mainly crooners and swing. When he brought the music he called 'rock and roll' to WINS in New York, Freed began a cultural revolution, in which white performers such as Bill Haley and the Comets began to *Rock Around the Clock* before middle class audiences with relatively large disposable incomes. Similarly, it was Radio Luxembourg and then the offshore pirates from 1964 to 1967 that brought important musical influences across the Atlantic to the United Kingdom and which, in turn, inspired the first teenage declarations of cultural independence by the 'beat generation' and the swinging sixties in their wake (Wall, 2003).

In the more competitive and faster maturing American radio market, other early popular radio formats included Adult Contemporary (AC), Adult Oriented Rock (AOR), Urban and Golden Oldie, as well as the more specialized Country, Easy Listening, Middle of the Road (MOR), Gospel, Soul and Latin. Variations on established formats included Soft AC, Contemporary Hit Radio (CHR) and Hot Country, as stations experimented with music **playlists** in order to shift the appeal of their output to particular **demographic** groups. The United Kingdom market has matured quickly since the 1990s, particularly with the development of **digital platforms**, and programmers now feel more confident about devising original formats – often borrowing elements from others – in order to create a demand for their own stations. For example, in 2002 the EMAP Group (now Bauer Media) launched niche digital services named after the *Smash Hits* and *Kerrang!* titles in their magazine publishing division.

Typically, the music policy is determined by the Head of Music, who reports to the Programme Controller, and until relatively recently – depending on the size and importance of the station – anyone involved in playing music could be subject to the attentions of promotion staff working for the record labels. Sometimes they offered inducements in addition to free copies of the records they were attempting to promote. The payola scandals of the 1950s and 1960s were widely reported in the press (Neer, 2001, 32–6), and Emperor Rosko described his involvement with record pluggers while at BBC Radio One (1976, 46–8), while Garfield found more recent evidence of heavy plugging there (1998, 230–1). Because of the influence of a national pop station on the sales charts, both presenters and producers are obvious targets for those whose livelihoods depend on promoting their product to the record-buying public.

Music policies vary from station to station – even those operating similar formats – according to the perceptions and preferences of the Head of Music. They are most effective, though, when they are based on common principles that allow the one programmer to control the sound of the station according to certain parameters intended to maximize its appeal to the target demographic. In most music stations this practice remains broadly unchanged since the 1950s. It is the manner in which it is operated which has undergone rapid change in the last two decades – change which has largely ended the original, permissive approach to the selection of music for playing in music sequences.

For example, in 1975 a Top Forty station might have begun each hour with a strong 'oldie' from a specified **era**, such as the 1960s. Commonly, formats use a **clock** (see Chapter 3) to express the placing of specified categories of music within each hour, and this was often to be seen pinned to the studio wall. The opening oldie might have been followed by an 'A-list' song, then a 'B-list', then an album track or some other category of music intended to broaden the range of music played and perhaps surprise the listener with its relative novelty value – before returning to the beginning of the cycle with another oldie. It was a **convention** for the oldie at the 'top of the hour' to be an **opener**: up-tempo, very recognizable to the **target audience**, and one which would get going without any long, rambling preamble to the introduction, in order to allow the music to quickly re-establish itself after the interruption of the news. Subsequent oldies in each hour did not need to meet such restrictive criteria, though, and any long **intros** could provide a useful vehicle for presenter **talkovers** (see Chapter 3).

The occurrence of individual discs in each category was broadly controlled by two different variables: the frequency with which the category occurred in the hour, and the number of discs in the category. Typically, the A-list contained fewer songs than the B-list, so if both categories were given equal emphasis, the A-list songs were played more frequently than those in the B-list. Classifying a song in the A-list gave it a considerable prominence in the overall station playlist, and so records in this category would be the strong, current hits which would appeal most to the target audience – probably including those with some momentum behind them in terms of their sales figures, television appearances on programmes such as *Top of the Pops* (BBC1) and other media coverage. As the B-list songs would by definition recur less frequently, they would include newer, less familiar material which suited the **station sound** and was likely to appeal to the target audience, even if too new to programme very frequently, for fear of losing listeners. Songs which had been in the A-list for some time, which were still popular with the target audience, but had begun to 'tire' – perhaps because of the over-exposure of remaining high in the sales charts for several weeks – could be demoted to the B-list and remain on the station, but with less prominence.

A station could quite easily vary the format and its effect on the station sound, according to the time of day or at weekends, simply by varying the clock. In the evenings, for example, the introduction of a C-list and the removal of some or all of the oldies could give a station a younger sound, to appeal more to teenagers listening while doing homework in their bedrooms. This was a common practice in the ILR network of the 1970s and 1980s which provided a broader service than the more narrowly focused stations they have since become. Specialist programmes, such as a folk hour or a country and western sequence in an off-peak **daypart**, could have their own clocks, or the Head of Music might relinquish all control over the music in deference to the producer or presenter's specialized knowledge (Starkey, 2011, 124–7).

In practice, the system allowed presenters considerable latitude in the day-to-day running of their own programmes. Playlisted singles would be kept in the studio, often in adapted wooden beer crates with cardboard dividers to separate the A-list from the B-list and so on. The most recently played would be at the back of each section, so the rule was to choose from the front two or three, returning each disc to the very back of the section afterwards. A set of prescribed oldies might have been provided in a box in the studio, in which case the same rule on **rotation** would apply. Alternatively, it may have been the responsibility of the presenter to choose oldies from the record library before the programme, or even to bring in appropriate songs from a personal collection at home, thus broadening the station's musical repertoire. To avoid repetition of oldies brought into the studio, conscientious presenters would scan through each other's music logs before going 'on air'. General rules would be applied and passed on via word of mouth, memos to on-air staff or entries in a station **style sheet**, such as 'no two female vocalists consecutively' or 'instrumentals only to be played up to the news'.

Presenters used all this relative freedom wisely if they wanted to remain 'on air', for straying from the programmer's notion of the station sound too far too often could result in being rescheduled in a less prominent daypart, or parting company with the station altogether. Presenters often possessed an encyclopaedic knowledge of the music they played, and it was common for them to foster audience impressions of their being 'music lovers' – an epithet which was more deserved in some cases than in others (Rosko, 1976, 37).

In practice, although it had many advantages, it was very common for presenters and producers to abuse the system. At the extremes, some presenters would play weaker songs at the end of a programme in order to sabotage the next one and its listening figures. Less cynically, it was very common for presenters to skip songs they didn't like – even those that were A-listed – and of course mistakes were made which on occasions meant a record was returned to the wrong part of the box and perhaps lost to the station sound until recovered. Sometimes oldies or album tracks would be repeated, even as soon as 20 minutes after their last appearance, because presenters changed shifts and not enough care was taken by the second one in checking what the first had played (Garfield, 1998, 104–6). If the status of Head of Music accorded a senior member of the programme team power and responsibility, the mechanics of the process eroded them both to the extent that programming a radio station's music was subject to the vagaries of chance and subversion.

More important in a commercial sense than any potential damage to someone's ego was the potential for inconsistency. If a currently important song went missing from the station sound for even a short period of time, it could have an impact on audience figures. Maverick presenters changing the sound during their own programmes by avoiding specific songs could also create a ripple effect on subsequent programmes, if they left those records at the front of the category every day. The occurrence of oldies was haphazard, and certain ones could be repeated deliberately or by accident very frequently, while others were not fully exploited, because easily accessible data on rotation was not available for even the most superficial analysis. The collection of data about what music was played, when and for how long, to report to licensing bodies in the form of **copyright returns** (see pages 102–3), was done manually and laboriously by the presenters or the producers, who neither enjoyed the task nor could be relied upon to work entirely accurately.

Exercise 4.1

Devise a music policy clock for a proposed radio station of your own, and then produce a playlist – divided into categories (A-list, B-list, etc.) – for your station. Discuss your answers in class, and be prepared to justify your choices by relating them to the target audience.

Scheduling software

Not surprisingly, it was the rise of the personal computer that was to bring about rapid change – yet it was not without resistance. In the

1980s a revolution began in the programming of music radio, which was to transform this aspect of the profession, when the US-based Radio Computing Services (founded in 1979 by Dr Andrew Economos) introduced computer software that would make the programming of music more systematic, and so – it is argued – more effective in targeting the station sound at the core audience. Selector was first deployed in the United Kingdom in 1986, at County Sound in Surrey, by its visionary Managing Director, Mike Powell. Even the BBC experimented with its own scheduling software, but Selector quickly established itself as leader in markets on both sides of the Atlantic that have more recently become increasingly competitive. Until its use became widespread, though, individual presenters and producers recognized scheduling software as a challenge to their own ability to choose the music on their 'own' programmes, and that it would result in a certain amount of deskilling because they no longer needed to know as much about music – although very tightly programmed stations existed long before Selector (Neer, 2001, 230–3). Some stations eased the introduction of computer scheduling by allowing individuals the flexibility of a number of 'free choice' slots in each hour, or the ability to swap the order of songs in the log if they preferred. Such concessions, although politically necessary at times, actually defeat the main object of using the software, because they disrupt the output by causing unintended repeats and allowing the introduction of songs which do not necessarily conform with the music policy.

In essence, computer-based music scheduling centralizes control of a station's music policy and places in the hands of the programmer a wide range of tools for honing the output according to a large number of variables. It can provide sophisticated data about the operation of the policy in order to further enhance that control – and it can be used for other commercial purposes, such as informing a sales pitch or a licence application (see page 100). The data can also be customized to provide accurate copyright returns, with comparatively little effort. It is now common for much or all of the pre-recorded **audio** that stations use regularly to be stored on a hard disk, and the most useful scheduling software interfaces with live **playout software**, such as Master Control by RCS, enabling the otherwise routine tasks of putting discs on and then returning them to their box or the shelf to be eliminated. Maverick action by presenters can still occur, but the potential for it is reduced.

Until RCS launched a Windows-based version in 2002, Selector continued to use the MS-DOS operating system, and some claimed this

Figure 4.1

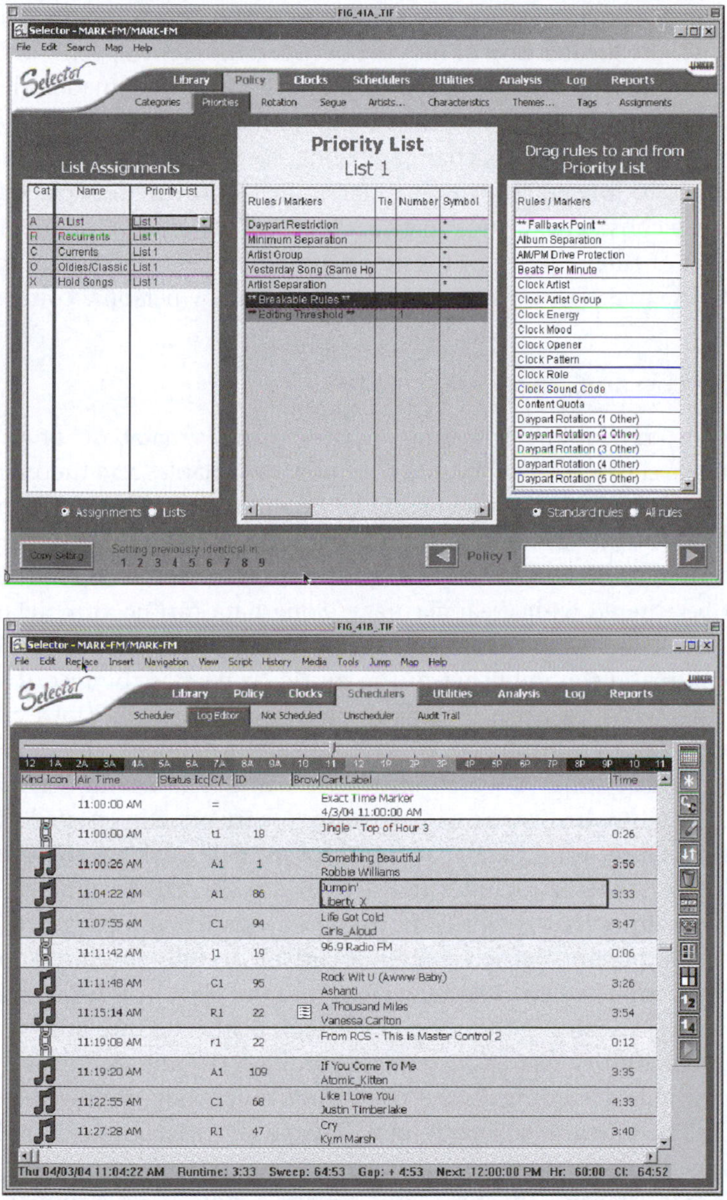

A **music policy screen (above) and part of a log (below) in Selector XV**, which brought Windows drag-and-drop functionality to the world's most widely used music scheduling software.

to be an advantage because of what they perceived to be the relative instability of Microsoft Windows. Undoubtedly, though, Selector lost market share to rival Windows-based alternatives, such as Powergold and AutoTrack Pro, because the simplicity of their drag-and-drop functionality, the greater ease of moving between different screens and the ability to navigate the on-screen display with a mouse, made Selector look old-fashioned for a while. In 2002, for instance, the Capital Radio Group announced it was changing from Selector to Powergold (*Radio Magazine*, 20 July 2002). However, being first in the market place gave Selector a considerable advantage, and in 2003 it was still the preferred software of the majority of music programmers, with RCS claiming it was in use in 85 per cent of stations scheduling by personal computer.

Using the software

Typically, scheduling software operates using a database of songs, which are classified according to a number of variables and then scheduled into a linear time sequence according to the music policy applied to them. As with any system for managing and retrieving data, for the results to be consistent and reliable the data on which it depends must itself be entered with great accuracy. Song data can be very detailed, from the title and the artist, to other **copyright** information, such as the writer and the publisher of the music, as well as the record label and the serial number under which it was released. However, if misspellings are introduced, or case sensitivity ignored, the data can itself be misleading. A search under the name 'The Beatles' can yield incomplete results if some of their songs are incorrectly entered under 'Beatles'. Other song data that the software will interpret in order to produce a schedule includes that which describes the sound of each song – qualities that are inherent to the way audiences hear music, but which computers themselves are not yet able to fully interpret alone.

For example, when creating a song card in Selector, it is possible to define in great detail the mood, the tempo, the texture and several other descriptors relating to the recording. Default definitions are customizable according to the user's preference, but in principle any scheduling software will work most effectively when these subjective judgements about how sound is represented on the system are also made consistently. In short, one person's notion of tempo being medium/fast may be another person's fast/fast. Inconsistency in a number of different variables could easily damage the system's performance, and for this reason music scheduling works best when operated by a single person. Although it may be tempting to allow several users access to the database, it makes good sense to set up a hierarchy of users with the power to make critical alterations only available to the supervisor. Conversely, a single person may schedule a number of stations, both in-house and at a distance, and simplify common actions by copying different elements between databases.

'Library management' involves classifying songs in categories, which may be called A-list, B-list, Recurrent, Resting or any other user-definable description, and categories may be further subdivided into different levels that allow certain songs within any category to rotate faster than others in the same category, depending on the level to which they are assigned. As songs rise and fall in their usefulness to the station (and the desirability of them being heard often alters in response to chart performance, promotion in other media, and so on), they can be moved between categories and levels at will, without the need to amend the song cards or the potentially very detailed data in them. Categories such as Christmas or Summer can reflect seasonal changes in tastes for back catalogue, and programmers who are sensitive to criticisms that computer-based scheduling makes stations sound formulaic and lacking in the innovation, interest and inspiration which the human element often used to give individual programmes, may want to use a Nuggets or a Surprise category to 'spice up' the schedules with appropriate but unusual songs for occasional use. While some stations operate very tight formats with just a few hundred songs, in the UK Saga Radio drew from a back catalogue of 5,000 songs, until it was re-branded Smooth (see **branding**, pages 103–5).

The music policy that is applied to the 'library' of available songs dictates not only the frequency of rotation, but also what type of song may follow any other. Just as the traditional model could accommodate a few basic rules such as those forbidding two consecutive female vocalists, the more sophisticated software can apply a wide range of '**segue** rules'. Severe jumps from, for example, a slow/slow song to a fast/medium song could be outlawed, just as easily as two songs from the same artist could be disallowed within any set time period. This could also prevent a Beatles song being followed by a John Lennon solo before an appropriate interval had elapsed (on the basis that he was himself a Beatle). However, if too many rules are applied at once, it may become impossible to schedule a time period without the software leaving gaps in the **running order**, so rules may be prioritized, with some being unbreakable and others being breakable according to an order of preference which is itself user-definable.

Once the music policy has been determined, clocks need to be created and assigned to different dayparts. Although very detailed in content, and often linear in appearance – more like a running order – the clock is a close relation of the former drawing pinned to the studio wall. It defines which category is to be played at each point in the hour that a song is to be heard. Selector interfaces with another RCS product, Linker, which schedules **idents** and non-musical items, such as **public service announcements**, commercials and even programme **feature** items which may be pre-recorded or live events. The clock is common to both programs. Generally, only a minority of songs have strong enough introductions and are recognizable enough to the target audience to be played as the first item after the news. So the first song position in the hour is usually an opener, defined on the clock as such and relatable by the software to only those song cards which have been given the opener descriptor. Each subsequent song position is assigned a category, with items other than songs being allocated between the songs. The system is more flexible than the traditional model, because potentially a different clock may be assigned to each hour in the week, allowing either subtle variations to reflect different dayparts or quite different formats for specialist programmes in the evening, for example.

Once the programmer has set all the different variables, the software will schedule all the hours in a given time period. Some programmers prefer to schedule close to transmission, in order to allow the most recent changes to the music library to be reflected in the output, and others prefer not to risk some unforeseen problem preventing them doing the job in time. Practically, a scheduled day can be re-scheduled later on if necessary. A careful programmer will read through the log produced, checking for any unscheduled positions (where the software has been unable to find an item in the library which meets all the rule criteria), imagining how the programmes are going to sound and ensuring that the segues will work. The computer can't spot unfortunate connections between song titles and current news items, and Absolute Radio, for example, would probably not like to accidentally play Dave Edmunds' *Crawling From The Wreckage* immediately after a news **bulletin** that reported a plane crash. The more radio output is computerized and automated, the greater is the potential for such potentially embarrassing mistakes. The best software will suggest the next best alternative for any position in the log, where its first choice is problematic. In examining the log, it is often helpful to interrogate the software for data as to when a particular song was last played, for instance, and this should be available in the history.

Exercise 4.2

Using appropriate scheduling software which has a demonstration data base associated with it, make a range of adjustments to the music policy, the songs and the clocks, in order to become familiar with its operation. Schedule a day's output, checking for anomalies and unscheduled positions, then print the log.

When there is a sudden death or a news event of great importance, the normal playlist – and indeed, much of a station's normal programming – may be replaced by something better suited to the public's response to what has happened. While closer regulation in the past meant that UK commercial radio stations were obliged to follow a set **obituary procedure** in the event of the death of certain predetermined categories of public figures, more enlightened attitudes are beginning to prevail, which allow stations more latitude to decide for themselves how they wish to respond to royal deaths. Logic dictates that this should be related to the target audience's likely wishes. For example, when Diana, Princess of Wales died in the shocking and tragic circumstances of a car crash in 1997 (Garfield, 1998, 170–4), younger listeners were more likely to be affected by the event than the passing away of the centenarian Queen Elizabeth the Queen Mother in 2002. Scheduling software allows a range of possibilities to be planned for in advance, by creating discrete categories for use in particular circumstances, and clocks that use them to a greater or lesser extent, depending on the station's intended response. They can remain dormant until needed.

Automation

Of course, at all times the music in the log the software produces must be available in the studio, and when automated playout software is being used, additions to the music library need to be recorded or ripped into the hard disk before they are needed. Similarly, live script reads and recorded idents and speech items also need to be available on time. The first radio station in the United Kingdom to use hard disk storage and playout of its audio was Pirate FM in Cornwall, where Mike Powell pioneered the use of automation in ILR, and the then innovative technology was featured on *Tomorrow's World* (BBC1). His overnight programming on 106.6 Star FM (Slough) and 96.4 The Eagle (Guildford) featured 'android' presenters named Twinkle and Talon respectively, who were in fact **processed** voice recordings of a range of different links that were then randomly scheduled by Linker and played out 'on air' by Master Control. Although both Talon and Twinkle made public appearances, as did their less unusual presenter colleagues, outside the radio stations they were in fact casual workers dressed in shiny plastic costumes tailored for the purpose. Powell's **franchise applications** to the then **regulator**, the Radio Authority, described their on-air work as 'intelligent **automation**', but until its replacement by Ofcom, the role of automation remained controversial (Starkey, 2011, 127–8).

Competitors have since appeared on the market, operating with varying levels of sophistication and reliability. Examples include Sound Box by Beaumont-Colson, Radioman the joint venture between IBM and Jutel adopted by the BBC in 2002, Myriad Playout by P Squared and SAM Broadcast, which is very popular with internet-only stations and is relatively cheap to purchase. Stations with tight budgets have even automated overnight using DAVE 2000 and the shareware Winamp. While Master Control and other reliable playout software offer great potential for pre-recording links and scheduling them into predetermined sequences, one widely felt concern is that less elaborate use of such systems can produce bland programming with few presenter voice links and little personality as a result.

Another possibility is that a small number of very successful presenters will broadcast programmes on a number of local or regional stations at once, sending links to the different studios via **ISDN** or the Internet, and only rarely even visiting the studios in the areas concerned. One useful alternative approach which may be less abusive of the listener's trust is for the breakfast presenter to present live from the studio in the morning, and then after that to **voice-track** a second, off-peak programme on the same station before going home around midday. Practically, if used without regulatory control, especially on internet-only stations, automation allows a whole radio station to broadcast without any presenters or technical operators at all, or to appear to have the same presenter broadcasting 24 hours a day. While non-stop music sequences have always been an option, common sense would suggest that listeners might quickly rumble the presenter who appears to be permanently 'on air' and never sleep.

In 2002 the Radio Authority's rules on daytime automation

restricted most FM stations to two hours and AM stations to four hours (Radio Authority, 2002). Many stations were using the technology around the clock, though, in a form of semi-automation called 'live assist', where all recorded audio was automated, but the presenter links were live and news and traffic bulletins were also inserted in real time. New stations, such as Life, Planet Rock and Mojo, transmitting via **DAB** and such loosely regulated platforms as Freeview and BSkyB used automation extensively to reduce start-up costs.

However, automation of a different kind was not new elsewhere in the world, predating hard disk storage by four decades. In the United States, regulation by the FCC is much less intrusive, and stations began to introduce automation systems – developed by Paul Schafer – in 1956. In his manual for American radio broadcasters, Holsopple featured a whole chapter on the subject (1988, 147–56) describing the use of early mechanical 'sequencers' which used several rack-mounted tape recorders and **cartridge** banks equipped with moving players sliding between different tape cartridges. Each item on tape or cartridge would have a pulse recorded after it, which would tell the system to begin the next event. Variety could be introduced by changing the spools of non-stop music or pre-recorded sequences on each tape machine and recording new links onto the cartridges.

Such systems were in use overseas by the British Forces Broadcasting Service in the early 1980s, and in their Gibraltar station otherwise apparently sane broadcasters and engineers referred to their automation system as 'Gladys'. This very human tendency to anthropomorphize an electronic substitute for paid staff who would otherwise have been working a night shift, may have masked anxieties about the consequences for them of further development of automation. The negative impact on employment has inspired at least suspicion of new technology since the Luddites reacted destructively to the introduction of machines in Nottinghamshire factories in 1811. Such anxieties do not always recognize the economics of situations where there might not have otherwise been a budget to employ staff to do the job, but there are valid concerns that overnight presentation is no longer a relatively easy way for beginners to gain valuable on-air experience, in spite of costing stations relatively very little compared with the fees paid to daytime presenters. The economics of automation do allow bespoke 24 hour broadcasting, where previously smaller stations would have been obliged to close down late at night, or to rebroadcast sustaining services provided by others, such as the Radio Radio service syndicated to ILR stations in the 1990s (Starkey, 2011, 155).

Copyright

Whether automated or not, the use of copyright music 'on air' must be reported to the various bodies that represent the owners of the original work done to create it. The more sophisticated software will produce printed or electronic declarations – copyright returns – in accordance with their requirements, saving producers and presenters literally hours of repetitive administrative work. Automation software should report not just which songs were scheduled, but how much of each song was actually put to air, again saving time on paperwork. Relations between radio stations and copyright bodies have not always been easy, and in the United Kingdom for example, the first ILR stations to broadcast on a 24 hours per day basis were restricted to only eight hours of 'needletime'. Even though the rest of their output included advertisements, news and traffic bulletins, interviews and so on, music radio stations found filling the rest of their broadcasting day without breaking the terms of the agreement rather difficult. Most played 'non-needletime' music from record labels that were not members of Phonographic Performance Limited (PPL), the body which represents record companies and performers. This meant that artists such as Johnny Coppin received more radio plays than their popularity with the public really deserved, although inevitably they would be heard more often in the middle of the night than in daytime. Some stations simply cheated, and declared less copyright music than they actually played – although evidence of that is understandably hard to find today. The returns they made to PPL differed significantly from those made to the Performing Right Society (PRS), who were less concerned

Figure 4.2

Artist	Title	Composer	Publisher	Label	Serial number	Duration used
Christina Aguilera	Beautiful	Linda Perry	Stuck in the Throat/Famous Music Corp.	RCA Records	7432 1961252	3'58"

An example of the information needed in copyright declarations when using music. Copyright declarations should include seven essential pieces of information about the track played, as shown above. Composers' names are often found in brackets on the label, and it is important not to confuse the publisher of the music with the record label.

about the total *amount* of music played than collecting royalties from stations and distributing them among their members, the composers. Some BBC local stations had only one hour per day of needletime allocated to them, although they broadcast more speech than the commercial sector.

In a landmark agreement, after long discussions with the radio industry to renegotiate the fees, PPL agreed to lift the restrictions on needletime, allowing commercial stations to progressively increase their reliance on music as the main ingredient in their output. Such agreements are elusive, because radio stations may have tight budgets and the copyright bodies want to earn as much money for their members as possible. This conflict of interests is mirrored by the debate over whether radio listening harms sales of music online and through retail outlets such as high street shops, or encourages music sales by promoting new releases and raising awareness of record companies' back catalogue. The Internet, being closely associated with past copyright battles over music sharing services such as Napster (Gibson, 2003a), presents particular difficulties. PRS and MCPS – a third body representing the owners of the recordings – began licensing Internet radio stations originating in the United Kingdom in 2001, but in the United States many Internet services were forced to suspend operations in 2002 because of the threat of high copyright fees and possible legal action against them by record companies who perceived them to be damaging their business (Harmon, 2002).

Branding

Increasingly, the music scheduled on individual stations and the key high-profile presenters who play it are seen as part of a **brand**. Marketing theorists usually consider that branding is one of the key elements in selling any product, from insurance to tinned beans, to potential customers (Godfrey and Herweg, 1997, 92). An appealing name and an attractive package can sell a product as effectively as the actual substance within the packaging, and some of the lessons of successful marketing have been learnt by those whose job it is to market radio stations to listeners and to advertisers. Marketing is vitally important to commercial stations, which derive their income from advertising, and so need as large an audience as possible to effectively sell on to their advertisers. That is, external bodies such as private companies or government agencies buy airtime on the station, to use to sell their own products or services to the listeners who have tuned in (see Chapter 6). In this sense, listeners are firstly sought after, then they themselves become a commodity to be bought and sold.

Public service radio stations also need to market themselves, because without large audiences their funding may be threatened. The BBC, for example, can run its expensive minority channel, Radio Three, on a national network of FM transmitters only because it forms part of a package with the Corporation's other national, regional and local stations. Together they achieve more than half of the radio listening in the United Kingdom, and often the message behind the BBC's marketing of its radio brands is one of quality and diversity of choice (Fleming, 2002, 52). This needs to be regularly reinforced in order to justify its continued funding from the mandatory television licence.

In the increasingly competitive environment of the UK radio industry, branding has become more important in marketing terms than ever before (Godfrey and Herweg, 1997, 64). The first Independent Local Radio stations were expected by the then Independent Broadcasting Authority to offer a 'full service' of music and news, with programming to appeal to different sections of their local communities – including the minority interest groups who would tune in especially to a folk hour on, for instance, a Tuesday evening (Starkey, 2011, 68–76). The best example of this mixed programming was Radio Clyde

Figure 4.3

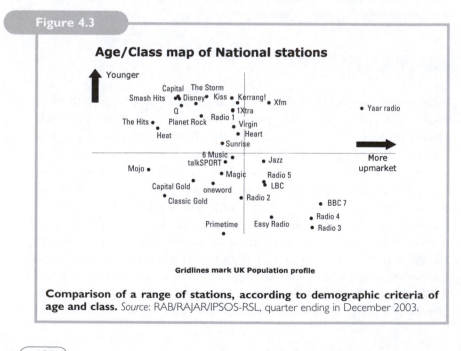

Comparison of a range of stations, according to demographic criteria of age and class. *Source:* RAB/RAJAR/IPSOS-RSL, quarter ending in December 2003.

in Glasgow, which continued to broadcast a wide variety of specialist programming on its AM service, Clyde 2, long after the demise of both the IBA and the Radio Authority.

Formats

With successive relaxations of the regulatory controls, and the removal of the full service commitment, UK commercial stations are now much freer to concentrate on serving a core target audience full time. In 2001 each station's individual Promise of Performance to the Radio Authority was replaced by an agreed Format document which described in a few sentences what would be the station's output. The huge growth in stations from 1990 onwards (Starkey, 2003a) saw the opening of many 'niche' stations, whose formats were very tightly targeted at quite narrow demographic groups. Examples in the London market alone were Jazz FM, Country 1035, London Greek Radio, the indie-label station XFM and Premier Christian Radio. Among the least successful was Liberty, which targeted a 'female' audience, but often found it hard to achieve even a 0.1 per cent share of listening in the capital.

With so many competitors 'on air', stations need to communicate effectively to what may be a small potential audience. Virgin Radio was an extension of the hugely successful Virgin brand created by Richard Branson when he set up his own independent record label in 1973. The brand is used to sell financial products, mobile phone services, and a cola drink, as well as the products in the Virgin Megastore retail sites, but it has had to struggle against often negative publicity from Virgin Trains. Although Branson's controlling stake in Virgin Radio was sold to Chris Evans in 1998 (Reece, 2002), it remained, because of the name and the **logo**, very strongly identifiable in the public mind as a station for people who appreciate rock music, probably grew up listening to such Virgin Records acts as Mike Oldfield, and had grown too old (or mature) to appreciate the kind of music played on the national youth station, BBC Radio One. This image compared with the station's agreed format statement, which committed the station to a particular mix of rock and contemporary music.

While Virgin Radio's target audience probably did coincide with part of the market for the financial products, there was a mismatch with the image of the high street Megastores, and further confusion resulted from the Virgin Trains connection: its customers were not

Figure 4.4

Logos from EMAP's Big City stations (left) and GWR's The Mix stations (right) in 2003. When Bauer Media acquired EMAP's stations, those logos remained largely unchanged. Global Radio, however, rebranded most of the former GWR stations Heart soon after acquiring them, while Beacon was sold and later became Free Radio.

determined by lifestyle, age or musical upbringing, but by their need to catch a train over a route on which that company has a monopoly.

A much clearer branding has been achieved by Classic FM, the first national commercial radio station to be licensed in the United Kingdom, which began broadcasting in 1992. Its agreed format commits it to providing a service of 'classical music, national and international news'. Since its launch, the station's interpretation of 'classical' has inevitably been driven by the commercial imperative to maximize audiences. 'Classic' is a deliberate misuse of the adjective 'classical' that more closely describes the mainly orchestral music it plays. Those who criticize it for playing only a relatively narrow selection of the best-known works and parts of works, compared with the much wider-ranging BBC network, Radio Three, are – consciously or not – acknowledging the very tight formatting of the station.

The small playlist and the relative predictability of its music repertoire means there are certain classical pieces that fit the station sound, and many more which would not. The station announces itself regularly as Classic FM, and the branding is reinforced by the repetition of the same musical **ident** arranged in a variety of different ways – each version sounding like a brief classical piece itself. While the brand has been successfully extended to a monthly consumer magazine on sale in newsagents and mostly concerned with classical music and recordings, as well as occasional 'best of' classical CD releases and – from 2002 – a television channel, it would seem very odd for it to be further extended to a fizzy drink or a train company.

Other examples of strong branding in the UK market include Saga, which operates in a number of different fields – from insurance to holidays – exclusively for the over-50s, and devised a radio format which it began to exploit through two regional licences in the Midlands from 2002. Galaxy targeted the youth market in a number of locations with stations playing exclusively 'dance' music, and in 2000 Guardian Media Group launched its first Real Radio station, in South Wales. It then revamped the failing Scot FM in the same **style** and won another regional licence, enabling it to set up a third regional station bearing the brand in Yorkshire, in 2002. Common to each of the stations within a brand are normally the music policy, the presentation style, news presentation and outside promotional events. In most cases the management is centralized too, in order to encourage conformity in each location to common house styles and practices. In 2011 Galaxy was re-branded Capital.

On occasions, the presenter can become the most successful part of the branding. For example, the press reported that speculation over the departure of Chris Tarrant from the Capital Radio breakfast show had caused the Capital Radio Group's share price to fall on the London Stock Exchange, and when he agreed to stay, it rose again (Milmo and Day, 2002). Part of BBC Radio One's difficulty in retaining its audience after the appointment of Matthew Bannister can be attributed to the disruption of the firmly established 'happy sound' branding of the station and a failure to replace it with much more than a succession of high-profile breakfast presenters, each of whose image seemed to be more important than the station as a whole (Garfield, 1998, 67–93, 128). It is arguable that the 'happy sound' had become outdated and too closely associated with the 'Smashie and Nicey' parody of egotistical and cliché-ridden DJs. However, it is not hard to imagine that alternative approaches to introducing change might well have been more successful in audience **ratings** terms.

Exercise 4.3

Continue the table below, filling in the blank spaces and adding more examples of strong branding by a range of radio stations that you can receive in your area. Discuss your answers in class – for example, does the image fit the content of the station, and how successful do you expect it to be? You could compare audience listening figures as evidence to support your conclusions.

Radio station and target audience	Your own description of the station's image	Comments on the station's branding
Absolute Radio, mainly lower middle class, the 'rock and roll generation' now grown up	Plays rock and pop for music lovers who have grown out of Radio One	Uses adaptation of familiar virgin logo from record label etc. Voiced idents and strap line.
BBC Radio Four, average age 53, middle class, educated, culturally aware, wanting 'intelligent' speech	Often rather stuffy: broadcasts many talks, but also comedy and a little music	Low key. No recorded idents, but continuity announcements in a similar style to BBC2 television. Has a logo in *Radio Times*.
BBC 1Xtra, 15–24, into latest music of black origin		

Launching a new station or a network of stations within a new brand needs careful thought and planning. Even a university, community or **Restricted Service Licence** station should be sufficiently distinguishable from the range of competing services its target audience might otherwise be inclined to listen to. The station name should **connote** something that the target audience will respond positively to, and market **research** can be a useful indicator of how different names are perceived. For example, the BBC's local radio stations each make clear geographical connections with their audiences with such names as Radio Leicester and Radio Merseyside. When Melody launched in London in 1990 its name was intended to evoke its musical content and so emphasize its potential appeal to a middle aged, middle class audience in a way that the New York pirate, the Voice of the Angry Bastard, would probably not have done. Melody became Magic in 1998.

Communicating the brand

The manner in which the name is conveyed – visually and 'on air' – is another important consideration. From the logo on stationery, studios, station vehicles and car stickers, to the font used on **rate cards**, press advertising and corporate literature, the 'look' of the station should be distinctive yet appropriate and appealing to the target audience (Fleming, 2002, 58–60). 'On air', except in exceptional circumstances, the name should be repeated in recorded idents – either sung or spoken – and the style should accord with the other elements of the station's **imaging** (see the section on idents, on pages 111–14). Individual presenters and programme items such as news bulletins, traffic and travel spots, the weather, competitions, **promos**, **trails** and regular features may all need their own identification elements such as **jingles** and **beds**, and on stations which intend to benefit the most from strong branding, these will probably have commonalities of style and sound which afford sufficient variety to sustain listener interest but which relate strongly to each other.

Such closely-linked elements of on-air branding are likely to form part of a 'package' (although here, the term has little in common with its use in Chapter 2). The fastest development of the **jingle package** was in the 1950s, when PAMS of Dallas, Texas became the market leaders in radio station imaging. In the United Kingdom, one of the earliest specialists in the production of jingle packages was Steve England, whose Manchester-based company, Alfasound, created sung idents,

shouts and instrumental beds to order and sold generic collections for use by low-budget stations, such as hospital radio. England also used the vocoder to create electronic-sounding voice idents, long before advances in technology made 'robot voices' achievable at the click of a mouse. The vibrating vocoder was held against the user's throat, and he or she then 'shaped' the sound it produced by articulating with the mouth the various vowel and consonant sounds which give voice its meaning.

In the 1990s, a trend in the United Kingdom was for sung jingles to be replaced by spoken idents, particularly on stations targeted at younger audiences. Radio One probably saw the move away from sung idents as part of its attempt to shake off its 'Smashie and Nicey' image. While Radio One was shedding listeners by the million (Wells, 2002a), the United Kingdom's most popular station, BBC Radio Two, persisted with melodic, sung jingles appropriate to the station's sound. When Piccadilly Radio 261 (now re-branded as Key 103) first launched, its Managing Director, Philip Birch, told *The Guardian* that one indicator of the new station's success in Greater Manchester was that listeners were singing the jingles to themselves on the street. More recently, the lesson to be learnt from Birch's observation has often been forgotten. Local and regional stations began to see the spoken ident as a convenient means of reinforcing their relevance to their own geographical market, running names of towns within the area alongside the more traditional station name and frequency information, in what became known as **sweepers**.

The voiced ident also easily accommodates a station **strap line**, another potentially powerful element to branding. This positions the station, making a clear and (in theory) memorable statement about the station's content, its supposed personality or its relevance to the audience. Strong examples used include 'today's better music mix' (GWR Group stations in the 1990s), 'Sunderland's most listened to radio station' (Sun FM) and 'exclusively Sunderland' (107 Spark FM). Strap lines are not a recent phenomenon, however, and lend themselves well to being sung, too. In the 1980s, for example, Radio One's 'the happy sound' was a catchy refrain, which regularly punctuated its programming, and PAMS sold such jingle packages as their 'My Kind of Music' to stations in many different US and overseas markets. Successful strap lines work because the listener learns to associate the brand with the statement in it, and as Pavlov demonstrated (see 2001), association can lead to the most powerful of responses. It is arguable that many people will have been convinced of the happiness of Radio One's sound (even where this contradicted the reality of any sad songs playlisted – or indeed the content of many news bulletins). However, it is debatable whether the PAMS singers should have used 'your' rather than 'my', or even 'our kind of music' in order to send out a more inclusive message to the listener.

Exercise 4.4

Devise the branding for a new radio station, or plan how an existing station could be re-branded. Identify the visual and aural elements that will make up your new brand, and show how they relate to each other and to the target audience. Explain your decisions and the research you carried out to find the best solutions in each case, explaining why you rejected any alternatives you may have considered and/or market tested with sample listeners.

Producing idents

Clearly, choosing the words that will send the correct message to the audience in any form of positioning statement is very important, and it needs to be done *before* the production **process** begins and the use of producers, studios, session singers or **voice-over artists** begins to incur costs. It is common for rough demos to be made where the budget will allow it, in order to market test alternatives. Where budgets are not generous, it is usual for packages to be adaptations of pre-existing beds and **stings**, which can be used in different locations where listeners are unlikely to be able to receive distant stations using the same material. The voices, either sung or spoken, can simply be added in **post-production.**

One sung phrase can be **mixed** and re-mixed with alternative arrangements of similar beds in a way that makes it very economical to produce a number of packages for small stations from one voice recording session. Groups of stations can achieve similar efficiencies by commissioning almost identical packages for all their own stations at once, if they broadcast in different markets. A station name, frequency, and strap line can each be extracted from the session, to produce differ-ent **a capella** versions – that is, the voice without any musical bed. Voiceovers can be used dry, and in the 1970s a number of UK ILR stations made extensive use of the deep, rasping voice of Bill Mitchell to identify themselves, inspired by the popularity of his hit record

spoof of a Telly Savalas version of the song *If* (1975). A dry voice or an a capella can lend itself to being played over the introduction to a song, because there is no bed to clash with the introduction itself. Similarly, a multi-voice shout can be used 'on air' in a variety of ways – although the popularity of the shout has declined over the past two decades – and it is relatively simple to produce using enthusiastic beginners rather than the talented vocalists needed to create sung jingles with any credibility.

To record voice work for idents of any kind requires a suitably soundproofed and acoustically-treated studio, preferably with the control room separated from the performance area by heavy glazing. Practically, a **microphone** and a portable recorder could be used in a location with suitable **acoustics** if resources are tight, although an obvious useful enhancement would be a **mic** stand to avoid **handling noise**. The session producer should have a clear idea of what is wanted, and each item should be clearly written down on a script – with copies for everyone involved. Producing the session means more than technical operation to ensure **levels** and microphone position are correct (see Chapter 1), and ticking off each recording made on the script. It also means directing the performers, making sure their intonation and pronunciation are correct, that they enunciate each sound clearly enough to be easily audible over any bed or electronic effects, and encouraging them to put as much effort into their performance as is required.

If singers are to follow particular musical notes, it will help them to hear the bed they are to sing along to in their headphones, and this is where an **auxiliary output** or **clean feed** off the **mixing desk** can help. This can be set up to allow them to hear the bed, while only their microphone **channel**s are on, faded up and so being recorded. Once the producer is satisfied with the recordings, the session comes to an end and the post-production begins, using either more traditional real-time mixing in the studio, or appropriate software such as SADiE or Adobe Audition (see Chapter 1).

Techniques that have been popularized in recent years by producers of spoken idents include using **reverb**, repetition of words or individual syllables and using processing effects such as **equalization** and phasing (or 'flanging') to add 'excitement' to the finished **product**. Many of these techniques can be mastered by experimental use of the more sophisticated functions of audio software programs, and as with any kind of creative effect, it is important to try them out and listen back critically to the results before settling for a finished product. As a full-time jingle producer would do, by getting **feedback** from the client, beginners should market test their own productions and **evaluate** their effectiveness before use 'on air'. Generally, a new jingle package should be introduced to an existing station all at once, and all elements of the previous package should be removed immediately, to prevent brand confusion or distortion of the station's message.

Exercise 4.5

Plan and produce a package of idents that will establish and reinforce the branding of either an existing radio station, or one you design yourself. Market test the results, evaluating your package and reconciling the individual elements of the package with the reactions of your audience sample.

Analysing idents

Idents may be short, but there are interesting conclusions to be drawn about how they are made and how they are used. Their importance lies in making statements about a station and the content it broadcasts – as well as the presenters who feature on it – so they should not be underestimated as objects of academic study. The conventions of the genre (see above) are not so rigid that new styles and approaches are discouraged, and as creativity is often acclaimed both within the radio station and in industry awards, individual producers and presenters may seek to find new and original ways of **signposting** elements within their own live sequences. Trends, such as that away from the sung jingle and towards the spoken sweeper (see page 110), arise out of innovation, as one original idea is copied and adapted many times by others who quickly perceive the worth of a new approach. **Codes** operate in the organization of idents around programme items – the news banner *before* the news, the sponsor credit *around* the weather, for instance – and in the way music, voices and effects are arranged within idents, too. It is worth considering the **semiotic** value (if any) of Capital Radio's regular punctuation of its mid-morning programmes in the 1980s with a school choir singing 'Michael Aspel makes your morning, Michael Aspel makes your day'. What message was it intended to convey, and to whom – and would the same station use a similar approach today?

Positioning statements within idents, repeated many times within the hour and over the broadcasting day, can be considered in the light of **audience theory**. Spurious claims, such as 'the best music', 'first with the news' and 'taking care of business' may sound superficially attractive to those who use them, and their clear, simple messages certainly lend themselves to a station's attempt to become the listeners' favourite. It is difficult to reconcile them, though, with notions of audiences as individual, active makers of meaning, each one **reading** media texts from different and experienced perspectives. For example, how could any selection of music be believed to be incontrovertibly 'the best', when most listeners know other people who have different musical tastes from their own?

Similarly, the reporters working for any one station would need superhuman powers to always be the first to broadcast every news item before any other media outlet. Some listeners may understand that the syndication of news services (by, for example, in the United States the three main networks and in the United Kingdom Independent Radio News) means that most stories are inevitably first broadcast simultaneously on several stations in their area. Commonly, embargoes orchestrate the simultaneous release of information by all interested news media, anyway. More functional statements, such as 'travel on the ones' accord more closely with the **uses and gratifications** theory, in that until 2003 listeners to London's News Direct 97.3FM may well have consciously tuned in at 1, 11, 21, 31, 41 and 51 minutes past the hour, because they knew travel bulletins were broadcast at those times and they wanted to hear the latest information available.

In terms of **ideology**, some might argue with some justification that the 'news' is only what a ruling elite wishes to tell us about the world, anyway, being biased and incomplete (Alleyne, 1997). The **narrative structure** of most idents will be **closed**, although those that precede such feature items as the weather may be **open** if they include a bed over which the presenter reads the forecast. **Closure** comes with the subsequent playing of a further ident which reinforces the identity of the item and perhaps includes a sponsor credit, or it may be that the presenter provides some closure by fading the ident and bed manually and making such a remark as 'and that's the weather'. It is hard, however, to imagine a growing trend towards idents with **multi-strand** narrative structures (see Chapter 1).

Measuring audiences

Audience research is commissioned regularly by most radio stations, to measure the size of the audience and to find out more about them and their perceptions of what they hear. Re-branding or reformatting a station is intended to increase audience share (see definitions, page 116) – or at least to stop it going down – so the hope will be that soon the figures justify the changes made. Even smaller changes, such as moving a programme or a sequence presenter to a different slot, can show up in more detailed research, as can the introduction or re-scheduling of particular programme items, including competitions, feature items and guest interviews. Commercial radio stations depend on audience research to demonstrate their usefulness to advertisers, in terms of how large an audience or what demographic groups they can deliver. The rate card consists of pricing information for advertisers, and usually presents figures in terms of the 'cost per thousand'. In the United States, the market leader in producing radio audience ratings is Arbitron. In the United Kingdom, most full-time radio stations subscribe to Radio Joint Audience Research Ltd (RAJAR), a company owned by the RadioCentre and the BBC on a 50:50 basis. Prior to 1992, the commercial and publicly owned sectors of the industry each made their own arrangements for audience research, and the Joint Industry Committee for Radio Audience Research (JICRAR) produced figures for ILR, while the BBC used a different methodology to produce their own. As both sets of figures rarely tallied, it was felt that a single body, using a single methodology, would produce results that could be accepted more widely by stations, advertisers and others – results which became known as the 'gold standard' because of their supposed reliability. A small number of stations led by Kelvin MacKenzie, Chief Executive of the Wireless Group (which included the third national commercial network, talkSPORT), became disillusioned with the diary system used by RAJAR and began a very public campaign for the introduction of electronic measurement, which they felt would improve their results (Starkey, 2003b, 43–68).

The listening diaries depend on listeners' ability to recall any listening they have done since the last time they wrote in them, and to note it down accurately. Because this is obviously done only by a sample of the potential audience in any **Total Survey Area** (**TSA**), even small discrepancies – such as a mis-match or a change in the sample – can have a considerable impact on the figures. Electronic measurement of radio listening, unlike with television, is complicated by the fact that on a typical day people may hear radio through a number of receivers in the house as well as in the car, on the bus, in shops, garages, offices and even leisure centres. The first devices for electronic measurement addressed this problem by being worn by each member of the sample,

like a wristwatch or a pager, from which data could then be transferred to the research centre for analysis. An experiment in Slough in
Berkshire produced results that greatly enhanced the ratings for
speech-based stations, including talkSPORT (Cassy, 2002). Large
differences between the figures produced by meters and by recall
confirm that audience measurement of any kind must be viewed with
some suspicion, but RAJAR began testing both Arbitron's Portable
People Meter and Radiocontrol's Audiometer in 2002, somewhat
inconclusively. One important question is why listeners should be
better able to recall listening to music stations than to speech stations
– and if they can't remember being within hearing of a talk station,
does it actually constitute listening (Starkey, 2003b, 66)? Whatever
the methodology, smaller sample sizes can distort figures considerably.

Interpreting audience research also requires understanding of the
terms used. RAJAR use the following definitions:

▸ Reach: how many people are said to have listened to a particular
  station or one of a set of stations for at least five minutes over a
  week. This is also expressed as a percentage.
▸ Average hours: the number of hours listened to a station or a set of
  stations during a week, averaged over the total number of listeners
  or the total number of people in the area, be they listeners to that
  service or not.
▸ Total hours: the overall number of hours listened to the station or
  set of stations.
▸ Share of listening: the percentage of listening done in the area, to
  the station or set of stations.

Reach and average hours are important indicators for any radio station,
because even if the audience is tuning in in large numbers, if they are
not listening for long the station's share of listening will suffer – and
comparative 'league' tables tend to be based on share. Programmers
will want to find ways of encouraging greater listener loyalty, perhaps
by **teasing** future items more, or running more features and competitions which require sustained or repeated listening to fully enjoy them
or take part in them. Just before the release of the latest figures, radio
stations can become very tense environments, especially when
managers and programme staff fear their own jobs may be jeopardized
by poor results. For Mark and Lard on the Radio One breakfast show,
consistently poor results meant 'demotion' to the afternoon (Garfield,
1998, 186–96).

A useful skill is being able to spot good news even in disappointing results: the audience reach and share may be down, but if listening hours are up, it may be worth publicizing this 'success' 'on air' and via a press release. Often, a station which has added listeners, and so has an increased reach, will find its average hours are down – but this may

Figure 4.5

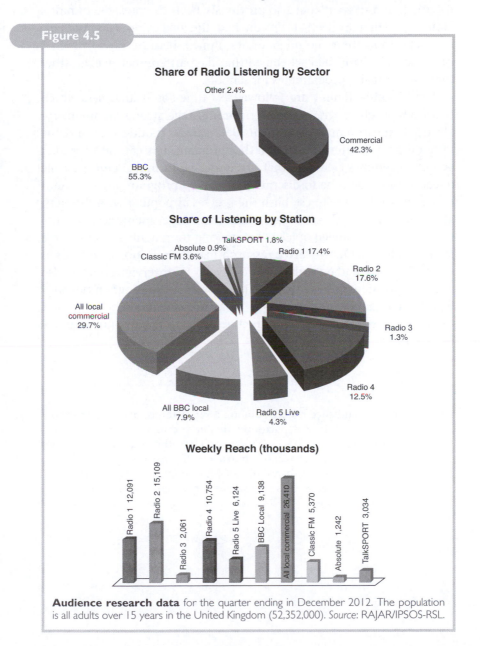

Audience research data for the quarter ending in December 2012. The population is all adults over 15 years in the United Kingdom (52,352,000). *Source:* RAJAR/IPSOS-RSL.

well be because the new listeners are not in the habit of listening for very long yet. The challenge to programmers is to keep them and get them listening longer. It may also be worth setting the figures in wider **contexts**. For example, in the United Kingdom, in the first quarter of 1983 the advent of breakfast television caused a considerable drop in listening, in a daypart that had previously been the preserve of radio. Similarly, when in 1988 ITV launched the magazine *This Morning*, most mid-morning radio programmes dipped, because it was the first time that television had scheduled that daypart competitively, rather than transmitting programmes for schools.

The headline figures are followed by time-based analyses, which show how each programme is performing. One strong argument for electronic measurement is that this data can be produced on a daily, rather than a quarterly, basis and that programmers can take speedier action to remove elements that are under-performing. One possible effect of this would be to discriminate against programmes and items which may take time to establish themselves as popular with listeners, although it may also encourage short-term experimentation because reactions can be gauged quickly, before long-term damage is done to a station's ratings. **Quantitative research** has its limitations, and just as the BBC's early audience data was collected by interviewers who also asked **respondents** about their feelings towards the programmes they heard, **qualitative research** that seeks impressions and considers listeners' interests can be used effectively to plan and improve programming.

Exercise 4.6

Carry out some audience research among a set of respondents, chosen to represent a clearly defined population either according to geographic area alone, or within certain demographic groups. Use either a diary method or a questionnaire to find out what stations they listen to over seven days, and for how long. Consider the validity of your sample when analysing the results and their implications for the stations included in your survey.

5 Magazine Programmes

In this chapter you will:

▸ learn how magazine programmes are made and used in radio
▸ research, plan and produce your own magazine programme
▸ consider ways of analysing magazines you hear and make yourself.

Magazines in context

The **genre** described as the radio magazine programme is in many ways just as a literal **reading** of the name suggests. While print magazines are collections of different items, all held together by a common theme or a target readership, so are magazines on radio broadly divisible into two similar categories. The 'common theme' magazine is one that includes a range of different items, which are all related to a particular subject – and just as a newsagent's shelves are loaded with magazines, each about music, gardening, hobbies or celebrities and so on, the possibilities for radio magazines are also many and varied. In the United Kingdom, recent examples from the BBC's main speech network, Radio Four, include *Medicine Now*, *You and Yours* and *Today* (see Chapter 3). *Today* soon metamorphosed into the country's most influential news and current affairs magazine, but when it began in 1957 the content was much more varied, and it even included keep fit exercises and recipes as recently as the 1970s (Luckhurst, 2001, 15). The original **proposal** characterized the programme as a 'morning miscellany' – the idea being that it would consist of a collection of miscellaneous items scheduled between the regular early morning news bulletins and only loosely connected to each other (ibid, 6–7).

Like the original *Today*, the second category of magazine unites a wider variety of subject matter around assumptions about the common interests of the **target audience**. In the United Kingdom, the best-known example is the BBC's *Woman's Hour*, which was first broadcast on 7 October 1946, and now runs five mornings a week on Radio Four, with a 'best of' compilation on Saturday afternoons. The unifying factor behind its content is its supposed interest to women, although the programme claims to welcome male listeners as well. As individual items aren't limited to a single subject, a typical programme may deal with topics as diverse as the early twentieth-century suffragettes, hormone replacement therapy, life as a single mother and widows' pensions. In 2010 the BBC launched a weekly *Men's Hour* on Radio Five Live, in the way that in print *GQ* may be said to complement *Cosmopolitan*, but those who defend the creation of this much more prominent women's interest 'ghetto' often justify it by describing the majority of radio output, including sport, business and motoring magazines, as intended for men (Mitchell, 2000, 12).

The characteristic which most closely defines magazines on radio is that each contains several different items rather than consisting of a single, linear **narrative**, in the way that a documentary deals with one particular issue over a longer **duration** and in greater depth (see Chapter 9). A common thread through each magazine programme is the linking material provided by one or more presenters, who introduce each item, add supplementary material between items and ensure listeners know what else is coming up before the end (**signposting**). Individual items may be delivered in different **styles**, too, and variety in approach as well as content is one of the magazine's strengths. A typical *Woman's Hour*, for instance, might include a speech **package** or two (see Chapter 2), a live interview with someone in a remote studio, a **'round table'** discussion between the presenter and two or three guests in the same studio, and an episode of a short, serialized drama in which a fictional story unfolds over a number of programmes. Until the introduction of the drama slot, the story was a simple prose reading by an actor or – occasionally – the author of a recently-published book.

Most often, though, the magazine deals exclusively with factual content and its production is essentially a journalistic activity – even if the journalism is often at the softer end of the spectrum. To continue the print analogy, most radio magazines contain feature material that would probably not be dealt with on the news pages. Topical items may be heard alongside others, which are relatively timeless in their appeal and which could have been broadcast in an earlier edition of the programme or equally held over until a future edition, without losing any of their impact. Magazine items often develop a current news story, by exploring the background to an event in the news **bulletin**, or by exploring hypothetical alternative outcomes. To add to the diversity of the genre, many stations carry news magazines, which can seem similar to extended news bulletins and concentrate on providing extended coverage of the day's hard news as well as a greater depth of analysis and further background to it.

Exercise 5.1

Continue the table below, adding more examples of radio magazine programmes. Discuss your answers in class – for example, are only men interested in football?

Magazine title, station and day/time of broadcast	Target audience	Examples of programme content
Front Row, BBC Radio Four, weekdays, 7.15 pm	Middle class, interested in arts, film and fairly 'highbrow' culture, average age 53	Discussion of theatre ticket pricing, preview of new ballet, interview with director
The Film Programme, BBC Radio Four, Sundays, 11.00 pm	As above, but interested in film	Review of *The Hobbit*, preview of new film and DVD releases

Producing magazine programmes

Creating a new magazine programme may involve the same kind of commissioning **process** as is described in Chapter 3 for live sequences. Certainly, if the series is to convey a clear sense of identity and **purpose** to the audience, there must be some firm decisions taken about the content and who it is aimed at, well before the first programme goes to air. A proposal should reconcile the two, preferably detailing some careful **research** into the nature of the audience, their likes and dislikes, and the kind of programming to which they already listen. A list of sample items is a good way to suggest what the proposed content might be, and this could be accompanied by a commentary indicating how the programme might react to different types of news events. A pilot programme might be required, as a demonstration of how a typical programme in the series could sound.

Knowing the audience and what they are interested in is vital in deciding what kind of items to include – and how to approach them. For instance, the daily magazine *You and Yours* is aimed at a general Radio Four audience who might be interested in consumer affairs, financial and social aspects of their own lives and the health and well-being of their families. It is scheduled at lunchtime, when there is a relatively large audience available and it would be unwise to alienate many of them by broadcasting a minority interest programme. So when dealing with a health item it must be accessible to the ordinary Radio Four listener, explaining unfamiliar medical terms in a way that will enable them to understand the item even if they don't already have any specialist knowledge of the subject beforehand. This contrasts strongly with the approach taken on the same network's *Medicine Now*, which was scheduled in the evening, and presupposed that the much smaller number of listeners tuning in regularly at that time were doing so because they had a particular interest in medicine – being, perhaps, involved professionally. The **mode of address** was quite different from that on *You and Yours*, because this audience had a greater prior knowledge of the issues being discussed, and a far better understanding of the medical terms and concepts forming part of the **discourse**. *Inside Health* targets a less specialized audience at 3.30 pm.

A useful means of conveying the nature of the magazine programme to its potential audience is its title, which must be sufficiently evocative of its subject matter and its approach to attract as many as possible of those who would be interested in hearing it, and might reasonably be expected to become regular listeners. Sometimes titles are easy to think of, although often producers rely on what have become clichés through overuse – an example being *Sunday Supplement*, which was in use on Bristol's Radio West in the 1980s and on many other stations before and since. Other titles are misleading, for example *Sunday Service* on Radio Five Live might have suggested a religious theme, when its content was mainly political. The title of Radio Four's *Today* might appear vague and unhelpful to those who haven't heard of the programme's agenda-setting reputation, and that it often alters the course of news reporting on the country's other radio and television services for the rest of the day.

Today runs for three hours, five days per week, with a two-hour long Saturday edition, which is unusually long for programming of this type, and so it has much in common with the live sequences described in Chapter 3. Half-hour or hour-long magazines are more common, largely because of the resource demands created by the need for a large number of speech packages (see Chapter 2). The specialized nature of many thematic magazines means they are likely to be broadcast only weekly. While the extended duration of *Today* and the topical nature of its content mean it could only be transmitted live, many shorter magazine programmes are pre-recorded up to a few days before they are broadcast.

Theme tunes, menus and signposting

Depending on the style of the station's programming, it is a **convention** of magazines that they begin and end with a short **theme tune** of a few seconds' duration – between 20 and 40 seconds may well be sufficient. Otherwise called a **signature tune**, the purpose of this music is to identify the programme, to set a particular mood in keeping with its content and approach, to **denote** its start and finish, and to be one of a number of hooks which might encourage listeners to tune in again on a regular basis. *Today* has no theme tune, and neither do Radio Four's other news and current affairs sequences – in fact, when the early evening *PM* programme used a signature tune, it was the cause of a sustained campaign of written complaints from a hard core of listeners who claimed to be irritated by it. The BBC eventually conceded victory to the letter writers, in what became an interesting example of how a group of very experienced broadcasters misjudged their audience and how a vocal minority forced the programme's producers to change their approach.

Choosing a theme tune can be a time-consuming task, but one that, if successful, can considerably enhance a magazine programme. A station with a large budget could commission an original composition, but it is more usual for most producers to choose from the wide range of **library music**, which is released by private companies for just this kind of purpose. Library music is also used extensively for commercial production (see Chapter 6). The major drawback with it, though, is the danger, however small, that the track chosen might turn out to be one already in use on another radio station or television channel which listeners in the same market might also be able to hear.

If the tune has a slow build to the introduction, starting softly or with little impact, the first section could be **edited** out, so the programme appears to begin more certainly than would be the case otherwise. Similarly, it is useful if the theme has a definite ending, rather than a simple fade out, which can seem rather lame as the final seconds of the programme. The total duration of the track in its original form is not an issue, because it is most likely to be faded out after the first 20 seconds or so – although it could be allowed to play for a while under a **talkover** introduction to the programme. If the theme is allowed to play for very long at the start, it might suggest that a music, rather than a speech, programme is beginning. Too much music at the end, and it can create the impression that the programme has run short of material. At the end of the programme, the final few bars can be faded up – and if the producer has correctly calculated the moment to start the tune playing, the definite ending will run neatly to fill the intended total duration. **Back timing** the end theme in this way sounds particularly effective when the programme runs up to the news, a commercial break before the top of the hour, or the Greenwich Time Signal many Radio Four listeners affectionately refer to as 'the pips'.

Once the opening **theme** has had sufficient time to establish itself, the presentation talent should welcome listeners to the programme and promote its contents as reasons to keep listening. This **menu** should perform much the same task as a menu in a restaurant, making the substance which is to come sound appealing and full of promise – after all, if the items in the programme sound unpalatable, who in the audience is going to keep listening to hear them? Of course, as only Internet forms of radio can include total interactivity, the listener usually has no choice over which of the actual items are served up: another very good reason for giving them a positive sell. It is possible to over-hype the menu, though, and it is important for the presenter to strike a balance between selling and subtlety so as to avoid alienating listeners instead of persuading them to stay tuned.

As with live sequences (Chapter 3), as the magazine programme progresses, it is important to **signpost** the items which are still to come, promoting forward at every reasonable opportunity so listeners are reminded of the reasons why they should want to keep listening. This also allows new listeners who have tuned in after the beginning of the programme to know what is coming up, and it is a more inclusive approach than one that loftily assumes they have all been there from the start. The appeal of some items later in the programme may even keep listeners tuned in through items they find less interesting, so the benefits to the producer of signposting are closely linked to audience figures (see Chapter 4).

Planning the content

When planning the **running order**, then, it is important to consider very carefully the placing of individual items in relation to each other and to the total duration of the programme. Depending on the nature of the material, it may make sense to run the most serious and hard-hitting items at the beginning, and to save the softer or most humorous item until last. If the magazine is longer than half an hour, though, it may be advisable to make sure there are regular bursts of light relief, or the audience may be too weary or traumatized after a while to carry on listening. Some items will, by their topicality, or their relevance to an item in the news bulletin that precedes the magazine, be most suited to an early position in the running order. Others – perhaps an interview with a celebrity – will be sufficiently appealing to keep the audience listening until near the end, just so they hear the interview.

Although generally factually oriented, it is not uncommon for magazines to include competitions for prizes, and these may be run either short or long, with answers and winners in the first type being announced before the end of the same programme, and the conclusion of the second being used as an enticement for listeners to tune in for the next edition. Of course, if the programme were pre-recorded, it would not be possible to include instant competitions without a certain degree of subterfuge, or contriving a live section to be inserted at the appropriate point – taking care not to allow the joins to become apparent.

Variety is one of the best ways of maintaining interest in radio programming, and the approach to each item can be varied in order to achieve it. A detailed analysis of *Today* showed that over a seven-week period in 1997 it broadcast more than twice as many live or 'as live' interviews as speech packages, by a ratio of 23:9. The programme also carried almost as many **two-way** discussions with reporters as speech packages, as well as straight script reads by regular contributors which included the daily newspaper reviews and the 'Thought for the Day' (Starkey, 2001: 236). Separating similar items and approaches can increase the appearance of variety, although there are of course instances where two items really need to be broadcast consecutively, because they are related. Often an effective formula, on *Today* and elsewhere, is to run a speech package (see Chapter 2), and then follow it up with an extended interview, which develops points raised in the package. This second item could otherwise be a two-way, a brief listener **phone-in** (see Chapter 3) or a round table discussion between two or three interested parties.

Devise the running order for a pilot magazine programme, of either 30 or 60 minutes in duration (minus the time any news bulletin and any advertisements would take up). You may not be ready to plan the actual content yet, but you should be able to identify the structure of the programme. Discuss your running order in class, explaining your decisions and the approach planned for each item.

Production roles

Deciding on which items to run, and how they should be presented, is ultimately the job of the producer or the editor of the programme. Depending on how ambitious the programme is, in terms of the number of editions per week and the duration of each programme, the production team could be fairly large for radio. Each edition of *Today*, for example, has two editors, who work under a series editor. The relative complexity and the economics of television mean that there are normally striking contrasts between the resource demands of the two different media, in terms of both budget and the number of personnel. Because finance is limited, some radio magazines will combine the roles of editor and producer into one, and it is very common for some members of the programme team to be volunteers, especially on local radio. Religious programmes are often coordinated by someone who is funded by the church, who is in turn assisted by members of that faith community.

Although the role of producer may be performed autocratically, the most productive working relationships are usually achieved when all the different members of the programme team feel they can contribute ideas and suggestions which influence, if not actually control, the content. The forum for planning the content is usually a production meeting, and these tend to be held as often as is practical, usually at least once a day for a daily programme, and once or twice per week for a weekly one. The meeting should be chaired, formally or informally as seems appropriate, by the editor. Luckhurst described in some detail the planning process behind *Today*, and how preparations for the next programme are supervised by a night editor. When the presenters arrive at around 4 am, most of the running order has been decided, although sometimes tensions remain over who should present which items (2001, 70).

The convention is for there to be one or two presenters on a magazine, and there may be a role for a third: for example *Today* occasionally sends one member of the presentation team to present part of the programme from a political party conference or from a foreign country where news is breaking. *You and Yours* has one. One obvious advantage of double-headed presentation is the scope it allows for two presenters to talk to each other – without making the audience feel excluded – and the variety it brings to the programme. Beginners working on magazine programmes as part of their radio studies often feel less exposed and less vulnerable to mishaps if they have a counterpart with whom to share the role. Filling to time, for example, is often easier – although it is one measure of a true professional to be able to *ad lib* up to the news when the script has run out without it sounding like there is anything wrong, and it is a skill to be developed though both practice and experience.

Other members of the production team include the technical operator (known in the BBC as the studio manager), who will need to know about any particularly complicated technical operations in the programme early in the planning stage. **Outside broadcasts** (see the section on **OBs**, on pages 134–5) involve particularly intricate planning, and even one or more contributors being on the telephone or in a remote studio adds its own level of complication. There may also be a number of researchers and reporters who contribute to the programme, and although the presenters may often suggest programme items for consideration at the planning meeting, it could be they who originate the most material. The basic distinction between researchers and reporters is that the researcher finds stories, checks facts and writes scripts and interview questions – as do reporters – but the researcher is generally not heard 'on air'. A reporter presents speech packages, carries out remote interviews either live or 'as live' and is interviewed by the presenters in 'two-way' discussions about specific subjects or events, either in the studio or from a related location.

Programme items

Once a magazine programme has become established, and the staff have been working on it for some time, it is likely that it will have developed a character of its own. That is, the programme team – and the regular listeners – will probably have an innate sense of what kinds of item will be suitable and what would sound out of place.

There is a danger, though, that it may become predictable, so there should always be room for items that bring originality and experimentation to the **format**, as long as they are handled in a way that doesn't clash too markedly with the rest. A new programme, and one which is being produced as a one-off, will rely more heavily on the initial proposal with its definition of the target audience and sample content.

A balance must be struck between the timeless and the topical. Timeless items are those that are of as much interest to the listener this week as they would be next month. They can be held in reserve in case another item has to be pulled at short notice or a technical breakdown means an item can't proceed as planned. If an item over-runs, or the programme wishes to respond at short notice to breaking news, then a timeless item can be delayed until a future edition, without all the work that went into it being wasted. A programme that includes little that is topical, though, can seem out of touch with the world around it (the external **diegesis**) and so, out of touch with the listeners' concerns and experience of everyday life. Topical items make good first items precisely because they begin the programme by **anchoring** it in the present.

While relatively timeless items can be planned days or even weeks in advance of transmission, topical items might seem to demand very short lead times between the initial idea and being broadcast. That is indeed the case when responding to quickly breaking news, but very often even topical items are planned some time ahead. Just as radio newsrooms each tend to keep a news diary, showing anniversaries of newsworthy events, recording the dates of future court appearances of those accused in interesting criminal cases, and so on, a well organized magazine production team will also keep an up to date diary of forthcoming dates of interest. There are other **sources** of interesting diary material, too, particularly on the Internet (for example www.on-this-day.com), and an excellent printed resource is *Whitaker's Almanack*.

Ideas may come from a variety of other sources, including the trade or specialist press which publishes material about the subject area, other areas of the broadcast media, books, press agencies, freelance reporters or **stringers** who find material and want to be commissioned to produce it for the programme, and even listeners, who may write or call in with leads which deserve following up. *You and Yours*, for example, because of its concern for consumer affairs, receives large numbers of requests from listeners who want issues to be taken up on their behalf. Most areas of the print and broadcast media are sent large numbers of press releases from organizations and even individuals who are attempting to gain either free or relatively cheap publicity for a product or service they are selling – and the publishing world is renowned for its eagerness to secure author interviews in order to boost book sales. In this way, the editor must assume the role of gatekeeper, sorting the press releases and email and telephone approaches which are worth following up, from those that would not benefit the programme, or for which there simply isn't enough time.

Of course, some approaches from publicists are accompanied by gifts or inducements, so the careful editor should take care not to infringe any policy the radio station might have on such matters – and should certainly not allow editorial decisions to become so compromised that the programme loses its appeal because it is covering the wrong items at the expense of others which would be better suited to the target audience. Not all inducements offered by publicists are insidious, though, and often a programme can enter into an arrangement where for a reasonable amount of publicity, there could be an attractive competition prize to give away 'on air', which would otherwise be far too expensive for the programme budget.

Exercise 5.3

Plan the individual items for your pilot magazine programme, considering where in the running order each item would fit best. Discuss your plans for the programme in class, explaining your decisions and the approach planned for each item.

Linking material

Scripting for magazines can be done so thoroughly that every word is planned in advance, and there is no need for the presenter to *ad lib* at any time. Some presenters will feel such an approach too constraining, though, and may prefer the freedom to talk around a list of bullet points instead – for example, when running through the menu and when signposting items still to come. Some presenters will sound more natural doing an *ad lib*, however, if the **link** becomes too rambling and begins to lack direction and focus, the programme can start to lose impact and even sound less than professional. For example, this opening from *You and Yours* (25 February 2003) is an efficient and welcoming beginning to the programme:

Continuity:	And now it's time for *You and Yours*, with John Waite and Liz Barclay.
Liz Barclay:	Hello and welcome to the programme.
John Waite:	Coming up on *You and Yours* today: good news – our charter airlines are finally reducing those annoying airport delays which so often get holidays off to such a bad start. We'll be speaking to one of the airlines that's improved the most.
	A new report today says government departments are still churning out regulations which tangle businesses in red tape. We'll be hearing from Michael Heseltine, who was asked as a minister to make a bonfire of regulations and ended up getting his fingers burned.
Audio (Michael Heseltine):	"The fact of the matter. . . they never did." 10"
John Waite:	Also today: the senior doctor suspended and later sacked, shortly after complaining about care standards at her hospital.
Liz Barclay:	And on *Call You and Yours* at around half past 12 it's marriage versus cohabiting. In a society where cohabiting is no longer seen as 'living in sin', and where marriage rates are at their lowest for a century, is it time to give non-married couples the same legal rights as married couples? Or would that further undermine the importance of the institution? Call us now with your views and experiences on 08700 100 444.

The different items in the magazine are arguably the most important aspects of it, for it is the content that is used to 'sell' the programme to the listeners. One radio producer likened the integration of each individual item into the whole programme as taking off and landing: the most crucial parts of any aeroplane journey, and the aspects of any flight on which a pilot must concentrate the most in order to avoid disaster. In his analysis, for each item the 'take off' is the point where the presenter directs the audience's attention from whatever preceded it, and on to the new subject. It must set the scene and provide any explanation and contextualization that are necessary to capture the audience's interest for the duration of the item. However scripted or spontaneous the rest of the programme may be, this **cue** needs to be both written and delivered flawlessly in such a way as to draw in the audience without allowing any confusion or indirection to detract from it. The 'landing' is the **back anno**, which is the follow-up to the item, and which leads the listeners smoothly from the item and back into the rest of the programme ready for some more signposting, an **ident** or some music, perhaps, and then the next item.

In Figure 2.4, (page 51) the cue to the package on euthanasia was delivered in just three concise sentences, which ended by identifying the reporter to whom the programme was effectively delegated for the 4 minutes and 57 seconds of the package. The back anno provided an opportunity to point the audience to a subsequent item, which would develop the theme – and this might well have resulted in some of them listening longer. In magazines each type of item, from the package to the live interview, the two-way and the live script read, needs integrating with the rest of the programme in this way.

Live interviews

Live interviews are particularly useful in making the programme run to time. While the package or the recorded interview may have a pre-determined **pot point** which would allow it to be cut off prematurely at a given point without it being obvious to the listener, a live piece may be shortened or lengthened at will. A programme which is over-running, but which has a live interview at or near the end, can be made to run to time by simply asking fewer questions or cutting short the interviewee's answers. Similarly, if the programme is under-running, the presenter can ask a number of supplementary questions to 'pad' the material. Of course, there are extremes in both cases, which no responsible producer would wish upon the presenter, the interviewee or even the audience, because an interview which is too short to convey much information will lack credibility and the guest may ask why he or she made the effort to get to the studio. An interview that drags on long after the main interest in the subject and the guest has subsided can cease to be an asset to the programme, and even cause the audience to tune away.

Woman's Hour **presenter Jenni Murray interviewing politician, broadcaster and novelist Edwina Currie.** Note the availability of several microphones for other contributors who may, from time to time, sit around the table. *Copyright* BBC.

Planning for a live interview should be done in much the same way as for a recorded interview (see Chapter 2), and many of the same considerations apply, from prior research and content to setting up the **microphone** and not moving about or knocking the studio table. Live interviews also involve the logistical considerations of how to get the guest into the studio and out again, without disturbing any live **mic** work that may precede or follow the item. If the interviewee is live, but in a remote studio or on the telephone, the arrangements must allow the connection to be established and any testing of the line to be carried out before the item goes live to air. Where a magazine involves live guests, the use of a studio/control room combination is most appropriate, rather than crowding all the participants into a single studio which also houses the control desk and the technical operator.

While greater risks can be taken with recorded interviews, though, it is important to consider the implications of interviewing someone live, who is unlikely to observe the minimum requirements of **taste and decency**. Both Liam Gallagher and Ali G have used language when being interviewed on BBC Radio One, which has brought the

Corporation into disrepute, although it is possible that in either case that youth-oriented network may have considered the resultant tabloid newspaper coverage to be more beneficial to it than harmful (Garfield, 1998, 247–53; Kelso, 2002). The large falls in the station's listening figures since Matthew Bannister became controller do not, however, suggest that their programming strategies have been entirely successful. Of course, just as with phone-in programmes, magazine programmes can make use of the **profanity delay**, if the studio is equipped with one (see Chapter 3).

The other major problem with even the most respectful of interviewees is that they may simply be overwhelmed by the experience and 'dry up', making any attempt to prolong the interview very difficult. For this reason, it is particularly important to help live guests to settle into the studio environment for a few minutes before the item begins – and their nerves may be calmed if they know what subject areas they will be asked about and what the first question will be. Knowing what the first question is will enable them to concentrate on formulating at least the beginnings of a response. If the mic isn't live, the final moments before the interview are a useful opportunity to check the pronunciation of the guest's name, if it is at all unusual, and to confirm his or her job title, if that is to form part of the cue. When an interviewee begins by correcting such basic details, it can have the effect of making the interviewer sound unprepared. There will be occasions when the interviewer doesn't want to fully brief the guest about the questions, or to feel obliged to avoid certain issues – the often intense political interviewing on *Today* is a good example. Sometimes in political interviewing, there will be agreement between live guest and presenter not to discuss a particular topic, but it is not unusual on *Today* for an argument to break out between interviewer and interviewee about the line of questioning and whether certain questions are legitimate or not (Luckhurst, 2001, 143–4).

When there are multiple guests participating in a single item – for example, a round-table discussion – the presenter needs to use particular skills to ensure the item runs smoothly. If more than one person speaks at the same time, the effect is to disorient the listener because it becomes difficult to discriminate between the participants and it may not be clear who is making which point. The voices may even become garbled. It is useful before going live with the item to establish a simple set of ground rules to which all participants should agree: that they allow the presenter to effectively chair the discussion, that they wait until they are asked to speak and that they respect the right of the others to be heard. Of course, they are unlikely to adhere to the rules if they perceive the airtime to be allocated unfairly – especially if they have been chosen to participate because they represent opposing perspectives on an issue. Providing what is said is audible, there are times when an argument getting overheated can produce some compelling radio, provided matters don't then get out of hand and studio discipline doesn't break down.

Exercise 5.4

Produce and record your magazine programme as live. Play back the programme in class, explaining how you dealt with any problems that occurred and evaluating the success of the production in the light of feedback from others.

Outside broadcasts

Just as individual items may involve remote studios or locations, radio magazines are often well suited to being wholly presented from somewhere that, because of its relevance to the subject matter, will enhance the programme in terms of its listener appeal and the availability of interviewees and even **atmosphere**. If the subject is health, a hospital might provide a suitable environment, a consumer programme might be broadcast from a shopping centre, and so on – as long as the connection is not too tenuous. Stations can turn the event into a marketing exercise, and increase their visibility among their potential audience, which can benefit audience **ratings**. However this can add to the organizational burden, and if there is any chance that very large numbers of listeners may attend, there are aspects of crowd control that may require coordination with the police – or security officials in the case of private property, such as at a county show. Choosing any location involves visiting the proposed site and carrying out a detailed **risk assessment**, identifying any health and safety considerations involved in the operation.

Even without the possibility of a live audience turning up, OBs always require more planning than the routine studio-based equivalent. The broadcast equipment will require power, which may require a generator on site – although it will need to be far enough away from the microphones to not be heard. The production team and any equipment will need protection from any rain, if outdoors. Simple logistical aspects such as refreshments and toilet facilities also need consideration. The signal from the portable **mixing desk** needs to be sent cleanly back to the studio, without interference or interruption, and this may be done in any of three ways. A direct link can be established using a relay transmitter and an aerial directed towards a receiver back at base – this may be most easily achieved by using the station's **radio car** or **OB** truck, but it does require testing in advance, to ensure that the signal will be strong enough and that there are no obstacles which may be a hazard when setting up the aerial. Where a radio link is impractical, **ISDN**, **music lines** or a reliable and relatively good quality **VoIP** (Voice over Internet Protocol) solution will be needed. ISDN uses digital encoding to send output down dedicated lines, and requires a **codec** (encoder/decoder) at each end. Before the advent of ISDN it was usual to request the temporary installation of music lines, which had a high enough capacity to accept analogue **audio** signals of sufficient bandwidth to prevent any deterioration of sound quality between the remote and the studio. Music lines are a much more expensive option than using ISDN (if available) or VoIP.

At the OB location the producer, presenters and technical operators need to hear the station's output, in order to pick up **cues** or audible prompts to begin broadcasting after news bulletins, commercial breaks or any other material that is to be inserted into the programme from the studio. ISDN and music lines can provide a return **clean feed** of studio output minus the OB material – or if the magazine is being broadcast live from within the transmission area, simply using personal FM radios with headphones or earpieces can be both efficient and cost-effective. Internet solutions can be unreliable and slow, introducing a confusing delay. Other considerations are the number of microphones needed, and how any recorded material is to be played into the programme, as well as whether any **PA** or public address system is required to relay the output to any live audience. An extra **effects microphone** can be useful where there is any atmosphere that will enhance the programme – for instance, from an audience or from an event that is taking place. There should also be some means of communicating easily with the studio, and mobile phones are a useful modern day means of doing this – if in range and fully charged.

In addition to the usual programme team, extra help from runners or 'gophers' can be very useful, as can the services of somebody who knows the location well, perhaps through belonging to the host organization. Gophers can 'go for' this and 'go for' that, passing messages and helping to ensure people are in place in time for their cues.

Plan the logistics of producing a magazine show as an OB. Discuss your plans for the programme in class, explaining your decisions and the approach planned for the event.

Analysing magazine programmes

Magazine programmes can share many of the characteristics of live sequences (see Chapter 3), particularly where the personality of the presenters is allowed to assume as great an importance as the actual content. Packages within magazines can be rich in material for **textual analysis** (see Chapter 2), as can **idents** (see Chapter 4). The various conventions of the genre, as described in this chapter, may be present to a greater or lesser extent in each individual text. Magazines may use different **narrative structures**. Most are simply **closed**, in that a discourse opens at the beginning of the programme and progresses – often erratically – through a number of different, related topics, after which an act of **closure** follows with farewells and a simple invitation to listeners to tune in for the next edition. If the ending includes an enigma, in the form of a competition question, or the posing of some problem that will be resolved in the following edition, the **structure** of the programme can reasonably be described as **open**, because of the similarity to the cliffhanger in a drama serial. A magazine may even be described as **multi-strand** if its content is so arranged that similar topics reappear at different points in the same edition – just as a package might be presented in several parts interspersed with other items, or studio guests might be repeatedly brought back into the discourse to comment on different items or to continue a running theme or topic. The Internet offers the potential for individual items to be accessed separately by the listener in the order of his or her own choosing, through 'listen again' or podcasts, and such a structure could be described as **investigative**, in the manner of the encyclopaedia or the dictionary (see Chapter 1). In fact, continuing the comparison with print magazines, begun in the introduction to this chapter, they are also more likely to be read erratically, rather than from cover to cover.

Even a signature or theme tune, if there is one, and any beds used deserve close scrutiny because of the roles they play in contributing to the discourse being constructed within the programme. They have usually been chosen by the producer or the presenter for their appropriateness to the programme, its subject matter and style, or for their appeal to the target audience, yet whatever meanings broadcasters might try to **encode**, audiences may well **decode** them in rogue or deviant ways. A tune that is light and melodic might be intended to create a light-hearted impression of the programme, to **connote** that it is positive and upbeat. A more melancholic feel might be better suited to a magazine that deals with consumer issues or financial advice. Some popular song lyrics evoke particular contexts, such as The Beatles' *Paperback Writer* (1966), while some music uses everyday objects to produce notes or to add to the percussion, such as the cash register in Pink Floyd's *Money* (1973). The one might be suited to a magazine focused on books, writing, or publishing, while the other might seem appropriate to a financial programme. While the instrumental introduction to the Pink Floyd track might connote to some listeners only the connection with money, though, it might be **symbolic** of something more sinister to those who know and remember the lyrics to the song, which criticize inequality and describe money as both criminal and the 'root of all evil'.

The various **models** of **audience theory** (see Chapter 1) can be used in considering audiences' listening to magazines. The **uses and gratifications** theory that people within audiences use the media to gain access to information they need does explain why someone who is concerned about the stock market might listen to a business programme, why a patient might tune into a medical programme and why a farmer might follow *Farming Today* (BBC Radio Four). The other ways in which listeners might use magazines to meet their own needs include diversion, companionship and for referencing their own ideas, values and experiences against those of others, as indicated by McQuail, Blumler and Brown (1972). One could also discuss the relevance of other models – **stimulus-response**, passive and **hypodermic needle** – for instance in determining why listeners might make a recipe they heard on a food programme, begin to accept different attitudes to alternative lifestyles featured in a religious magazine, or go to see a film which was discussed on *The Film Programme* (Radio Four).

Magazines can raise various issues around **representation**, particularly because the speech content is inevitably relatively high, compared to other radio genres, such as music sequences. While the pejoratively termed 'DJ patter' – as parodied in the United Kingdom in comedian Harry Enfield's 'Smashie and Nicey' misrepresentation of 'deejays' – can deliberately avoid controversy and concentrate instead on 'simple' dedications and what's ons, magazines frequently court controversy. *Today* regularly makes the newspaper headlines because it challenges politicians live 'on air' to justify their actions and statements. A motoring magazine may attract attention because it unfavourably compares the cars produced by one manufacturer with those of another, or reveals a safety hazard with a particular **brand** of tyre. This raises issues of balance and bias – because a political party that feels it is being unfairly represented, or a tyre manufacturer who is criticized but does not get a chance to reply might be justified in making a complaint. In some territories there are strict **codes of practice** governing **impartiality** (see Chapter 9), but the existence of rules does not necessarily mean they are effectively adhered to (Starkey, 2007).

In considering the choice of presenters, of regular and irregular contributors, and of other interviewees, both producers and academics face questions of who they are, and from which gender, ethnic group and region they originate. Their age, class, religion and sexual orientation may be problematic, too, although the last two may be less easily apparent from the sound of their voices, than from what they say or the way in which they are introduced. Luckhurst reported some of the very recent controversies over both gender and regional origin concerning *Today* presenters (2001, 49–53). The first presenter of *Woman's Hour* was a man called Alan Ivieson, a production decision by its creator Norman Collins that can seem absurd as well as reactionary in these relatively egalitarian times, and probably a mistake which the BBC has been cautious about repeating. However, at the time, the predominantly male broadcasting establishment was breaking with convention in even broadcasting such a programme.

Neither gender, nor any other **demographic** descriptor, should necessarily exclude a person from particular roles on radio, though. Just as some television programmes (such as in the United States, Playboy Channel, and in the United Kingdom, Men and Motors) use female presenters to interest male viewers, one role of the presenter may justifiably be to excite, rather than to empathize. Condescension, though, rarely works as an audience puller, and *Woman's Hour* soon chose instead to empathize with its target audience: one of the key decisions behind its subsequent longevity. In textual analysis, it is important to consider not only the production motives behind such choices, but also the effects those choices may have on the **product** and its audiences.

Representation may also be affected by **ideology**. Just as many of the academic perspectives on *Woman's Hour* in Mitchell (2000) are driven by an interest in feminism, the programme makers themselves soon discarded early notions that they should cover only matters concerned with the domestic and personal routines of housewives, and began to include items that accorded with the feminist agenda. The programme has, however, managed to balance the hostility to men which is implicit in some feminist thinking with more accommodating stances over gender, to such an extent that men constitute up to a third of its audience. Conservative ideology, in its broadest sense, is more resistant to such an inclusive approach, and right-wing politicians who campaign for 'family values' such as monogamy, marriage and heterosexuality may have been appalled by the programme's occasional discussion of lesbianism. Other magazines that have challenged attitudes include *Out this Week* (BBC Radio Five Live) and *Gaytalk* (BBC GMR), both being targeted specifically at the gay communities in their own TSAs.

As 'common interest' magazines may target niche audiences made up of individual listeners who are likely to share common values, they are often ideologically charged rather than neutral over issues and beliefs that would be more controversial in other **contexts**. In more tolerant and democratic societies this is regarded as axiomatic of the relative freedom of speech they espouse, and there is no serious 'men's' campaign to silence *Woman's Hour* any more than animal rights campaigners visibly conspire against fishing programmes. However, these freedoms are not universally enjoyed, and interesting comparisons can be drawn between the magazine programme output of, for instance, the Voice of America or the BBC World Service and the international services of different authoritarian regimes.

It is difficult to imagine domestic broadcasters in such countries railing on behalf of the disabled against 'government bureaucracy' in the manner of *You and Yours* (Radio Four, 6 Nov 2002). Even in relatively benign contexts such as western democracies, the gatekeeping role of producers and contributors is decisive in controlling which items and viewpoints get to air – and therefore, which perspectives and beliefs are allowed to inform the discourse being articulated and to shape the representations of the world being constructed. Every day, producers are deluged with press releases and other approaches from organizations and individuals who wish to influence the content of their programmes, and it is only a producer's own notion of which items and perspectives will be appropriate to their programme and target audience that distinguishes between those that get through and those that are spiked. Inevitably, the close involvement of the BBC's Disability Affairs Correspondent, Peter White, in the production of *You and Yours* as one of the presenters makes certain perspectives on disability more likely to get through – because he is blind.

The way in which interviewers, particularly in live situations, treat their interviewees can be an indicator of their own ideological positioning, however much they may insist that they are 'impartial' – or, at least, we are entitled to speculate as to how they might be influenced by their own positioning. For example, *Today* presenter John Humphrys told the former media magazine programme, *Medium Wave*, that he leaves his political views 'outside the studio door' before going inside to broadcast (Radio Four, 28 Jan 1996). However, the seriousness with which he regards his 'impartiality' does not prevent him from contributing opinionated and provocative articles to the press. Because the BBC considered the *Today* programme's then editor, Rod Liddle to have compromised his own impartiality by also writing for the press, Liddle was removed from the programme in a flurry of media coverage (Plunkett and Cozens, 2002). Certainly, the nature of interviewing means it involves so many variables that it is practically impossible for two different interviewees to be given equal 'treatment' by even the same interviewer (Starkey, 2007, 105–14).

Various techniques of **discourse analysis** can be used to examine and compare interviews and the ways in which they are conducted – whether they are in an acutely political context like *Today*, or an apparently benign environment such as a leisure or cultural magazine. The more obvious issues include tone, which may be aggressive, light-hearted, friendly, sceptical, dismissive or any other that connotes any other type of emotional response to the interviewee. A sceptical tone, for instance, may suggest to listeners that an interviewee's evidence or opinion is not valued as highly as that of an opponent. One laugh may have a completely different **semiotic** value to another, as may a sigh or any other paralinguistic element of the interviewer's discourse (Argyle, 1988). Interruption can be indicative of the amount of latitude given to interviewees to speak according to their own agenda: politicians in particular may wish to be 'on message' in that they have a number of points they wish to make, whatever questions are asked of them, and they don't want to be diverted from their own preferred discourse. Although some listeners complain of 'rudeness' by interviewers who interrupt their guests, others feel evasive interviewees should be pursued aggressively (Starkey, 2007, 110–14), and to treat them unequally can be read as creating an imbalance. Timing the responses between questions and counting the number of interruptions can produce some interesting and valuable **quantitative research** data, which may begin to justify some harsh conclusions about the way different interviewees are treated in a text.

The questions asked deserve to be scrutinized, too. Using a systematic approach to question analysis can reinforce superficial notions of 'hard' questions and 'easy' ones. Categorizing questions according to a logical analysis of their effects on the dialogue provides a framework for such an approach. For example, asking an **open question**, rather than a closed one can in itself allow the interviewee more latitude (see Chapter 2) in the way that 'Will you raise taxes?' can be read as more insistent than a question that asks for impressions or feelings about taxation. Multiple questions – such as 'Which taxes are going up, why and how do you feel about that?' – can be unclear and allow interviewees considerable freedom to ignore the awkward parts and focus on those they would rather answer, particularly as listeners will soon forget exactly what the question was asking. Non-questions don't begin with the usual interrogatives, but they are mere statements put forward by the interviewer for confirmation or rebuttal, or as prompts to begin talking on a subject, for example 'Taxes will be going up'. Categories used for this type of analysis can be complementary, as well as the mutually exclusive ones above. Closed, open and multiple questions can also be 'leading' questions. These are loaded with possibly incorrect assumptions that the interviewee must either accept or deny – a classic example is 'When did you stop beating your spouse?' – and McLeish considered them to be lazy, inexperienced or malicious by nature (2005, 89). Feeling the need to deny the allegation in the question can disadvantage the interviewee, who might have to come 'off message' to do so; and, furthermore, the loading of a question can actively position the interviewer on an issue.

Bell and van Leeuwen's analysis of complementary question types (1994, 149–55) offered greater sophistication because it considered the interviewer's motives behind each one. *Soliciting opinion* involves 'cooperative' questions, lacking in challenge, and typified by the opening 'What do you think of . . .?'. The interviewee's views are being sought and it is usually clear they are valued. *Checking questions* are less cooperative, as they demand only affirmation of specific facts or opinions. Usually closed, they will seek a polarized response, as in 'Are interest rates coming down then?' *Challenging questions* share some characteristics with checking questions, which can also involve confrontation. The interviewer contradicts or confronts the interviewee, who in turn may need to dispute assumptions in the question. Bell and van Leeuwen identify *entrapment questions* as best demonstrating the power of the interviewer: '[they are] unanswerable challenges, statements with which interviewees can neither agree nor disagree without losing face, or . . . to which they can neither say "yes" nor "no" without contradicting themselves' (1994, 155). Finally, *release questions* are deliberately soft, and common after confrontation or entrapment. As in the narrative convention of return to equilibrium, even very tough interviews often end with an opportunity for interviewees to re-establish their authority.

6 Advertisements and Trails

In this chapter you will:

▶ learn how advertisements and trails are made and used in radio
▶ research, plan and produce your own advertising campaign
▶ consider ways of analysing adverts or trails you hear and make yourself.

Advertisements in context

Advertisements are arguably the most important elements in a commercial radio station's output. Without them, such stations would be deprived of their main source of income, and the news and programming departments would soon cease to exist. They can take up large amounts of airtime, yet ironically the vast majority of listeners will have tuned in to hear something else, which might be music, news, traffic and travel, or just for company. **Trails** are of less importance, but without them, listeners would be less likely to hear about other programmes at other times, which they might enjoy – and encouraging listener loyalty, getting them to listen for longer, is vital to audience **rating** success.

As launch presenter *and* Managing Director of Century 105 in northwest England, John Myers welcomed listeners to the station, played the first advert and (after fading down the studio **microphone**) told the watching audience to the television documentary *Trouble at the Top* (BBC1): 'I like this bit the best. This is the money!' It was a good joke, at an exciting time, but how cynical *is* the commercial radio sector, when it needs to earn money to survive? Successive British governments resisted the introduction of commercial radio until the passing of the Sound (Broadcasting) Act 1970, largely because its opponents argued that programming quality would be subordinate to making money. The first **regulator**, the Independent Broadcasting Authority, controlled the nature and the amount of advertising so tightly and set so many programming rules that those fears initially proved to be unfounded. Under its successors, the Radio Authority, and now Ofcom, the regulatory environment has become much more benign. Stations have much more freedom now than at the launch of the first **ILR** station in 1973. However, most listeners probably still perceive the advertising they hear to be of secondary importance. As Myers's candid moment revealed, though, the investors, shareholders, and managers in commercial radio have a very different perspective.

For its first 20 years, ILR suffered from very low penetration of the advertising market, taking only a 2.8 per cent share in 1992. The birth of three national stations, Classic FM, Virgin and Talk Radio (later talkSPORT) in the 1990s, and then rapid growth in local and regional provision, allowed radio to achieve a 6.6 per cent share by 2002 (RAB, 2002). Enjoying what has at times been a lucrative business, some of the major interests in commercial radio have made big profits, with the Capital Group reporting a profit of £27.8 millions from a turnover of £120 millions in 2001–2 (Capital, 2002). However, the subsequent recession turned profits into losses (Sweney, 2012).

One irony for a commercial station in deriving the greatest income from selling its airtime to advertisers is that too much advertising, or the wrong kind of advertising, might drive away the very listeners the station is 'selling'. Advertising cannot, however, be unobtrusive, because if it's not noticed, it's unlikely to be effective. An exception was in the cinema, where subliminal frame advertising was apparent only to the viewer's subconscious mind – but this was soon outlawed in the United Kingdom, because it suggested a response, without the viewer being able to question whether or not to follow it. Advertising on radio cannot use the subliminal frame effect, or even the visual media's ability to flash legal 'small print' onto the screen without it detracting from the artistic and entertainment value of the production. In fact, one of the main disincentives for advertisers of financial services to use radio is the requirement to actually voice in real time legal warnings and detailed examples of credit agreements, giving them far greater prominence than they assume in television or press advertising.

So, commercial producers in radio must make adverts which sell but don't repel, which are persuasive but not invasive and which will ideally enhance the listening experience, rather than detracting from it. This is a lot to ask of busy people who may work on a dozen or more ads at a time, and often have small production budgets. Many clients in local radio run small businesses and they have been persuaded to try radio advertising for the first time, but they are unsure of how well it will work for them. They may, as a result, be unwilling to commit large sums to production, when they have already paid for the airtime. As some of the best commercial producers and radio salespeople recognize, if that airtime is to be used effectively, it is worth developing an effective commercial to fill it.

At the opposite end of the spectrum are national advertisers, who already spend much more on relatively expensive television advertising, and who have decided to increase the impact of their existing **campaigns** by exploiting the synergies which are made possible by using the two media together. In the 1980s, Radio Luxembourg produced **research** that suggested that the message in a television campaign persisted much longer in the audience's minds if combined with subsequent radio advertising, which carried on the campaign theme. Although a fairly obvious point, its importance lies in the relative cheapness of radio, which allows a tight budget to stretch much further over time by first establishing the message on television, and then reinforcing it over a longer period on radio. The Radio Advertising Bureau was set up in 1992 by the United Kingdom's commercial radio sector to develop and exploit such research data, later confirming the Luxembourg findings (RAB, 2000). Its web site (at www.rab.co.uk) offers advertisers assistance in planning campaigns, including cost per thousand listener analyses, **demographic** and rating information and examples of successful advertising campaigns. There is also a very useful archive of creative adverts that have proven to be successful.

It is worth noting that an advertising campaign may consist of several different adverts in the same medium, which are united by a common aim or a theme that runs through them. If a client is

Exercise 6.1

Continue the table below, filling in the blank space and adding more examples of radio adverts. Discuss your answers in class.

Product or advertiser	Target audience	Style
Autoglass	Car owners	Windscreen repair technician explains chip repair then catchy jingle plays
Carphone Warehouse		Bernard Cribbins then voice-over artist; Wombles theme under

prepared to pay for it, the added variety of a series of ads can enhance the campaign considerably, because listeners are less likely to bore of a series of ads, than they are of just one, which is played more often. Different ads may feature different products from the same retailer, or different characteristics of the same product or service, or they may simply use common characters in different **scenarios** in order to invite the same listener response. The scheduling of ads can be sophisticated enough to accommodate different ads for different weather conditions, or relate the content to a particular **daypart**.

Planning a campaign

The first stage in the creation of any ad is the initial contact between the sales executive and the client – and this relationship, if successful, can be a lasting and profitable one, especially for the executive, who will probably be working on a commission basis. Many advertisers have also reaped great benefits from using radio, either exclusively or as a key element in their marketing mix. The commission provides a considerable incentive for the sales executive to give the client the best possible advice, because a satisfied client is more likely to give the station repeat business. Conversely, if the client is poorly advised and later perceives the advertising to have been a waste of money, the station – and the executive – will probably lose the client to a competing station or medium. As in the United Kingdom most businesses' first experience of advertising is likely to be through the local newspaper or the internet, it can only harm the radio industry if they try radio and find the experience unsatisfactory.

The executive needs to find out certain information from the client, and this will form a major part of the client brief. Firstly, *who* is the advert aimed at? This is a fundamental question, which influences radio production in any **genre**, and concerns **target audience**. If the advertiser wishes to influence young men to buy a particular lager, for instance, then a station such as Gold – which targets the over-forties – simply can't deliver. A station's **audience research**, and even some common sense, might suggest that a typical CHR station (see the section in Chapter 4 about music formats) is listened to by large numbers of young men, and that during the Saturday afternoon sports coverage they are proportionately well represented in the audience. Directing the client's advertising spend towards Saturday afternoon on such a station, then, can make the campaign particularly effective, and make the client feel the money has been well spent. Audience research data (see Chapter 4) can be analysed in such a way as to indicate a cost per thousand listeners in different dayparts and on different days, on an 'all listeners' basis and according to different demographic descriptors.

Secondly, what does the client want the target audience to *do*? It may be to buy a particular lager, or it may be to buy it from a particular retailer, who is also involved in paying for the campaign. Sometimes the client just wants the listeners to try the product – for instance, coming into a car showroom and taking a test drive – and then the client's own salespeople can begin a harder sell, on an individual basis. Either formally or informally, retailers measure footfall – that is, the number of people who walk onto their premises – which can be done by sophisticated counting devices at the entrances, linked to a computer, or just by gauging whether they have had a 'busy' or a 'quiet' day. Either way, they probably want to increase footfall, because the more people who come into the premises, the more will actually buy something, or at least, return another day to make an actual purchase.

Increasingly, there are also clients who wish to change people's behaviour. For example, a health promotion organization might want to discourage smoking, to encourage safer sex, or to educate people about healthier diets. A local council might want people to make sure they register themselves on the electoral roll of those who are entitled to vote, and the police might want to discourage drink driving or warn of new speed cameras on the motorway. This kind of advertising is very similar to the traditional **public service announcement** which non-commercial stations such as BBC local radio broadcast free of charge in the interests of the community. To a commercial radio station, these publicly-funded bodies can be just another client with money to spend – and sometimes plenty of it.

Thirdly, *why* should the target audience do what the advertiser wants? The answer to this may simply be that the product is the cheapest, that the retailer is the friendliest, or that not following the healthier lifestyle can have tragic consequences. Whatever it is, this reason must be clear and compelling, otherwise listeners will be ambivalent about following the advice. Where a product or a service is in competition with others, which the listeners could buy instead, the main advantage it has over the others is called its unique selling point. Sometimes the sales executive needs to work with the client to find out what the USP is, and it may be that the client needs to devise a special offer that will give the client's product or service a competitive edge. In a **PSA**, the USP may be so blunt as the grim reality that anyone who doesn't stop drinking and driving may cause a fatal accident.

The fourth question is: what first step does the client want the target audience to actually *take*? This should also be clear and straightforward, because if it is too complicated or difficult to remember, listeners can easily forget or become confused as to how to follow the advice in the advert. Because many clients' first experiences of advertising are of placing display ads in the local newspaper, they are used to including their telephone number in their advertising. On radio, complicated numbers are not easily remembered by listeners who may be driving the car, cutting someone's hair or engaged in any other activity which prevents them immediately reaching for a pen and paper. Some phone numbers are, of course, memorable because they have several noughts in them or they repeat particular numbers or patterns of numbers, and the listener has a better chance of retaining these. There are also ways of making a number more memorable, for example by singing it in a **jingle** or finding words which rhyme with it, but in the United Kingdom too many local radio adverts end with phone numbers, and the clients should be asked to consider whether picking up the telephone is really the most desirable response to the advert anyway.

Often the client really wants footfall, so the response sought should be to go to the premises. It is likely to be easier to remember a location, particularly one that uses local landmarks, than to remember a phone number. Sometimes a client wants to be better able to judge the effectiveness of a particular advertising campaign, by finding out which customers have responded to the radio campaign, as opposed to any simultaneous press, television or billboard advertising. Then it may be useful to build distinguishing incentives into the advert, such as: 'For an extra five per cent off, come in and tell us Capital sent you'. The client must, of course, be aware of the financial implications of such an offer.

Exercise 6.2

Negotiate a client brief with a local advertiser, by agreeing the nature of a radio advertising campaign for a real product or service. This may involve role-play in class. You will be scripting and producing ads to meet this brief in later exercises.

Scripting advertisements

After agreeing the client brief, the next stage is undertaken by the creative or commercial production department (once widely known as 'Com Prod'), where a proposed script is written and then sent back for the client to consider. As commercial production costs time and money, in terms of the human effort and studio resources taken up by it, the script must be agreed by the client and signed off as part of a binding agreement before any further work is done on it. Scripting may be done by a dedicated **copywriter** who is a permanent member of the creative team, or by someone who undertakes a number of production roles. As increasing numbers of smaller commercial stations were launched in the United Kingdom in the 1990s and 2000s, it became more common for stations to contract out their commercial production to specialist production houses, such as S2Blue (www.s2blue.com) or Airforce (www.airforce.co.uk), who produce ads for several stations at a time. The large radio groups may also choose to centralize production at one of their locations, just as GWR Group

Figure 6.1

National	£ million
1 COI Communications	15.81
2 BSkyB	9.27
3 British Gas	8.33
4 Autoglass	7.93
5 Unilever	6.64
6 Volkswagen	6.26
7 Vodafone	5.82
8 Blockbuster	5.61
9 Lloyds TSB	4.66
10 Carphone Warehouse	4.54

UK top ten national advertisers in the year 2011. *Source*: RAB, Nielsen Media Research.

moved all its creative production to Bristol in 1993. This can have the effect of very similar ads being broadcast for similar, yet unconnected clients in different markets, simply because there was an already written script that just needed some minor changes, before it could be used again on a different station.

Large national clients, who have much bigger budgets than the average local business, can afford to use prestigious producers, and ask for more creative adverts than many other clients have to settle for. When budgets are more generous, proposed scripts can be tested through the production of rough demos. If the client likes the **demo**, it can then be recreated to a better standard – with, for example, the celebrity **voice-over** it would have been too costly to record onto the trial version. One of the best-known British radio adverts featured the voice of actor Griff Rhys Jones, for the television and **audio** equipment manufacturer Philips, which he deliberately mispronounced as 'Firips'. Although this was produced in 1981, it was still being discussed in the *Radio Magazine* in August 2002 (Calvert, 2002). The Radio Advertising Bureau makes available on its web site some of the most creative and memorable radio adverts, in order to stimulate present and new advertisers, and to encourage use of the medium (www.rab.co.uk).

Some creative producers are very critical of unadventurous radio adverts that use clichéd or routine scripts to convey their sales messages. The vast majority of local radio ads use a simple voice over a piece of music, which may include sung elements peculiar to the advertiser – the name, a slogan and perhaps a phone number. However, radio drama in its simplest form lends itself well to commercial production (see Chapter 8). Generally, though, such simple and formulaic adverts work, and because they are relatively cheap to produce, the clients tend to be happy with them. Time and budgetary constraints mean that few producers are able to create many campaigns that have the impact of Firips to tight deadlines and when they have heavy workloads to manage.

Scripting effective radio advertisements requires the copywriter to balance the requirements of the client brief with a sense of what makes good radio. If commercials aren't to be a turn-off, they need to be at least listenable – and if possible, positively enjoyable. This is one reason why copywriters use humour a lot, in the belief that an amusing ad is a memorable one – at least for a while. Some jokes have a longer shelf-life than others, though, and a corny punch-line, or a silly scenario which may be heard repeatedly by many listeners over an extended period, can actually begin to work against the client's interests, because listeners may begin to resent the advert.

The irritant factor can sometimes work *for* the client, though, as demonstrated by the reactions of commercial radio listeners in northeast England, who when asked in informal surveys to recall the names of advertisers using radio, will frequently cite Frank's Factory Flooring. Voiced by 'Frank' himself, this long-running campaign for cut-price carpets uses a simple monologue detailing the latest deals on offer, delivered in a manner with all the subtlety of a shouting market trader. This approach works for the business's real owner, Frank, and the stations in the region that carry the ads have not yet decided that the benefits of receiving his money are outweighed by any tune-out factor among irritated listeners. Imagine, though, if every advert on these stations mimicked Frank's, rather than contrasting in **style** and approach. As Classic FM's programming is largely 'relaxing' classical music, if Frank's business were to expand, it is difficult to imagine his ads being acceptable in style to that particular national network.

Whatever the style of delivery, writing for radio should always follow the basic rule that it is for the *spoken* word, rather than to be read off a page by the end consumer (see Chapter 2). A monologue should normally be addressed to the individual listener, and should balance informality with authority. Scripted dialogue between two or more characters should sound natural, as if it were a real conversation – and except in the case of a **spoof**, characters should seem real enough to carry conviction. Comedy of the absurd can work well, often making a simple point effectively, and as a student the author played the price-smashing neanderthal 'Rocky Bottom' in an advert for a furniture warehouse in Bristol. That such ancient cave-dwellers must have died out hundreds of thousands of years before didn't matter to the audience – the only claims made in the advert which had to be literally true were those about the prices and the nature of the furniture in the sale. Where simple **dramatizations** are used in adverts, there is much that is relevant in Chapter 8.

Even silence may have a role to play. Because airtime has to be paid for by advertisers, not using some of it may be a superficially unattractive proposition to them, but silence, as in other radio genres, can be particularly effective in advertising: at least so long as it remains unusual. As radio – particularly music radio – rarely falls silent except in the case of a technical breakdown, an advert using the following formula can usually be relied upon to grab listeners' attention:

```
mvo:    Listen. . .

(4" silence)

mvo:    Yes, the world outside seems quieter - with quality
        double glazing from ABC.
```

With a total **duration** of just ten seconds, the **copy** makes an important point simply. If the silence were instead broken by an alarm clock, a slice of bacon sizzling in a pan or some other effect, it could be used just as effectively for a different product or service. However, programmers' nervousness about silence is reflected in the use of silence sensors both in the station and at transmission sites, and if the detection parameters are set too tightly, the script above could cause failsafe devices to begin playing alternatives.

The more complicated the scenario, though, or the more sophisticated the message, the less effective radio ads can become because of the greater demands made of the listener. Creativity and originality work best for the client when the concept is simple and easy to convey in words, sounds and music. A further disincentive to making elaborate ads is the greater cost involved in production. Each **voice-over artist** must be paid for, and so must **copyright** music and sound effects, so there can be budgetary implications to adding layers of sophistication. Studio and **post-production** time must be accounted

---

Figure 6.2

Script, single voice-over, non-MCPS library
music, and up to 3 fx: £125
- for each additional voice-over artist: add £40 per voice
- with jingle over a syndicated backing track: add £500
- with jingle over a custom backing track: add £700–800

Price includes delivery by ISDN or Internet, but is subject to VAT.

A remake fee of 50% applies if client wants changes after completion.

Sample pricing information for a radio advert made by a production house for a single local station. Note that some companies charge higher rates and stations may add commission, or charge their clients more if producing the ad in-house. The fee for a single voice-over artist rises to £450 for use on a single national station.

---

for, too, as must time spent searching for particular pieces of music or sound effects that meet creative criteria – and not every elaborate advert with high **production values** will be as cost-effective as Frank's.

Legal and regulatory constraints

All copy must also satisfy the many legal and regulatory constraints on advertising. As with television, in the United Kingdom the regulator's **code of practice** (Ofcom, 2011) is binding on commercial radio contractors and there are penalties for breaking the rules. This contrasts with press and billboard advertising, where the Advertising Standards Authority (ASA) operates a voluntary system of self-regulation, and with the Internet, where there is no common system of regulation, either voluntary or statutory. It follows that a radio station which broadcasts exclusively on the Internet has fewer rules to follow – and, for example, could broadcast unlimited amounts of advertising if it wanted to. There are laws, though, which relate to the conduct of business, and it would be an unwise trader who advertised low mileage secondhand cars, knowing that the odometer had been turned back to deceive the customer over their true mileage.

Ofcom's radio advertising code (see page 154) has been enforced under contract by the ASA since 2004. There is an advice line, but the RadioCentre operates a central copy clearance service for its member stations, Radio Advertising Clearance Centre (racc.co.uk). Most types of advertising are quite straightforward, but certain categories require central copy clearance. The use of children in adverts, for example, is strictly controlled, as is any advertising that is aimed at children. Alcoholic drinks, medicines and treatments, as well as gambling, charities and religious organizations are particularly tightly controlled. Some services, such as prostitution, are obviously illegal, and cannot therefore be advertised, while cigarette advertising became subject to a legal ban from commercial television in 1965 anyway – also being banned in the United States in 1972 (Godfrey and Herweg, 1997, 64). Copy for financial services, such as investment advisors, credit card accounts, loans and mortgages, must include certain statements and disclaimers under the code, and even the offer of credit on a big purchase, such as a car, could require by law further details of the interest rate, the APR and the total amount payable. The local trading standards service will usually offer free advice on the legal controls on traders, if needed – and any adverts broadcast that they consider to break the law may have to be withdrawn and remade. The Office of Fair Trading web site is a useful resource (www.oft.gov.uk), and the Ofcom code is also accessible on line (www.ofcom.org.uk).

Exercise 6.3

Write scripts for at least two adverts that fulfil your agreed client brief. Get feedback from others as to their suitability and effectiveness, and then present them to the 'client' for approval.

Producing advertisements

In a busy in-house commercial production department, a voice session could involve the recording of a dozen or more scripts, and that could take as long as an hour, depending on the complexity of the work, and how many scripts are recorded in just one or two takes. The busy commercial producer may book two or more voice sessions per week, either through agencies or with the voice-over artists themselves, but because radio adverts can be booked, written, produced, passed by the advertiser and put 'on air' in a matter of hours, rather than days, it is useful to have someone in-house who can voice ads at short notice. Often this will be someone in the creative production department or one of the station's presenters. The most successful voice-over artists work for a large number of stations, either touring the country or working from a central base and using the Internet or **ISDN** to send studio-quality audio from their own studio to the radio station (Shaw, 2000, 143–60).

An experienced voice-over artist will require little direction from the producer, and may add a further layer of creative interpretation to a script that allows it. Ultimately, though, the producer has the responsibility to produce an effective and listenable ad which fits the client's brief, and so the voice-over artist has to be able to accept direction (Shaw, 2000, 6–33). When an ad has been over-written, in that there is a little too much copy for the total duration, it will require an increase in pace on the next take – although neither the producer nor the client will prosper from ads which are read too quickly and so garble their message. As airtime is normally sold in multiples of ten seconds, ads must run to the exact duration that the client is paying for. Thirty seconds is a common duration, which is affordable enough for the client to book a reasonable campaign in terms of how many times it will be played, yet long enough to allow it to clearly express the client's message.

Some producers record the voice dry – that is, without using any backing track or sound effects that the script calls for. They can be effectively added in post-production, after the voice-over artist has left the building. Others record a voice over the **bed** in real time, doing the **mix** on the studio **mixer** and ensuring the **levels** are consistent with each other – especially if there are predetermined points in the music around which the voice must fit, or if there is a sung element to the bed, which shouldn't be talked over. The producer must listen carefully and critically to the voice, spotting any accidental microphone **popping** or **ambient sound** (see Chapter 1) that could spoil the recording, as well as any stumbles or fluffs made by the voice-over artist. The script should also be read with the utmost clarity, with an appropriate amount of expression in the voice – including contrasts of light and shade, of happy and sad, of reassurance and surprise – without, of course, being too exaggerated to be taken seriously by the listener (Beck, 1997, 137–44). The advert will be heard by a relatively cynical and media-literate audience, and while the offer of 'buy one, get one half price' would be truly astonishing if applied to a brand new car, it would seem much less remarkable if the product were a packet of crisps.

A commercial producer needs to know how product names and places should be pronounced, and then to make sure the voice-over gets them right. Recording ads for Heart (formerly MFM) in Wrexham, for instance, may mean saying Llay, Cefn-y-Bedd and Rhosllanerchrugog correctly. In Cornwall, even the seemingly innocuous Mousehole, and in Cheshire, Cholmondeley can be problematic. The BBC's newsreaders make extensive use of the Corporation's Pronunciation Unit, as well as the *BBC Pronouncing Dictionary of British Names* (Pointon, 1983).

Where a script uses dialogue, it is not necessary for both voices to be present at the same recording session, or to be in the same location. The producer, or an assistant, can provide the other half of a conversation through the first voice-over artist's headphones if necessary, in order to help the dialogue flow. The second voice is then added in a later session. Just as the scripting should be as realistic as possible, so the actual voice work should make dialogue sound real – except in the case of a spoof, in which comic effect may depend on an element of absurdity.

Using music and effects

Choosing music for radio advertising can be time-consuming and therefore expensive. Most ads use **library music**, which is created for radio and television producers to use when budgets won't stretch to an original composition, performed especially for the particular production, or when a more familiar, commercially produced recording is unavailable. The economics of radio advertising, particularly on a local or regional basis, mean that budgets don't often stretch very far at all. An advertiser may want to use the James Bond **theme**, for example, because men wearing clothing from his shop will attract the attention of desirable women, but in the United Kingdom the Copyright, Designs and Patents Act 1988 forbids unauthorized use of the music. There are no blanket agreements between the copyright bodies, PPL, PRS for Music and MCPS, and the radio industry for the use of music on adverts, unlike those for music programming (see Chapter 4), so getting written permission to use the track on an advert involves contacting the owners of the copyright on both the composition *and* the recording, and agreeing what is likely to be a large fee.

The advertiser need not be completely disappointed, though, as there will inevitably be a library music track which sounds rather like the James Bond theme, in its style, sound and feel, without using a similar enough arrangement of musical notes to land the production house which recorded it in court for infringement of copyright. The collections of library music (some of them supplied free, some of them supplied on a subscription basis) normally have detailed descriptions of each track on the CD cover. Some collections boast searchable databases, either on CD-ROM or the Internet (for example, at unippm.co.uk), which can make finding a suitable track easier. Usually descriptions such as 'pastoral', 'industrial', 'dynamic' and 'action', coupled with references to tempo and instrumentation are insufficient indicators as to how a given track will sound, so searching for the best track for a particular advert can be painstaking and frustrating. There is no real substitute for listening to a track and deciding whether or not it fits the **purpose**.

Use of a library track must be declared and paid for, but it almost always represents considerable savings of time and money over securing the rights to more mainstream music. Some collections are sold on a buy out basis, whereby the purchase of the discs also buys the right to use them in specified circumstances, such as in radio advertising.

Others require declarations (**copyright returns**) to be made to the production company or MCPS (now part of PRS for Music) when they are used, and this information is normally found on the sleeve.

Much cheaper than using commercial recordings of popular, recognizable songs, yet more expensive than using an anonymous library recording, is the option of commissioning a sung jingle or bed which identifies the product or the advertiser, and may also include a sung slogan and a telephone number. Usually pre-existing tracks will be customized by a production house, who will arrange for session singers to record the vocals to order, over a bed which may have been used many times before in different markets. Costs are reduced by economies of scale when several recordings are made in a single session.

Sound effects can present similar problems, although when the exact sound effect a producer wants is not readily available on a compilation disc or via a searchable database, it can be more time efficient to create it. Common sound effects, such as car door slams, footsteps and doorbells are highly recordable, if care is taken over microphone position,

Figure 6.3

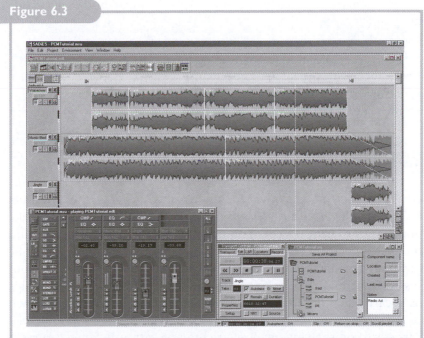

A screenshot of a simple advertisement in post-production on SADiE. Different stereo pairs of 'streams' are being used for the bed, voice-over and terminal jingle.

acoustics, microphone handling and the presence of unwanted ambient sound (see Chapter 1) and there really are hairdryers out there that sound on radio like spaceships taking off, particularly if subject to some **processing** in post-production (see Chapter 8). The Ofcom code of practice warns, though, of using car sounds indiscriminately in advertising, because they may startle drivers listening in heavy traffic, into reacting dangerously on the road.

However simple or complicated the production, the producer must exercise skill and judgement in deciding on the correct mix of all voice tracks, music and sound effects, as well as the nature and extent of any processing, such as **equalization**. Computer applications such as SADiE and Adobe Audition can enable skilled operators to create very polished productions, but it is still possible to mix and process effectively to quite high levels of sophistication using a number of sound **sources** in a production studio, and controlling their levels in real time through the mixer. Recording in stages, and **editing** tightly together each stage, or mixing a voice over another previously recorded mix, are techniques which served the radio industry well for decades before the arrival on the scene of the personal computer.

Exercise 6.4

Produce your advertisements, according to the scripts previously agreed with the client. Get informal and formal feedback, especially from the client, about how well they suit the original brief.

Transmission

Getting the client's approval for the finished advert is not the final stage before it gets to air. When time is scarce, playing it down the telephone to the client is a common practice, although some stations and producers insist on written approval before use. Next, the ad must be physically made available to the studio and any automated playout system that may have to broadcast it. Until the 1990s most studios used **cart machines** to play shorter items off tape **cartridges**, and each of the current ads in use was recorded individually onto a numbered **cart** stored on shelving often referred to as a cart wall. Some cart racks were round, and if pushed, rotated around a central axis, so they were called carousels. Each cart had to be labelled carefully in order to avoid them becoming mixed up, or the wrong ads being played, with the label showing the duration and the **out-cue**. The cart started to become obsolete with the advent of hard disk storage, although initially some stations found **MiniDiscs** or 'hot key' devices such as the Instant Replay by 360 Systems to be more reliable than computer-based solutions. The department that schedules adverts is called **traffic** (although it has no involvement in traffic and travel **bulletins**), and its function is to ensure that the advert is broadcast at the correct times on the correct number of occasions, according to the contract between the station and the client. Traffic may use software such as Airwaves by RCS (see Chapter 4) to do this. It will then prepare transmission reports and billing information to be sent to the client.

Making trails

Making programme trails bears a number of similarities with commercial production, with the notable distinction that there isn't an outside client to directly pay for the production time and effort spent on them. The product is a specific programme on the same – or a related – station. The target audience is a sub-group of the station's regular audience, who may be tempted to listen at a given time, for some specialized content or the coverage of an event. The intended reaction is that they will find the programme being promoted appealing enough to tune in then. The financial constraint of not having a paying client may not be insurmountable, either. While some voice-over artists will often voice additional trails free of charge, it is usually more appropriate for the programme presenter to be featured on the trail. In environments where production costs are closely monitored, such as the BBC networks, programme budgets may include a cost heading for promotion, and some BBC local stations have staff whose duties include trail production. A further advantage is that most of the copyright restrictions which apply to adverts, don't apply to trails, which can be considered to be part of the station's normal programming and so covered by arrangements such as those with PRS, PPL and MCPS (see Chapter 4).

The need to make clear to the audience what the trail is for and when the programme is broadcast is essential to any trail. On commercial stations the programme may be sponsored, and there may be a tag line associated with the sponsor's name to include. Again, there are strict rules about what may be sponsored and by whom, particularly when there is an obvious connection between the sponsor's business and the programme content. Some copy will require central clearance, or may even be disallowed under the code. Sponsor credits may render music copyright as problematic as with discrete adverts, depending on the licensing agreements in place.

As with adverts, trails may be very simple, and consist of a dry voice or a voice over a single bed. Alternatively, they may be much more creative, even using drama to create interest in the programme. A daily magazine programme (see Chapter 5) may require a new trail each day, each listing the content of the next edition. In the 1980s John Peel created a cult following for his trails on the British Forces Broadcasting Service, with his bizarre weekly episodes about a dysfunctional family. Only an oblique reference to the programme being promoted actually related the trail to the next opportunity to hear *John Peel's Music*. As few broadcasters are blessed with the dry wit and deadpan delivery of John Peel, most trails need to relate more overtly to the programme and its content. Listeners should ideally get a flavour of the programme itself, hear some compelling reasons to listen to it and become well aware of the day and time of broadcast. Before he died in 2004, Peel began regularly voicing witty, content-rich trails for the weekly magazine *Home Truths* on BBC Radio Four.

There is no set length for a trail – it must be long enough to be effective, yet not too long to alienate audiences through repeated exposure to it. Between 20 and 40 seconds will usually suffice, and presenters who create overlong trails for their own programmes may find them being quietly dropped from other presenters' programmes, because they resent a colleague taking too much of their airtime.

Since the mid-1990s a number of stations have exploited the 'previously on' formula reminiscent of television series which recap past episodes at the start of the next one. This consists of brief clips of entertaining **links** or parts of links, edited together over a single bed or station **ident**. This can be effective, but the principal risks are of individual clips being insufficiently distinguished from the others, and so sounding confused, and of the material being far less funny when taken out of **context** than it may have seemed in the studio at the time. In order to **anchor** the trail within the intended context, there need to be clear and unambiguous announcements at the start and at the end, which use such copy as: 'Previously on the breakfast show' and 'Don't miss the next breakfast show, tomorrow from six to ten'.

Analysing advertisements and trails

In terms of **ideology**, most radio commercials inevitably position them-selves and the contexts in which they are broadcast firmly within the capitalist paradigm. Capitalism values economic activity based on money and the enjoyment of wealth, as well as the right of the indi-vidual and the corporation to amass capital – or assets – for present and future exploitation. Based on the assumption that investment and economic growth benefit society as a whole, capitalism operates through local, regional and global markets within certain limited rules which proscribe extreme practices that may be harmful to workforces and consumers. The notion of a (mostly) 'free' market that operates legally in all but the most controversial sectors, such as illegal drugs, prostitution and human organs, is reflected in the kind of regulation which controls advertising in even the most liberal of western democ-racies. In the United Kingdom, Ofcom's code of advertising practice (see pages 153–4) prohibits the advertising of certain goods and services, and tightly controls others, while in the United States regulation by the FCC is more permissive. Competing ideologies, such as socialism (which seeks to organize the distribution of wealth more evenly), and communism (which centrally coordinates production and distribution according to a controlling elite's perception of need and merit), are generally less tolerant of the principle that private assets should be used to gain commercial advantage, and hence increase profit.

Every time a radio commercial extols the virtues of owning a new car or buying something on credit, it reinforces capitalist principles through **naturalization** – just as television's 'window on the world' presents a version of life which can seem comprehensive but which is really a highly selective construct (Hall, 1982). This explains why, although in the United States commercial radio has long dominated the industry, in the United Kingdom Labour governments remained opposed to it until 1997. However it doesn't explain why Conservative governments also resisted legalizing commercial radio until the offshore pirates of the 1960s again demonstrated the demand for self-financing, privately owned stations (see Chapter 1). When the new ILR network began under Edward Heath in 1973, the return of Labour in 1974 (Street, 2002, 127) saw initial plans for 60 stations cut back to just 19. That commercial radio should have been an ideological battle-ground for so long surprised few commentators at the time, but the fight was decisively won in the Thatcher era (Hendy, 2000, 24–5).

However, many paid-for PSAs can reasonably be perceived as socialist instruments of state interventionism, because it is most commonly taxpayers' money that is used to finance such campaigns. As higher earners inevitably pay more tax than poorer citizens, and it is often the less fortunate who suffer disproportionately from the negative effects of poor diets, drug, alcohol and nicotine addiction, inner-city crime and ill health, there is here a certain element of wealth redistribution.

Representation in advertisements and trails extends beyond the legalities of whether or not a product, service or programme has been fairly described or not. Trails that give misleading impressions of future programmes are likely to cause disappointment, but problematic adverts for goods and services can infringe broadcasting licence conditions or even lead to prosecution. Close **textual analysis** can also consider the choice of voices used, particularly as copywriters often reach for **stereotypes** in order to convey the quite complex meanings they might wish to **encode** in a more creative treatment, for example. Of particular interest are the further meanings also being suggested, particularly when, through the **process** of naturalization, they might be harmful to particular demographic groups. With luck, the days of exclusively *black* villains, stupid *Irish* people, and only accident-prone *women* drivers are long gone, such is the pervasiveness of relatively recent **conventions** of political correctness, but negative images of regional origin persist in British media – to such an extent that opinion surveys indicate varying levels of trust towards, for instance, Liverpudlians and Scots (Hill, 2002). In Northern Ireland, a mistake over religious allegiance could easily inflame sectarian tension. Few ethnic minorities are represented in substantial numbers in the ranks of voice-over artists in the United Kingdom, yet barriers of language and ethnicity operate on the margins of the industry, where stations targeting minorities need voice-overs that reflect their own special circumstances. There is, as a result, little mobility between such stations as London's Asian Sunrise Radio and more mainstream stations – even though people from ethnic minorities do not live and work exclusively in ghettos, but are widely visible (and audible) in a range of different roles. Thus, most radio advertising contributes to unrealistic representations of the societies in which we live.

Wherever radio advertising uses drama – however simplistic – it encodes information into both sounds and silence that relies upon their **semiotic** value to create meaning (see Chapter 8). Various **codes** may be evident: for example the enthusiasm of many voice-overs, communicated as much by the tone of the voice-over artist as by the written copy, is easily understood by most listeners as an endorsement of the product. More sophisticated use of tone in a simple dialogue may suggest one character is dubious about the product's virtues, until reassured by the other, who has put it to the test. The inclusion of a telephone number, without the *specific* instruction to dial it, can be relied upon to generally suggest that listeners should do so if they want further information, to arrange a test drive and so on. Where copywriters use superlatives to describe products, as the 'best', the 'greatest' or the 'fastest', the experienced listener may have heard such claims so often as to read them in different ways from those intended, and treat them with either suspicion or indifference. They might have lost much of their original value through overuse, so elements within verbal codes can develop new meanings, and copywriters might in the future decide such superlatives only have a role to play in spoof or humour-driven advertising.

Narrative structure in advertisements and trails can usually be considered to be **closed** or **open**, depending on the level of sophistication of the analysis. While most texts end decisively within the time allowed, and creative scenarios involve quick establishment, disruption and resolution, without any suggestion of future episodes to come later, the essence of all advertising is that it is intended to affect future behaviour on the listener's part. An invitation to arrange a test drive or to come in for a haircut is a clear suggestion that the **narrative** will only end when the listener becomes a part of it, by following the course of action suggested. Of course, the clear implication is that the narrative will then be resolved satisfactorily, without cause for complaint. Certainly, the use of **multi-strand** narratives in adverts and trails is usually impractical, given the short durations involved and the need for a campaign to quickly demonstrate its commercial worth to the advertiser, in time for the first payments to be made with confidence that the financial outlay represents money well spent.

The various **models** of **audience theory** are particularly relevant to advertising and trails, because of the focus on behaviour. If audiences were merely passive receptors of media messages, or inclined to react predictably *en masse* in the manner of **stimulus-response**, then running radio ads or trails would be very profitable in terms of achieving intended outcomes. Although radio advertising has shown itself to be very effective, and there are numerous testimonials to suggest it can represent excellent value for advertisers' money (including at www.rab.co.uk), experience suggests that announcing the existence of a 'great offer on Ford cars' or giving dire warnings about the toxicity of cigarettes just doesn't have the same effect on everyone. More likely, audiences are made up of individuals who will read these messages in different ways (see Chapter 1), either because they prefer Japanese cars or they know people who have smoked into their nineties, or because of an infinite number of other factors and variables which constitute their own set of experiences and attitudes.

At best, advertisers and stations can hope that such active responses to broadcast stimuli might be positive: in the manner of **uses and gratifications**. A trail might suggest to some listeners that there is enjoyment to be gained from listening to a future programme, for example, or that an advert on the radio provides opportunities to hear about bargains and business premises worth visiting. Certainly, behind the concept of image advertising there lies the hope that listeners will want to affirm their own personal identities as wearers of clothing, perfume, and so on that meets the aspirations of others (McQuail, 1972). Maslow's hierarchy of needs (1954) explained human behaviour in terms of the desire to secure basic life essentials first (food, water, sleep, sex, security), then to acquire increasingly inessential extras as resources allow, culminating for some in the most expensive of luxury goods. Every advertiser's products and services will be situated somewhere in this hierarchy, which explains why the desire for the test drive in a new Ford may be limited in the case of someone who cannot afford to eat properly. It also explains why selling such products as cars, clothing and perfume (but not normally double glazing) is often associated with the suggestion that they may enhance people's chances of getting sex. This appeal to listeners' baser instincts does, of course, have to comply with all legal and regulatory constraints on broadcasters and traders – and in the United Kingdom for instance, Ofcom's code of advertising practice (2011) is most specific about such claims.

Light Entertainment

Light entertainment in context

Much of radio's early success was built on the popularity of its light entertainment output. While news, drama, serious talks and performances of 'classical' music quickly established themselves as important fixtures in the programme schedules, some of the biggest audiences were for programmes which unashamedly set out to entertain. Home entertainment had been limited to singsongs around the piano or parlour games, so the arrival of a new mass medium that could be experienced by the whole family gathered around the 'wireless' in the living room quickly caught the public's imagination. Early influences were the music halls, situated in many towns and cities, which had developed a popular repertoire of often noisy and colourful songs, dance routines and stand-up comedy acts. To early radio producers, such as Eric Maschwitz, bringing the music hall to the home was a natural development of radio's ability to 'take' listeners to distant locations, and although stripped of the literal colour and spectacle, much of the material lent itself to adaptation for this new, electronically delivered medium. Relays of music hall performances began in 1923, and in the United States, New York's Radio City Music Hall later became one of the most famous venues for the developing light entertainment **genre**, with NBC radio programming under the control of the head of RCA, David Sarnoff (see Chapter 1). Wertheim's history of American radio comedy (1979) traced its development from song and patter to the comic routines of Jack Benny and Bob Hope.

In the United Kingdom, even Reith's relatively austere BBC included regular light entertainment in its schedules (Crisell, 1994, 19; 1997, 14,

33–5), but its importance was highlighted by the success of the foreign-owned commercial stations, such as Radios Luxembourg and Normandy, which broadcast popular programming that drew largely from the genre and regularly achieved bigger audiences than the BBC, despite the greater distances their radio signals had to travel (see Chapter 1). In 1936, Luxembourg was achieving audience share figures of up to 45.7 per cent (see Chapter 4), and the foreign commercial stations combined took a share of 80 per cent at certain times on Sundays (Briggs, 1985).

Original programming often drew elements from the music halls, such as the compere, the resident orchestra (playing 'dance' music, of course: big band, swing and ballroom), comedy routines and audience reactions. Comedians soon found that in the radio studio they needed an audience in order to 'time' their gags correctly. A vocal group called the Ovaltineys led singsongs amongst listeners to Radio Luxembourg, while promoting the milky drink product that sponsored the show, beginning in 1934. With the closure of the continental broadcasters at the outbreak of the Second World War, domestic audiences soon retuned to the BBC's new Forces Programme, a service that began to entertain British troops at home and abroad on 7 January 1940. The demand this highlighted, for popular, light entertainment programming, could not be stifled, and in response, on 29 July 1945 the Corporation introduced the Light Programme, in direct competition with its own more serious Home Service. The BBC's biggest stars of the post-war period included Arthur Askey and Billy Cotton, host of the *Billy Cotton Band Show*, which began in 1949 and featured his catchphrase, 'Wakey wakey!'. *Workers' Playtime* (1941–64) successfully took entertainers to perform to appreciative audiences at factory canteens.

Inevitably, though, the arrival of television and its gradual victory in the evening **ratings** battle (Crisell, 1997, 76) heralded the end of the 'Golden Age' of light entertainment, as the peak audiences for radio became the transient, daytime listeners who were more likely to be listening while getting up in the morning, working, driving, shopping or engaged in some other primary activity alongside the newly portable transistor radio (Crisell, 1994, 14). The development of popular music radio as the dominant genre in most territories (see Chapter 4) relegated light entertainment to minority status – and of course, the much smaller budgets of the 1960s offshore pirate stations, as well as **ILR** and even the United Kingdom's three national commercial stations, meant that they were largely unable and unwilling to develop much light entertainment programming to rival that of the BBC.

Within the wider genre, though, emerged such **sub-genres** as the situation comedy, the sketch show, the quiz programme and the panel game. Radio comedy exists today in many forms, from the simple recording of the stand-up comedian, to topical sketches performed by impressionists, and comedy **drop-ins** between songs in live sequences (see Chapter 3). A number of radio **sitcoms** transferred with varying degrees of success to television, such as *Hancock's Half-Hour* (on radio from 1954–9), *The Clitheroe Kid* (1952–72), *The Glums* (1948–59) and *Second Thoughts* (1988–92), just as the BBC have successfully broadcast on radio versions of such television hits as *Dad's Army* (McCann, 2001), *Steptoe and Son* and *To the Manor Born*. *It's That Man Again* (*ITMA*) ran on radio for ten years from 1939, and became a big-screen hit in the cinema, too. Another long-running radio sitcom was *The Navy Lark* (1959–77), which featured the antics of the 'crew' of HMS Troutbridge.

Another popular sub-genre is the comedy sketch show, and Peter Sellers, Harry Secombe, Michael Bentine and Spike Milligan are fondly remembered as stars of *The Goon Show* (1951–60) by a generation who particularly enjoyed their comic references to life in the armed services, because they resonated with their own experiences of conscription. The anarchic comedy of *The Goon Show* inspired other British producers and comedy writers, and shows such as *I'm Sorry, I'll Read that Again* (1964–73) and *Round the Horne* (1965–9) also won large and appreciative audiences, both at home and during the recordings. A hybrid of the sitcom and the sketch show may be the **spoof** commercial radio station created by Angus Deayton and others in *Radio Active* (1981–87), and recreated in a special anniversary edition in 2002.

Many quiz programmes and panel games are also performed before live audiences, and the BBC's Radio Theatre has been the venue for an impressive list of live recordings. Early panel games included *What's My Line* (1951–62), in which panel members asked questions to identify a profession. Resurgent after the studios' liberation from the Nazis, Radio Luxembourg again commanded large evening audiences in the early 1950s with *Take Your Pick* and *Double your Money* – game shows whose popularity ensured they soon transferred to the new Independent Television (ITV), as did *What's My Line*, in 1984. A number of other radio quiz and panel game **formats** have been redeveloped for television, just as Radio Four's *The News Quiz* (1977–) spawned *Have I Got News for You* (BBC1) and *I'm Sorry, I Haven't a Clue* (1972–) may have inspired parts of *Whose Line is it Anyway?* (Channel Four and ABC in the United States). The BBC's longest-running panel

game, *Just a Minute,* has been playing to both domestic and international audiences since 1967. Much of the BBC's classic comedy output
has been subsequently marketed on cassette and CD, and in 2002 the
digital station BBC7 (now Radio Four Extra) began regular rebroadcasts
of some of the more popular material (see Chapter 1). Fuller descriptions of most of the above programmes can be found in Street (2002).

Exercise 7.1

Continue the table below, filling in the blank spaces and adding more
examples of radio light entertainment and the audiences targeted. Discuss
your answers in class – for example, could some of these programmes be
popular with other demographic groups, if used in other contexts?

Title, day, time, and station	Target audience	Brief decription
Mark Steel's in Town, 6.30 pm Wednesday, Radio Four	Middle aged, middle class, relatively wealthy	Stand-up comedian recorded live on location with audience reactions
The Now Show, 12.30 pm Saturday, Radio Four	Middle aged, middle class, relatively wealthy	Impersonations of politicians, showbiz personalities and Radio Four announcers, in topical sketches
Comedy drop-in, during breakfast show, my local commercial station		
I'm Sorry, I Haven't a Clue, Radio Four		

Producing light entertainment

Some people have a gift for writing comedy, and – of course – skills in
acting and direction then become important in turning the comedy
script into a workable radio programme. The many and varied possibilities of radio drama (see Chapter 8) mean that imaginative situations
can be created in a well-equipped studio, even on very tight budgets –
although fees for scriptwriters, actors and the use of any **copyright**
material can be considerable. Success depends on an ability to turn the
spark of an idea into a sketch or a sitcom that will make the **target**

audience laugh – perhaps at someone else or, often more effectively, at themselves. Wertheim (1979) identified several major categories of humour, including song and patter (page 7), zany (113), insult (143), fall guy (131), ethnic stereotypes (26) and running gags (224). Today, ethnic and even regional stereotyping is widely regarded as unsuitable material for comedy, although it may not yet be politically incorrect for Jewish people to use 'masochistic' Jewish humour (132). Because humour is so subjective, not everyone can learn comedy writing, in the same way as through practice they may become skilled at operating equipment, or reading out a script. Some of us may have a talent for comedy that is currently lying dormant, just waiting for the moment when some catalytic experience will wake it up. Others may have already been experimenting with humour in some other way, perhaps by sending short comedy script items in to the BBC. The few talented individuals whose comedy actually works 'on air' are in great demand, not least because television, with its bigger budgets, regularly poaches both people and ideas from radio. However, many radio and television comedy programmes have been spectacular disasters, particularly when audiences have been slow to warm to the characters and situations they depict, and the networks have been impatient to see their investment translated into ratings success.

Many sequence programmes use comedy inserts – or drop-ins – that have been produced by a specialist production house and then syndicated to a number of stations in different markets. Examples in the United Kingdom include *TX Media Suite* from Murf Media (fmjocks.com) and the *Quackers Pack* from Dave Glass Productions (daveglass.co.uk), who supply programming items which include both timeless and topical material. Internet technology now allows fast turnaround times, because new material can be quickly downloaded from secure web sites and put to air according to a station's requirements, and the high **production values** of some of this material allows even smaller stations to benefit from writing, performance and production skills well beyond the reach of theirown resources if they were to attempt to produce comedy in-house.At the time of publication, demos were downloadable at both www.fmjock.com and www.daveglass.co.uk. Syndicated programming of this kind is not a particularly new development, though, because earlier distribution media included the reel-to-reel tape, the vinyl disc, CDs and **MiniDisc**.

Quiz programmes and panel games may be more realistic propositions for smaller stations and for beginners to produce – and the spontaneous humour engendered by their relative informality can be just as amusing. Even commercial music stations may consider recording a festive special edition of a quiz programme, perhaps using the station's presenters or local celebrities as the contestants. In the United Kingdom, BBC Local Radio stations such as Radio Kent, and even medium-sized ILR stations such as Marcher, have run series of quiz programmes in which teams from their local communities have competed for modest prizes. *The Marcher Pub Quiz* (1986) was, appropriately, recorded in local pubs, and cast sequence presenter Trevor James as the question master. Recording on location in a community centre or a church hall increases a station's visibility, and it is one way of being seen to be actively involved with the area. BBC Radio Four often records *Just a Minute* from high-profile venues and events, such as the Edinburgh Festival, and the value to a national network of making forays into some of the more remote parts of its **TSA** may outweigh the extra costs and the logistical issues raised by mounting an **OB** several hundred miles away from its base in London (see Chapter 5).

Figure 7.1

Just a Minute **being recorded on location at the Playhouse Theatre in London.** Seated next to host Nicholas Parsons (centre) is a broadcast assistant. Note the use of the individual microphones to ensure the best possible audio capture, and gaffer tape to secure wires to the stage. *Copyright* BBC.

Planning a quiz or a panel game

This kind of programme is most effective when the underlying concept is simple, so easily understood by its audiences at home and, if there is one, at the recording. In *Just a Minute*, two teams compete to score as many points as they can over the 27 minutes of the programme's duration, taking turns to try to speak for 60 seconds on a subject given them by host Nicholas Parsons. Once the stopwatch begins to count away the 60 seconds, any member of the opposing team may interrupt with a challenge, alleging hesitation, deviation or repetition – each of which is contrary to the rules. If Parsons rules the challenge to be correct, the challenger takes over the subject and must try to speak on the subject for the remainder of the time, until the blow of a whistle signals that the 60 seconds are up. The most success-ful contestants can speak both spontaneously and amusingly on whatever subject they are given, as well as responding quickly and amusingly to opportunities to challenge and challenges from others. Among the most fondly remembered regular panellists are the comic actors Kenneth Williams and Derek Nimmo, and more recently younger comedians such as Paul Merton and Graham Norton (both pictured in Figure 7.1) have been contributing their own topical and ready wit.

Devising a new game format with the simplicity and appeal of *Just a Minute* can be quite a challenge, but if successful, it may be one that can be sold to a broadcaster such as the BBC. A quiz should also be simple in concept, because if its operation involves convoluted expla-nations and inaccessible procedures, it risks alienating its audiences because they find it hard to follow. The BBC's *Brain of Britain* (1953–) asks individual contestants questions about general knowledge and special topics in a series of heats and finals leading to the declaration of the overall winner as 'Brain of Britain'. A programme change at Radio Four, following the appointment of James Boyle as Controller in 1996, created a lunchtime half-hour slot (at the expense of the news and current affairs magazine, *The World at One*) which, until 2011, lent itself to series of weekly quiz shows. A number of specialized quizzes were broadcast, each one being wholly themed around partic-ular subjects such as legal issues, politics and even the history of the BBC. Some of these were so specialized that few listeners will have found them accessible enough to sustain their interest for the full dura-tion – partly because listeners who find most questions in a programme to be beyond them will also feel alienated.

A solution to the problem of accessibility may be to vary the content of different rounds, and to deal with specialisms only briefly. Variety of approach may also provide the stimulation needed to retain audiences, and different rounds may involve contestants in supplying missing words to a phrase, or singing the next line of a song, for example. Some rounds could use recorded stimuli, such as speeded up or slowed down extracts from popular songs, or phrases spoken in foreign languages, which contestants have to identify. Identifying mystery voices or continuing famous phrases spoken by celebrities or historical figures can also prove interesting and inclusive, as well as providing opportunities for humorous responses from contestants. Provided each round is simple and clearly explained, and roughly equal in duration, it should be practical to structure a coherent programme around a simple game of points collection by two rival teams, and to present it as a clear proposal to a commissioning editor – if necessary, with a fully costed budget.

Exercise 7.2

Devise a proposal for a quiz programme or a panel game for a specific context and target audience. Indicate how the programme will be structured, the title of the programme and how the title and any of the content relate to each other and to any theme, if there is one. Discuss your proposals in class.

Practical issues

The personnel required for a simple quiz programme include a producer, a presenter or host, and a technical operator to drive the **mixing desk** during the recording and to take responsibility for the recording itself. A production assistant ('broadcast assistant' in the BBC) may take on an extra role of scorer, and if unheard 'on air', this role may include signalling scores to the presenter. There is a considerable amount of work involved in **pre-production: researching** suitable questions and answers, finding and making available any **audio** clips that are needed and scripting material for the presenter to use at such key points as the beginning and end of the programme, and even between rounds. This may be done by the existing production team, or it may be that others are recruited into the roles of researcher and scriptwriter. Ideally a studio recording will be made in a studio where a separate control room allows communication between the production team even when **mics** are live on the other side of the glass, and there is **talkback** to the presenter's headphones. Otherwise, it is possible to crowd everyone into a single studio space, but in order for the recording to be broadcastable, studio discipline must be maximized – especially among the contestants.

Choosing a presenter and the contestants bears comparison with casting for a drama. Ideally, all their voices should sound good on radio. In addition to the normal presentation skills, the presenter needs to be able to command the respect of the contestants, and assert a reasonable amount of authority over the proceedings, in order to ensure they run smoothly. In a quiz, contestants need to be knowledgeable enough to answer a majority of the questions, and in both quizzes and panel games they should be quick-witted enough to respond coherently and entertainingly to the game as it develops – especially if there is a 'finger-on-the-buzzer' round. They may also be funny. However, contestants do need the maturity to respond positively to a short briefing from the producer or a production assistant before the recording begins, over common sense issues of studio discipline. As well as avoiding the frequent use of language that would have to be **edited** out in order to meet consensual or regulatory standards of **taste and decency**, they need to understand that speaking over others is likely to render sections of the recording unbroadcastable. Because participants in a radio quiz are not on camera in the same way that they would be on television, it is possible to attract the attention of others (very effectively) with a hand signal, and so, be given a chance to interject. Certainly each contestant must accept the authority of the presenter as the final arbiter in any dispute, and in granting 'permission' to different participants, in turn, to speak. It is also important to maintain a correct position in front of a **microphone**, as explained in respect of live interviews in Chapter 3, no matter how entertaining and animated the recording session may become.

Rounds which are open to both teams and depend on speed of response may require contestants to have access to a simple 'buzzer' to attract the attention of the presenter – and most importantly, to give listeners an audible indication of their being the first to respond. Different sounds for different teams make it clearer which has responded first, and productions on a tight budget may make use of everyday items such as bells, whistles or even football rattles rather than finding an electronic solution. The sounds used may even be comic ones, and issuing, for example, duck whistles to one team and children's party blowers to the other can add to the amusement.

Technical operation needs to reflect the complexity of a production that requires an unusually large number of mics. Restricting teams to just two contestants each reduces the demands on both the resources and the actual operation of them. Careful attention to microphone position and to encouraging contestants to avoid knocking any mic stands or a table in front of them should reap rewards in the quality of the finished **product**. For stereo recordings, the presenter should be placed centrally, and each team's microphones should be **panned** to different sides of the centre, in order to create a **stereo image** similar to that in Figure 7.1. If contestants are expected to listen to audio inserts in particular rounds, either they will need headphones, or the mics will have to be cut during the inserts to allow them to be heard through the studio monitor. Lining up the inserts and playing them immediately on each **cue** from the presenter further complicates the job of technical operation. Because the programme is being recorded, any pauses to set up the next round can be edited out, but the producer or the production assistant should use a stopwatch to keep accurate timings of how much usable material has actually been recorded, listening very critically to the quality of the material, so as to exclude unusable material from the timings.

A number of student productions have suffered in the past, because they finished recording and let the contestants leave before they were sure they had sufficient material. It is always far easier to cut back this kind of material in **post-production**, than it is to generate more in order to fill the timeslot according to the original brief. In post-production the producer should listen very critically to the recordings to ensure that what seemed like interesting, stimulating radio in the studio is actually going to come across as such to the target audience listening through their radios. Any editing should respect the scoring, otherwise listeners who are paying attention may be surprised if scores inexplicably change dramatically because material has been cut out, or it has been rearranged. As with any recorded programme, a **cue sheet** should be generated and supplied with the recording before transmission. It should include continuity announcements to be read live before and after the actual broadcast, just as a speech package is preceded by an introduction and followed by a **back anno** (see Chapter 2). **Metadata** may also be required – such as a short description.

Exercise 7.3

Plan the logistics of your programme, including originating the content, casting for a host and contestants, and booking and setting up a studio. Record and post-produce your programme, and submit it for 'transmission' with a cue sheet.

Analysing light entertainment

It is unusual for programming in these various sub-genres to depart widely from their own **conventions**, even though the BBC did describe *I'm Sorry, I Haven't a Clue* as 'the antidote to panel games'. Quiz programmes without presenters to link them, ask questions and bring order to the proceedings may subvert conventional approaches just a little too much to be broadcastable – although it may be that some formula could be found which would allow this to happen. Subversion of generic conventions is not only a way of appearing to be avant-garde as a producer; it can also be a useful method of academic analysis, as an aid to **deconstruction** (Norris, 1982). While the aim of most quiz contestants is to accumulate points in order to achieve the highest total, someone who seemed to be trying *not* to win could raise important issues about the desirability of competition and whether it actually fosters in human beings the most productive and harmonious of relations. In terms of **ideology**, there are competitive elements to the accumulation of assets that is inherent in capitalism, which contrast sharply with alternative perspectives, including socialism, communism and the Cooperative Movement. A quiz or a panel game structured around financial **contexts**, where monetary tokens are valued as indicative of the winning team's 'success' and the relative poverty of the 'losers', is likely to reinforce a capitalist perspective through **naturalization**. The notion of competition as 'just for fun' is one which is more readily accepted by those listeners who are accustomed to success, than by those for whom success is seldom an outcome. This may seem a pedantic argument, but in essence naturalization, where it occurs, is by its very nature insidious – acting most effectively where to challenge its existence seems most unreasonable because the object of criticism is widely considered to be 'just the way things are'.

By convention, quizzes, panel games and the range of other forms of light entertainment are all rich in their use of **codes**. For example, laughter is often added to programmes by producers who wish to signal to their radio audiences that the preceding line is funny. The warm-up before a recording with a live audience often includes an exhortation to 'show appreciation' and to 'let the listeners know what you think': 'Don't just smile, laugh out loud!' This juxtaposing of joke and laughter makes a statement to listeners, that would be completely lost if the joke were to follow the laughter. Audience applause and, sometimes, brief musical interludes can be **signifiers** of changes of round, sketch or scene. Because both producers and audiences under-stand them in this way, they can be important elements in the estab-lishment and **signposting** of programme structure. The bells or buzzers in a quiz or a game show signify more than the mere presence of bells and buzzers. The **semiotic** value of one sound may become **indexical** of the individuals in one team and the collective to which they briefly belong, and another sound may similarly represent their rivals. A tick-ing clock may represent the increasing urgency of the need to respond (according to Ferdinand de Saussure (1916), the **signified**), rather than just its own mechanical operation (the signifier) or the mere passage of time. Failure – to answer a question correctly, or to answer in time – may be signified by a bong, or the blowing of a raspberry, while success is more likely to be **connoted** by fanfares, cheers or simple applause. In this way, few of the sounds used in such programming are semioti-cally neutral. Sketches, sitcoms and drop-ins have much in common with the other forms of radio drama discussed in Chapter 8.

The **narrative structure** of most light entertainment may be **closed**, but if a quiz is a heat in a championship such as *Brain of Britain* it may be considered to be **open** because the only definitive act of **closure** will come on the declaration of the overall champion at the end of the series. A convention of the **situation comedy** is its return to equilib-rium at the end of each programme, but the narrative structure of a sketch show which switches between a number of already established characters and situations and new ones, returning at intervals to reprise certain themes or situations within and beyond the same programme, bears close comparison with the **multi-strand** structure of a soap (see Chapter 8).

Light entertainment can raise a number of issues around **represen-tation**. For example, the humour in sitcoms, variety shows, quizzes and panel games largely reflects the common attitudes and accepted values of the era in which they were produced. The homosexual **stereotypes** of Julian and Sandy – two regular characters in *Round the Horne* – might be considered inappropriate today, whereas in the 1960s a sketch had only to begin with the sound of a door opening and the words 'Hello, I'm Julian and this is my friend Sandy' to apparently reduce audiences to gales of uncontrollable laughter. Similarly, the class representations in both *The Glums* and *The Clitheroe Kid* of family life in Northern England may today be considered harmful and misleading stereotypes likely to reinforce any lingering impressions in the south of the country that northerners are both unintelligent and preoccupied with the mundane – and to associate their accents with those negative qualities. In *The Goon Show*, few women or members of ethnic minorities were likely to enjoy equal status with the white male British stars, and the scripts made occasional references to 'coons'. By comparison, today even the humour of most stand-up club comedians displays a generally more enlightened attitude to differences within societies – which compares strikingly with the insensitivity apparent in such output as *The White Coons' Concert Party* broadcast by the BBC from 1932–6 (Crisell, 1997, 34). A number of interesting representational issues are raised by the original radio productions of *On the Town with the League of Gentlemen* (1997) and *Little Britain* (2001–2), both of which transferred successfully from Radio Four to BBC television.

The civilian response to the creation of the wartime Forces Programme by the BBC resonates with that **audience theory** which considers active responses according to various **uses and gratifications** – because for many, light entertainment provided a valuable relief from the pessimism of a long and disruptive war. There was also a strongly escapist element to such programmes as *Workers' Playtime*, which provided a distraction from the drudgery of routine production-line work in the large, labour-intensive factories of wartime and the post-war era – as well as from the constraints of housework experienced at the time by many women who in today's culturally and practically more liberating environment would instead be pursuing careers. Initial reactions to the launch of BBC7 included seeking out its relatively inaccessible digital-only transmissions in order to access its repertoire of archive material, much of it fondly remembered by middle-aged listeners from its original, analogue broadcast – and because of the heavy launch publicity the new network enjoyed on other BBC radio and television outlets, this contributed to the virtual sell-out of portable **DAB** sets in the United Kingdom over Christmas 2002 (Barnett, 2002 and Berry, 2004, 283–96).

8 Drama

In this chapter you will:

▸ learn how drama productions are made and used in radio
▸ research, plan and produce your own play for radio
▸ consider ways of analysing radio drama you hear and make yourself.

Radio drama in context

Dictionary definitions of drama generally suggest **representations** of life, either real or imagined. There are clear differences in print, screen and live performance media between **narratives** that are described and those that are enacted, and although often blurred, those differences translate coherently to radio **contexts**. For example, the novel often positions a narrator as the sole communicator of description and analysis to the reader, while the printed text of a play uses a minimum of description and stage directions to provide readers, directors and performers with a preferred contextualization of the dialogue that constitutes the bulk of the writing. Both in the cinema and on television, there are widely shared perceptions of drama as being distinct from the monologue of the news report, the newsreel, the documentary and the routine of the stand-up comedian. Central to these differences is the way drama attempts a portrayal of events – however faithful – that actively involves representatives of the people and events concerned.

A theatre may be filled with spectators enjoying a performance, but it is the nature of the performance that determines whether many would describe it as drama. On stage there may be a single musician or a whole orchestra, yet unless they enact some discernible narrative beyond the playing of a musical composition, it is called a concert. Alternatively a storyteller may recount a narrative with such dramatic characteristics as suspense or pathos, but if sitting, otherwise motionless, with no costume or props, it would stretch the most widely accepted definitions of drama to label it as such.

Similarly, radio may feature the organized **discourse** of a news report, a documentary, a travel **bulletin** or the reading out of a novel, but it is only at the extremes that such forms may assume the status of drama. The news report that includes **actuality** from the scene of an event is assumed by listeners to have required little intervention by the reporter, beyond capturing the sounds produced by others. Even if the actuality is a substitute from a collection of sound effects, used in the same manner as television often relies upon library pictures, few listeners would describe it as drama. If, however, the documentary contains elements of **dramatization**, in order to allow listeners to hear reconstructions of claimed actuality, it positions itself within the **sub-genre** generally accepted as 'drama-documentary', 'docudrama' or 'dramadoc'. If the travel bulletin overtly pretends to be live from a helicopter, when listeners are aware the noise of the rotor blades is a sound effect added in the studio, it assumes an element of **spoof**. Depending on the dominant genre in which a radio text is placed, audience **readings** can differ widely: the approach in the news report described above may create an impression of **'realism'**, while the fake helicopter is more likely to cast doubt on the accuracy of the information about road works and hold-ups.

This potential for ambiguity has afforded radio drama some spectacular opportunities to impact hard on its audience. In 1938, Orson Welles and his Mercury Theatre Company terrorized much of their American radio audience with a dramatization of the H. G. Wells novel, *War of the Worlds*. They broadcast spoof news reports of strange objects arriving from Mars, as interruptions to a live concert performance, in an unfolding narrative that progressed to descriptions of Martian invaders attacking Americans in their homes and streets. In the panic reaction which followed, as many as 6 million people jammed highways as they fled what they thought was a real alien invasion. Although clearly announced as a Mercury Theatre Company production at the start of the broadcast, listeners tuning in late were so convinced of the reality of Welles' subversion of the then fledgling rolling news genre, that they thought it was real. Although predated by the BBC's own *Broadcasting from the Barricades* in 1926, which convinced many listeners that a revolution was beginning in London, Welles' triumph was in realizing the ultimate goal of those who would present drama as realism as opposed to its diametric opposite, **surrealism**, or its more common relation, the simply improbable – neither of which would be so believable (see the section on **textual analysis**, on pages 201–2).

A common reaction to the proposition that they should produce drama, among students working with radio early in their careers, is surprise that anyone should even contemplate such an activity. Although inevitably exposed to various short forms of drama in their own listening, in, for example, radio advertisements (see Chapter 6) they do not always perceive radio's potential for longer works of 90 minutes or more. The **sitcom** is arguably a sub-genre of drama, because it bears all of the characteristics of the dramatized narrative, as well as some of its own, such as the **conventions** of the half-hour **duration**, the **closed narrative structure** in each episode and the **diegetic** persistence of the same characters and situations across whole series. In the United Kingdom, radio has spawned numerous translations of its own sitcom successes into television, such as *Second Thoughts* (see Chapter 7), which may not necessarily have gone unnoticed by younger audiences, but if their provenance has not been clearly articulated, it is not surprising that their origins on BBC Radio Four may not have been apparent – targeted as it is at an older audience.

BBC television's 1981 adaptation of the Douglas Adams series *The Hitchhiker's Guide to the Galaxy* created a new audience among science fiction fans for the original radio series, which had been first broadcast on Radio Four in 1978. A comparison of the techniques of dramatization used by the two different media reveals one of the main advantages radio has over television: audience visualizations of radio's two-headed character, Zaphod Beeblebrox, were commonly far more durable than the television representation, which really did look like a human being wearing a sculpted prosthetic head on one shoulder. When the Theatr Clwyd company took a stage version of the story on tour, they were further hindered by the practicalities of 'realistic' portrayal of unreal phenomena, not even having at their disposal many of the special effects available to television and film producers. Although computer animation has since then produced remarkable advances in the quality of special visual effects, radio remains a very cost-effective way of creating durable images in listeners' minds, which would be far more expensive to create on the screen.

As a genre, then, drama lends itself well to radio. There will always be those who decry the absence of given images as symptomatic of inferiority, but the 'blindness' of the radio listener (see Chapter 1) can also be attributed to the reader of a novel. Among the truly literate there are few who will deny the power of the printed text to conjure up images of characters, objects, locations and actions. Furthermore, despite the potential of a single image on the front cover to narrow the range of possible interpretations of descriptions within the text, most readers' visualizations of them are personal and unique, sharing only some characteristics with those of other readers. They customize their own previous experiences of the visible, to produce versions that match their own readings of elements within the narrative, adapting them as they progress though the book and then encounter further criteria to interpret. While film and television may provide viewers with predetermined, less controvertible images and sounds, they leave the other three senses of smell, taste and touch as much to the imagination, as radio leaves the listener's sight.

Within the wider genre, radio drama programmes exist in a variety of forms:

▸ The *single play* creates characters and situations that are not necessarily intended to be reprised in any future sequel or episode. It is a one-off, and its narrative structure may therefore be closed. Among the first single plays on radio were *Danger*, a story about two people trapped in a mine, and an adaptation of Shakespeare's *Julius Caesar*, both broadcast by the BBC in 1923. In the United States, dozens of Hollywood movies, such as *Casablanca* (1943) and *The Maltese Falcon* (1943), were adapted for radio broadcasting, often using such original stars as Humphrey Bogart and Ingrid Bergman.

▸ The drama *series* features some common characters and situations that return in each programme, without there necessarily being any plot development across the series, other than the stories that are begun and ended each week. A good example is the BBC's various series of *The Adventures of Sherlock Holmes*, beginning in 1930, in which Holmes and Watson solved different mysteries in each episode. Each programme ends with an element of **closure**.

▸ The drama *serial*, by contrast, involves the unfolding of a single core narrative over a number of episodes, each one having an **open** structure, but with the final episode ending in closure. Examples include *Dick Barton – Special Agent*, which became the BBC's first daily serial, running from 1946 to 1951; a serialization of *The Gemini Apes* in 2002 (see below); and the public radio adaptations in the United States of *Star Wars* (Daley, 1996).

▸ The *soap opera* consists of multiple episodes, each one being typically **multi-strand** – in that a number of different narratives run in parallel across several episodes, opening and closing at different times and without any particular connection between them other than the commonality of characters and locations.

The first 'soap', so-called because of its sponsorship by Colgate-Palmolive-Peet, was *Clara, Lu, 'N Em* (NBC) which first aired on 27 January 1931 in the United States. *The Archers* enjoys considerable fame as the United Kingdom's longest running soap opera, having begun its daily chronicle of life in the fictitious English village of Ambridge on 1 January 1951, predating the arrival of Independent Television by five years. The programme's longevity lies in its ability to change with the times: in the final quarter of 2002, a 'racy plot about sex and lies' drew a record audience of 5 million listeners (Day, 2003). No other British soap has fared so well. *Mrs Dale's Diary* was broadcast on the BBC Light Programme from 1948, before later becoming *The Dales* and then ending its run in 1969. The 2,824 episodes of BBC Radio Two's *Waggoners Walk* ran from 1969 to 1980, and Radio Four made a brief attempt to broaden the range and appeal of its soap output in 1987 with the ill-fated *Citizens* (Street, 2002, 123). **ILR's** early foray into soap opera, Capital Radio's *Bedsitter* starred comedy actress Peggy Mount and only lasted a few months.

A common convention is the enigmatic ending, designed to bring audiences back for the next episode in order to hear how it was resolved. In its most extreme form, this is commonly referred to as a cliffhanger. The main exceptions to the multi-strand narrative structure of the soap tend to be the first and last episodes, each of which requires at least an element of opening and closure respectively.

While the conventional length for British radio soaps is the quarter-hour, it is a form which adapts well to inclusion within programmes in other genres – for example, music sequences (see Chapter 3) can be considerably enhanced by the inclusion of brief drama inserts of, say two or three minutes. The **drop-in** is a brief and usually comic punctuation item, used by presenters to add humour and variety to their

Figure 8.1

11.30 The Change		7.00 The Archers				9.00 The Friday Play: After Dark – Night on the Town

11.30 The Change
Written by Jan Etherington and Gavin Petrie.
Starring Lynda Bellingham
2: Carol is enjoying spending time on her own, having found out that George, her husband of 25 years, would rather be called Georgina. It's just that her family seem to need her more than ever …

Carol	Lynda Bellingham	Sonia	Emma Kennedy
George	Chris Ellison	Jerry	Barnaby Kay
Violet	Sylvia Syms	Dave	Mark Powley
Maureen	Maureen Beattie	Man	Andrew Westfield
Ken	James Vaughan		

Producer Elizabeth Freestone

7.00 The Archers
Brian says it with flowers.

Phil	Norman Painting	Peggy	June Spencer
Jill	Patricia Greene	Sid	Alan Devereux
Kenton	Richard Attlee	Kathy	Heidi Niklaus
Shula	Judy Bennett	Eddie	Trevor Harrison
David	Timothy Bentinck	Ed	Barry Farrimond
Ruth	Felicity Finch	Roy	Ian Pepperell
Elizabeth	Alison Dowling	Hayley	Lucy Davis
Tom	Tom Graham	Mrs Antrobus	Margot Boyd
Brian	Charles Collingwood	Kirsty	Annabelle Dowler
Jennifer	Angela Piper	Heather	Joyce Gibbs
Debbie	Tamsin Greig	Chaba	Mate Haumann

Written by Simon Frith Director Julie Beckett Editor Vanessa Whitburn
ARCHERS ADDICTS FAN CLUB: send an SAE to PO Box 1951, Moseley, Birmingham, B13 9DD

9.00 The Friday Play: After Dark – Night on the Town
By Martin Jameson. A dark psychological thriller in which a lonely man goes out for a drink one night and is "befriended" by a couple who ask him back to their Manchester flat. They then empty his wallet and later his back account. Why doesn't he run away?

Tony	Tim Dantay	Babatunde/Shaun	
Sian	Jo Macinnes		Vincent Davies
DC Self/Clive	David Crellin	Bev/Cath	Jo-Anne Knowles
DC Fallon	Graeme Hawley	Sheila	Siobhan Finneran
Mash/Driver	Daniel Poyser		

Director Susan Roberts

Radio Times **listings for a sitcom, a soap and a single play, all broadcast on the same day in 2003 on BBC Radio Four.** The radio listings pages in this weekly magazine provide extensive coverage of BBC national networks and local and regional stations.

programmes between songs, and if not originated in-house they are frequently syndicated to users of such production houses as Dave Glass Productions (see Chapter 7). On Radio One, *Steve Wright in the Afternoon* (Garfield, 1998, 81) featured a range of comic interventions by such original characters as Mr Angry (1981–94), and Adrian Juste's Saturday lunchtime programmes interspersed clips from the BBC's archive of sitcoms between the records (1978–94). Depending on the nature of the drop-in, it may also have an open or a closed narrative structure. Sequence programmes also lend themselves to the inclusion of more systematic drama series – for example, Dirk Maggs's adaptation for Radio One of the comic superhero stories in *The Adventures of Superman* (Street, 2002, 142) which were first broadcast in 1994. Crook (1999) discusses the nature and the possibilities of radio drama in greater detail than is possible here.

Exercise 8.1

Continue the table below, filling in the blank spaces and adding more examples of radio drama, their target audiences and their narrative structures. Discuss your answers in class – for example, can the advert be an open narrative?

Title, day, time, and station	Target audience	Narrative structure and brief description
The Archers, daily, 2.02 pm and 7.02 pm, BBC Radio Four	Middle aged, middle class, relatively wealthy	Multi-strand soap opera, set in rural village of Ambridge
Advertisements for Budweiser beer	Young males, 18–35	Closed, funny conversation, ends with a tag line
Afternoon Play, Radio Four		

Developing a scenario

Before any detailed scriptwriting is begun, it is usual to set out certain information about the drama. The duration, the time slot of the first broadcast and any subsequent repeats, and the sub-genre are likely to be predetermined, as is the **target audience**. The **purpose** of the drama may be simply to entertain, or it may also be to persuade, educate or inform (see Chapter 1). At this stage, a soap opera that is to run over many episodes will need a considerable amount of forward planning – of character and plot developments – whereas for a single play it may suffice to create a **scenario** and make certain decisions about the **style** and the perspective from which the drama is to be presented. When writing any drama, there is a chance that it could **libel** a living person or an organization (see Chapter 9), even if the story and characters are entirely fictitious – so care should be taken over the use of names and scenarios which bear some resemblance to real life.

Although English libel law offers little protection to the dead, producers do have a responsibility to be truthful, otherwise they are deceiving the audience and quite possibly causing offence to the deceased's family. For example, relatives of the 1950s singer Alma Cogan tried in the High Court to prevent the BBC from broadcasting *Stage Mother, Sequined Daughter* (Radio Four, 29 July 2002) because they disagreed with the portrayal of her (Ezard, 2002).

Radio drama often uses a narrator, in order to convey certain key information effectively and quickly. Without a narrator, complex relationships between time, place, and characters can be very difficult to express, but once such obstacles are overcome, the audience is exposed to the narrative as if watching, unseen, from the seating in a theatre. Events unfold before them, yet they play no role in them, and they have no effect on their progress. The presence of a narrator alters audience perspectives in that now their presence is acknowledged, yet only by a single person who has a developing relationship with them. The narrator can be one of the characters taking part in the plot, and known to some or all of the other characters, or an omniscient figure who has no involvement in the narrative, but might plausibly have an ability to know about and describe events taking place perhaps even simultaneously, but in different locations. There are similarities between the omniscient narrator and a deity, because he or she can be aware of characters' thoughts, memories and intentions.

With so much potential at the disposal of the radio playwright, it is clear that creating original drama for radio can be an exciting and rewarding activity. The BBC's drama output earned it the epithet 'The National Theatre of the Air' – the majority of it broadcast on Radio Four, but Radio Three also features some experimental and more traditional drama. The BBC Writersroom (bbc.co.uk/writersroom), despite its lacking an apostrophe, encourages new writers to submit work for possible development, and the independent production sector also makes a sizeable contribution. Drama is not always totally original, of course, and adaptations of existing stories can be popular, as evidenced by the *Classic Serial* strand, which has produced new interpretations of such popular narratives as *Wuthering Heights* (1995) and *The Pallisers* (2004). There are, of course, **copyright** implications to using someone else's work in part, or in whole, which do not apply to developing one's own original idea. Written permission of the copyright holders is needed, in order to use their intellectual property, and they may not approve of the creative **treatment** being given it. There are collections of previously published scripts in book form (such as Carter, 1996; and Daley, 1996) and available on the Internet (for example at simplyscripts.com), but although useful to students of radio drama, there are also copyright implications to using them in productions or for broadcast.

Radio audiences, just like other consumers of mass media **products**, demonstrably like to hear a good story, if they have time to listen – which is less likely in the morning and evening 'drive' **dayparts**, when attention spans are necessarily shorter. The audiences for Radio Four's *Afternoon Play* will never approach the 9 million who regularly listened to the evening output of BBC radio before the arrival of television (Crisell, 1997, 76), but in this multimedia age, figures in the hundreds of thousands are respectable enough to justify the relatively large budgets spent on them. It is, of course, much more expensive per minute to produce a 45 minute radio drama than, for example, a presenter-led sequence programme, but the cost is still a fraction of that of making a television drama of the same duration.

Any **proposal** for an extended drama production should be fully costed, with a detailed budget, which reflects the **pre-production**, production and **post-production** stages. One of the principal costs in a professionally produced drama will be the acting talent needed, and time taken up by casting (see page 196) and rehearsal. As they are unseen by the audience, actors may work from written scripts, providing they are careful to avoid rustling the pages – and the most versatile of them may also play several parts in the same production. Student work often has to rely on members of the class to voice the different roles, but it is sometimes possible to recruit willing volunteers from local amateur dramatic groups. The use of copyright material of any kind may have to be paid for, including scripts, music and sound effects, and budgets should reflect this. Even studio time must be accounted for, and inevitably at least some further work will be necessary in post-production. A producer is likely to require technical assistance from studio managers during the recording.

Some producers prefer to work on location, and the costs of trans-port and refreshment, together with the time spent on reconnaissance and getting permissions from the owners of private property, can make this expensive. The advantages of location work relate mainly to **acoustics** and **atmosphere** (see Chapter 1), but many of these charac-teristics can be imitated in a well equipped drama studio. One of the biggest cost savings in radio drama derives from the ability to create 'virtual scenery' in the listeners' minds, rather than having to travel to distant locations with a whole cast and crew. However, if a suitable studio (see pages 197–8) isn't available for a student production, the

Figure 8.2

	£ (GROSS)
Writers' fees – new commissions	3,500
Cast	3,200
Executive Producer/Senior Producer	1,500
Broadcast Assistant	220
Secretary	350
Studios	1,960
Studio Managers	1,950
Post-production (studios)	1,220
Post-production (Studio Managers)	780
Location & travel	250
Accommodation, IT, Telephony	250
Other overheads	1,000
Production fee	1,500
TOTAL COST OF PRODUCTION	17,680

Budget for a typical 45-minute *Afternoon Play* on BBC Radio Four. Note that, depending on the nature of different productions, they are likely to be costed differently – and they may include other cost headings, such as for use of copyright music or for additional production personnel.

ready availability of atmosphere and acoustics can represent considerable economies of time – while still presenting appropriate levels of challenge.

Writing drama scripts

The radio drama can convey information to listeners through voices and through sounds. Their 'blindness' (see Chapter 1) means they must work harder than television viewers or cinemagoers, in order to interpret what they hear – and the more information they are given, the more the text itself can restrict listeners' capacity to make **alternative readings** of a drama. Where the information is contradictory – or at least ambiguous – the more enigmatic the drama becomes, and the greater the chance of alternative readings being produced. Too much ambiguity, or too little clarity of meaning and direction, and audiences may become alienated as they struggle to make 'sense' of what they are hearing. There is a balance to be struck between creating drama that is too formulaic and predictable, leaving little to the listeners' imagination, and trying too hard to innovate, by challenging listeners' inclination to follow a narrative which may be confusing or vague. Radio listeners find it much easier to tune away or turn off, than theatregoers do to walk out of a performance, with the risk that that entails of causing offence and creating a disturbance (Crisell, 1994, 145).

The necessity for radio drama to describe more, in words as well as sounds, inspired Timothy West's spoof play, *This Gun in my Left Hand is Loaded*. The unnaturally precise description of what it is that the character is holding – and in which hand it is being held – satirizes the often adverb and adjective-laden dialogue which radio playwrights can produce. However, without the absurdly comic extremes of the **transcodifiers** in West's dialogue, a more explicit mode of expression can be vital to providing the radio audience with sufficient clues as to what people, places, events and things look like. Just as the novelist may digress from the unfolding narrative in order to provide the reader with a description to interpret, the additional information which can be inserted into the dialogue in a radio play may be seen as a necessary digression in order to orientate listeners and increase the likelihood of their making the writer's **preferred** reading of the **audio** text.

Therefore, the line: 'What are you doing in here?' can be much more explicit if rendered as: 'And what's John doing in my study at one o'clock in the morning?' The content-rich approach of the second line provides the listener with a much clearer picture, identifying not only the identity of one character, but also the location, the obviously inappropriate time of day, and the element of intrusion implicit in John's presence. Even if the scene were never developed beyond that sentence, the existence of confrontation has already been firmly established for all but the most insensitive of listeners.

The plot is the working out of the narrative, from the beginning of the drama to the end. Some analyses identify commonalities of narrative construction, which suggest that the classic story begins with a predetermined equilibrium, consisting of a situation and a set of characters within it. Soon this equilibrium is disrupted by an event that produces a disequilibrium, the resolution of which provides the main focus of interest in the story. If there is to be an act of closure at the end, this involves a return to the previous equilibrium – or at least a new, settled stasis – which invokes a shared sense of satisfaction among both participants and audience (Berger, 1997). Where a narrative ends without every controversy in the plot settled, there is an element of enigma which – because of the persistence of audience intrigue it can create – can also provide an enjoyable, if perhaps less satisfying, ending. By contrast it is a convention of some types of detective mysteries, such as those by Agatha Christie, for all unresolved questions to be answered in a final confrontation with a number of suspects – a construct known as the dénouement. There is far less interest, and so listener satisfaction, in a predictable ending, and in whatever sub-genre the drama is situated, the element of surprise – the 'twist' – is a useful device.

Some avant-garde drama may avoid using a discernible plot, just as in literature James Joyce's *Ulysses* is commonly described as a stream of consciousness, and others such as surrealist writers and filmmakers Alain Robbe-Grillet and Luis Buñuel may subvert the traditional linear development of a plot from a clear beginning through a middle to a conclusion (Durozoi and Anderson, 2002). However, unlike in written texts, a radio listener who is struggling to make sense of a very challenging play cannot refer back to something heard earlier – unless, exceptionally, listening to a recording. Admittedly it is a disadvantage of radio that the potential for disorienting listeners and still retaining their attention is much less than in television, where the presence of visual clues may be enough to encourage a greater persistence of effort. That is, a blind person is more likely to become bewildered in an unfamiliar location than a sighted one.

Concerns about listeners' ability to follow more challenging narrative structures do not exclude the possibility of including a small number of sub-plots, provided the production is of a long enough duration to allow them to be established alongside the main plot, and to develop to some degree of sophistication. Similarly, most listeners to radio drama readily understand the **flashback** to be a device for exploring the history of a character or a situation, even though it disrupts the normally linear progression of a narrative. It is the choice and use of various **symbolic codes** to suggest such disruptions of the normal passage of time that will determine how successfully flashbacks are incorporated into the radio play.

Exercise 8.2

Devise the scenario for a new single play. It should be clearly aimed at your choice of radio station and target audience. Identify the plot, any sub-plot, the main characters and any secondary characters. Present your ideas to the class, explaining your decisions.

Time and place

The passage of time is most commonly indicated by a change of scene, and often achieved by the fading down of one scene, a pause, then the fading up of the next. This has a clear resonance with the dimming of the stage lighting in a theatre, fading briefly to black on television, and leaving a gap of two or three lines on the page of a novel. As a change of scene usually implies movement to a different time or place, an unusually longer passage of time may be **connoted** by a longer pause, of perhaps three or four seconds. If the amount of time that has passed is significant, or if the new time is a flashback, it may be important to the plot that it is immediately apparent, and so some means is needed of communicating to the audience the advance or the turning back of time. This may be done bluntly through narration if it has already been established that there is a narrator, or if not, more subtly through the dialogue: so a character might be required to comment on how things have changed, or to lament the passage of time.

There are other means of indicating a change of scene, and this is one area in which drama producers continue to innovate. The sound of a harp being stroked may be a cliché, but in some circumstances it could be an effective one. A musical phrase, faded in and out at each change of scene will quickly establish itself as a recognizable **signifier**. It is important, though, whatever the code used in a particular play or series, that it is used consistently – otherwise the message will become confused.

Characterization

Dialogue may also contribute to **characterization**. Without discernible characters, with whom listeners may empathize, there is a danger that they will fail to engage with the narrative – not caring what might happen to any of the different individuals portrayed. The role of other characters may be to incite antipathy – audiences can love to hate a villain, and the binary opposition of the good guy versus the bad guy, as representatives of good and evil, is very common in story-telling. Most narratives also require secondary characters whose pres-ence is fundamental to the development of the plot – the butler who opens the door, or the doctor who advises of a dire prognosis, for example – and, although less fully developed, they have a role to play. Empathy may cross gender boundaries, and – it follows – the artificial divisions of religion, class and ethnicity. In deciding for themselves, though, with whom they empathize and with whom they don't, listeners need information about the different characters. Every one who speaks displays **demographic** characteristics inherent to them-selves – such as the age of the voice and its gender – and actors can introduce other vocal characteristics that relate to region, race and social background, which further describe the nature of the characters they are playing. Further alterations to the voice can suggest a range of emotions, worry, tension, fear, loathing, love, excitement, passion, surprise, and relief being just a few examples. Most of these emotional characteristics are transitory, and they will both rise and fall in inten-sity in response to events in the narrative to which characters are react-ing.

Beyond the voice, though, and how the actor might use it, descrip-tion can be conveyed convincingly in the scripted dialogue. For exam-ple, one character might describe another as a 'bit of a joker' and, unless contested, this could contribute to the listeners' perception of one or both of the characters in the scene, without any joke having been articulated. Similarly, two characters might discuss another who is not present. A narrator, whether involved in the plot or omniscient, might be expected to have a personality, too – and there is no rule that says he or she should necessarily be telling the truth all the time. When characters know something another character doesn't, or the listeners know something none of the characters know the drama can become very compelling. This technique is called dramatic irony.

In West's play, the clear implication of saying 'This gun in my left hand is loaded' is that the speaker is prepared to use it. Listeners will inevitably compare that information with their prior experience of the character, and expect to be able to draw reasonable conclusions about whether or not to believe him. Where a character behaves inconsistently with those audience expectations, it should be because of some identifiable factor within the play – otherwise the credibility of the characterization begins to break down. One considerable challenge for writers of shorter dramas is to establish meaningful characters quickly, whereas in a longer production aspects of their personalities may be revealed more slowly and in response to the developing narrative.

A key convention of most drama production within the **realist paradigm** is that characters are believable. If they are not, they actively erode the realism that is intended. There is, of course, a role for the unbelievable in a spoof, but fans of science fiction may enjoy that subgenre because they want to believe in the *possibility* of what they are hearing. Similarly, the BBC's 1981 dramatization of *The Lord of the Rings* (Radio Four) was enjoyed not by listeners who believed Tolkein's hobbits and dragons really exist, but by large numbers of people who wanted to enjoy the escapism of a world they knew to be fantastic, but to which they were willing to be transported by a combination of the narrative and their own imagination (Street, 2002, 136). Since the possibilities of plot and characterization in radio drama are infinitely variable, there is plenty of room for the play where the characters and situations are implausible, and the narrative unlikely – provided the audience consents to the contrivance and is willing to persist in listening to it. When conventions are subverted so much that the end product fails to retain a sufficiently large audience to satisfy those who are paying the costs of production and transmission, then it is reasonable to question the appropriateness of innovation.

Developing a narrative

In order for a narrative to progress beyond the initial equilibrium, there must be some action. Action can be portrayed through dialogue, as well as the use of other sounds. It is possible for all the action in a play to be indirect, or reported, in that the audience needn't actually hear anything *happening*, just characters describing events they have previously witnessed. Each new scene can contain further references to new developments of which they have become aware. Such is the essence of the Alan Bennett monologues *Talking Heads* which, although – rather surprisingly – originally written for television, translated very effectively into radio and were very well received in both media. However, and notwithstanding the success of Bennett's work, listeners may feel a sense of disappointment at not being able to witness the actual events. Such an approach certainly doesn't exploit radio's ability to portray fictional events cheaply and convincingly, and one of the surest ways to make interesting radio is to include a variety of sound.

The sound effect can describe something succinctly and quickly, using airtime economically because it can release precious seconds for something else. It may also produce meaning simultaneously with other sound effects, or with dialogue, and the listener's capacity to **decode** complex **mixes** is already highly developed from early childhood, because human beings exist in polysonic environments (McWhinnie, 1959, 23). Various academics have discussed the ability of radio to deceive the human ear, by contextualizing one sound in such a way as to make the brain perceive it to be something else (for example Crisell, 1994, 47). In this way, the banging together of empty coconut halves in certain rhythms and at certain speeds can simulate the sound of horses' hooves on a hard surface – but not, of course, on gravel. Without the visual reference of seeing the coconuts or indeed any hooves, radio listeners may be convinced of either scenario, depending on the nature of any accompanying contextualization provided. So a character shouting 'Hi ho Silver, away!' might suggest he is a masked man on horseback – especially to anyone who has previously been exposed to the stories of the Lone Ranger. The same voice saying softly, 'These coconut halves sound a bit like horses' hooves' would probably inspire a totally different reading in most listeners' minds.

It may at first appear obvious that sounds may be long or short, persistent or fleeting, sustained or contained, but a common distinction in radio drama is between those that are **atmospheric effects** and those that are **spot effects**. Atmospheric sounds most often describe location – the roar of traffic suggesting the proximity of a nearby road, the cawing of crows evoking a field in the countryside, and the wash of gentle waves on sand **denoting** a beach. To each of these may be added other atmospheric effects, such as a pneumatic drill, a combine harvester, and the braying of donkeys, respectively. To do so is to alter each image considerably, and in each case listeners' readings would almost certainly be altered, too. As well as place, atmosphere can suggest time, or era: tooth brushing is most commonly performed on getting up and at bedtime, while the steam engine is associated with the hundred or so years before the arrival of the diesel train. Music may play a part, too, if it sounds as though it is being produced at the location: that is, as **diegetic sound** as opposed to incidental music. A lone accordion being played among the general hustle and bustle of people in a busy market might effectively situate a scene in nineteenth century Paris. If snatches of their conversation were discernible, though, they would have to be in French, or the image would become confused.

Spot effects are dropped into an ongoing scene to describe action, or at least as a precursor of it. The waves lapping on the beach will continue to lap for some time after a thunderclap has broken the idyll and introduced a sense of expectation to the scene. The cawing of the crows in the countryside, though, would reasonably be expected to react to a gunshot, and the traffic sounds would probably subside soon after the noise of a collision. If characters are present, they too would be expected to react to each of the spot effects above. Some situations and actions will require a number of spot effects in sequence, or some may overlap. The producer has to make editorial judgements over the timing of each one in relation to the others, and, of course, over the relative **levels** at which they are heard. An effect may be required in a scene, but only very quietly, in order to be heard but not to intrude. At times realism must give way to pragmatism, when using sounds in drama – some sounds will be unpleasant and tiring for the audience if allowed to persist for longer than they will find comfortable. For example a pneumatic drill, or a siren, may be so intrinsically irritating that an element of realism in the representation has to be compromised in order to retain an audience.

The brief scene in Figure 8.3 uses both dialogue and effects to create an initial scenario and then action, to which the characters react. There are brief directions for the acting talent to follow, as well as instructions relating to the use of effects. The layout separates the dialogue from the labels on the left, and the sound effects ('fx') are underlined to make them more easily discernible from the rest. In longer scripts, each line of speech may be numbered to allow the cast and the production team to navigate more easily around the text. In this script, the characters display traits that, despite the brief duration, suggest some basic characterization.

Figure 8.3

```
Girl:   John, what're you reading?
Boy:    Oh, some story about a couple lost on a paradise
        island.
Girl:   What's it like?
```
<u>Fx: waves lapping on beach (hold under)</u>
```
Boy:    Blue skies, palm trees, coconuts and so many
        fish in the sea you can just put your hand in
        and pull one out.
Girl:   What do they do all day?
```
<u>Fx: thunderclap 2"</u>
```
Boy:    Well, they build themselves a shelter and...
```
<u>Fx: heavy rain and wind (hold under)</u>
```
Boy (shouting):
        ...it blows down when a tropical storm comes, so
        they get soaked to the skin until...
```
<u>Fx: herd of elephants stampeding 3" (then quick fade
        out of all fx)</u>
```
Boy:    ...they get trampled to death.
GIRL (SARCASTICALLY):
        mmm... sounds lovely! but don't you need
        pictures to enjoy a good story?
```

A short drama script, illustrating the main conventions of layout, including the underlining of effects and the use of tabs for clarity

Care should be taken over perspective. A character inside a house, complaining about roadworks outside, should seem to be louder than the offending noise, which in turn should have been muffled by the walls and windows between them. This places the listener inside, *with* the character, and creates a more realistic image than one that contains a number of different elements, but doesn't acknowledge the existence of any spatial relationships between them. Just as in television, where the camera is active and may move from one location to another, the radio audience may move around, according to the dictates of the script and the scenario it depicts. The annoyed resident, having complained bitterly about the noise outside, may decide to go out there and remonstrate with the road workers. The audience may remain inside, and hear his dialogue through the wall and windows, or they may be taken out with him – in which case footsteps, the opening of the front door, and footsteps on the gravel drive may be accompanied by a change in the roadwork noise as the door opens and everyone steps outside.

Acoustics differ, too, between locations. The presence of hard, reflective surfaces, and their distance from the original sound will alter it (see Chapter 1), whereas outdoors there are usually no reflective surfaces nearby, and so there is no **reverb** on the voice. Therefore, the voice of a character talking while moving from inside a cathedral to the outside will change. If the listener is moving too, accompanying the character, the volume of the voice will be unchanged. If the listener remains inside, though, the voice should recede as it alters in acoustic treatment. Among the production directions on the script should be clear instructions as to what kind of acoustic is to be used.

It is difficult to tell from the look of a script how long it will last 'on air'. The pace of delivery should be neither rushed nor too ponderous, so it is important to know before beginning production that there will be the correct amount of material for the slot. Writers and producers can do timed read-throughs, speaking the dialogue for the acting talent and pausing for the intended duration of any music or effects. Although rehearsals with the acting talent in place are not essential in radio, depending on their experience and ability to 'sight read', they can provide useful indications of how well the material fits the times-lot, and whether or not additional material may be needed. The use of incidental music and, perhaps, music at the beginning and end of a drama – if it is appropriate – can be used to 'pad' a little, but overuse of music can sound rather obviously like a lack of substance. It is conventional for a radio drama to end with spoken credits for the writer, the performers, and the production team, and it should begin with at least an announcement of the title and the name of the author. This may be recorded into the programme and spoken by a cast member or a separate announcer. Alternatively, such information can be written into continuity announcements to be read live before and after the recorded material by the duty announcer. In this case, they should be supplied on the **cue sheet**.

Exercise 8.3

Write the script for your play, paying attention to your earlier decisions about plot and characterization.

Interpreting a drama script

Just as the expression of a narrative on paper is an act of interpretation by the writer, turning an idea into a fully worked-out script, so the realization of that script into a broadcastable piece of audio involves a further layer of interpretation (McWhinnie, 1959, 35). Where the writer is able to work with the production team, there is a better chance that the finished product might resemble what was originally envisaged, but a producer may want to let his or her own aesthetic values influence the outcome. The acting talent may also have opinions about how the script should be performed, and one of the strengths they bring to the production can often be their creative input. They must, however, be able to accept direction. One crucial stage in pre-production is the casting, when decisions about who should play each role can have major consequences for the success of the production (Beck, 1997, 2–3).

A common problem with student productions is that they often use only actors from within their own group or their wider circle of friends. Apart from their lack of acting experience, their voices may not sound appropriate to the parts they play. With practice, and the right kind of direction, they can often perform well in their roles, but their voices may not have the maturity that is needed to evoke, for instance, a middle-aged woman or a senior citizen. There are also discernible differences between accents of class, region and ethnicity, which should be reflected in the casting. Because listeners piece together all the information they hear in a drama, to create pictures in their minds, that information should normally be clear, not contradictory. One solution is to write scripts very narrowly, using only characters from a similar demographic to the student group, but another, more challenging one is to cast more adventurously, using contacts, relations of friends, and even approaching amateur theatre groups.

A useful procedure in casting is to record the actor's voice performing a number of typical lines from the script – this is the audio equivalent of the screen test. Listen back to it, eyes closed, and try to imagine how listeners might perceive the character. In radio, actors' voices are disconnected from their true appearance, allowing some very creative casting decisions to be made. An exception to this rule is when they are to be seen by audiences in publicity shots and, in the case of *The Archers*, at public events such as the Archers weekends that regularly draw large numbers of people to 'meet' the fictional residents of Ambridge.

Production techniques

The well-equipped drama studio has a separate control room, with a large, soundproofed window into the performance area. This is the centre of operations during recording, and the producer oversees each session, using the **talkback** system when necessary to communicate with the acting talent and any technical assistants on the other side of the glass. In the control room is a **mixing desk** large enough to handle the output from a number of **microphones** in the performance area, as well as a range of playback **sources** such as CDs and a computer. The **mixer** will be flexible enough to perform some complex **processing** tasks, including **equalization**, and there may be a real-time effects generator which can add reverb to any **channel** routed though it and alter sound in ways which will meet the requirements of even the most demanding science fiction productions. There will also be recording facilities, which may include specialized computer hardware and software, such as SADiE or Pro-Tools. An important advantage of SADiE, over a budget PC application such as Adobe Audition, is its multi-channel input capability through an advanced **breakout box**, enabling sounds which are simultaneously produced to be recorded as separate tracks for individual manipulation later in post-production.

The performance area of the studio may be divided into different areas, depending on the amount of space available. There will be sufficient soundproofing and acoustic treatment of the whole space to prevent unwanted sound entering the studio from outside, or from the control room, and to reduce the amount of reverb to a minimum level. A 'dead' area may have received additional acoustic treatment in order to reduce reverb to imperceptible levels, so that outdoor scenes may be recorded there with an outdoor acoustic. This enables characters from *The Archers* to discuss the weather while shearing sheep, without the scene sounding like it is taking place in the bathroom at Grey Gables. Other areas may be divided from the rest of the space by portable screens, and these are often used to prevent one actor's voice being picked up with another's, if both **mics** are live. For example, a telephone conversation may be heard from the perspective of one of the callers, and the other voice is processed to make it sound as if it is

Figure 8.4

Ideally, a drama recording studio should have separate control room and performance areas, with talkback and a window allowing verbal and non-verbal communication between them.

coming down the phone line. It is important in creating the effect that the 'telephone' voice doesn't also leak into the other mic, and avoid the processing being applied to the 'caller'.

Separation of sounds in the studio is also important when different microphone channels are to be **panned** in the mixing desk in order to create a **stereo image**. Two characters conversing in a shop are not likely to be standing in exactly the same place, and so, for listeners hearing the drama in stereo, sitting between twin speakers in front of them, a more 'realistic' image can be created by placing the two voices slightly apart, just to the left and to the right of the centre. Imagine the stereo image as a line drawn between the left and right speakers, on which any number of different sound sources may be placed separately. The conversation – taking place just to the left and right of the centre of this scene – might be interrupted by someone else entering the shop hard over to the right side of the image, making the door bang and a bell ring on the way in. It follows that the door and the doorbell would also be placed hard over to the right – otherwise the image would be confused and disorienting if the voice and the door were on different sides of this 'virtual' shop.

As characters move around, their voices should move with them, and this may be achieved by altering the pan control as they speak. If the tracks have been recorded separately, as opposed to being mixed before recording, then panning can be done in post-production. Another method of creating realistic movement around the stereo image, and one which is achievable with only limited studio resources, involves a crossed pair of **unidirectional** microphones on a single stand, feeding separate channels on the mixer – one panned to the right, the other panned a similar amount to the left. With no acoustic separation placed between them, each mic will clearly pick up a voice in front of it *as well as* picking up another voice to the side – although the secondary voice will in each case sound **off mic**. The two voices in a conversation will appear either side of the centre, until one of them moves around to the other side, or away, out of the centre of the image altogether, becoming progressively more off mic – and sounding more distant – as it moves. Similar effects can be achieved using a single, stereo microphone that has two separate outputs: left and right channels (see Chapter 1). This technique can be used to create stereo recordings on location without taking a mixer, provided the left and right microphone leads are connected to separate inputs on a stereo recording device, such as a solid-state recorder.

Figure 8.5

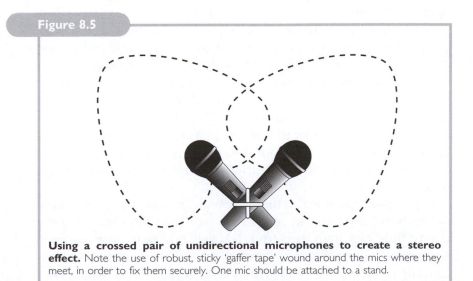

Using a crossed pair of unidirectional microphones to create a stereo effect. Note the use of robust, sticky 'gaffer tape' wound around the mics where they meet, in order to fix them securely. One mic should be attached to a stand.

Creative approaches

A popular technique in radio drama is to speak very softly into a very close microphone ('close micing'), taking care not to pop or to touch the mic in any way. Because the voice is close, the **gain** control on the channel will need to be adjusted down to keep its level consistent with the others, and so a bassy, more thoughtful voice is produced, which connotes the thoughts inside the character's head. This can also allow the character to assume the role of narrator, whose direct address to the audience can suggest artificiality.

Sound effects and incidental music may be added live to the recording, or inserted in post-production. It is important to get the levels right, and especially so when they are being mixed live through a mixer, as they will not be separable from the rest of the audio later. Some effects, music and voices may be heard only quietly, if that is what the script and the scenario demand. A radio playing in the background of a conversation should not be so loud that it makes the conversation inaudible or it distracts listeners from the dialogue. Similarly, it is possible to clutter a scene with too much added ambience, and for this reason movement by actors is often not accompanied by the sound of their footsteps as they move around. Sometimes, though, slow footsteps can heighten suspense – as at the start of *The Whistler*, which was broadcast weekly in the United States on the CBS network (1942–55), conjuring up the murky world of fog, smoke and shadows in which were set its detective stories.

Sound effects may be pre-recorded, or created live – and a well-equipped performance area may have a range of opening and closing doors, doorbells and buzzers, telephone handsets and crockery, so that the acting talent or an assistant can pick them up and put them down, knock on the doors and slam them shut, all on **cue** and to time. Two or three gravel trays can each contain different sizes of gravel, which can be walked on in order to simulate footsteps on a path or a drive. Separate mics will be needed for the quieter sounds, but a slamming door a short distance from a character's microphone might suit a script well.

In post-production, tracks that have been recorded separately can be **edited** before mixing – so actors who fluff their lines should begin again a little back from their error. It is very unwise to allow actors to leave before the producer is satisfied that all their lines have been correctly recorded, clearly and with the right expression. Re-takes at a later date may not bear the same acoustic properties, if adjustments have been made to the studio or the equipment, and so they may sound obviously like additions. The recording should be monitored and timed to ensure it is neither under-running nor over-running. At all times, in production and in post-production, the producer has to make editorial judgements about how the finished product is to sound – and make decisions accordingly. This may mean increasing or decreasing the amount of reverb or equalization on a channel, altering the amount of panning on a voice or an effect, or even ruthlessly throwing out less essential material in the event of an over-run.

Exercise 8.4

Produce your drama. Play your drama to the class, and evaluate their reactions.

Analysing radio drama

Drama that makes fantasy seem real, such as *War of the Worlds* (1938), tends to be an exception, whereas drama that purports to recreate elements of someone's experience of real life is much more common. Audiences frequently accept drama as 'realistic' because they recognize in it elements which accord with their own experiences, or at least, that resonate with other information they have gained by proxy from other people or other media artefacts. The essence of popular culture lies in the **intertextuality** of referencing one text against another, rather than against one's own personal experience (Barthes, 1973). However, producers and listeners who imagine a representation constructed through drama in any medium to be anything more than at best an interpretation, and at worst a distortion, are surprisingly naïve. This deception was exposed in 1890 by Edmund Gosse, in his article *The Limits of Realism in Fiction,* when he wrote of 'the inherent disproportion which exists between the small flat surface of a book and the vast arch of life which it undertakes to mirror' (in Becker, 1963, 390). Although predating film, radio and television, Gosse's argument against the possibility of the novel ever reflecting a true and complete picture of events it attempts to portray is just as applicable to the electronic media of today. Early last century, both painters and composers began to recognize the limitations of their own media in communicating exactitudes to their audiences, because realism is 'not only a technical but also a philosophical impossibility' (Grant, 1970, 64–5). Barthes saw '**myth**' as a way in which the bourgeoisie protects its own privileged status by constructing images of 'reality' which accommodate these contradictions to its own advantage (1973).

In the cinema, and more for legal reasons than a concern for ethics, the small print in film titles often distances texts from 'real events and persons, living or dead' – but there is no such disclaimer broadcast either before or after the vast majority of radio dramas which also pretend to portray 'real' life. The media do, though, wield immense power to convince audiences of the accuracy of their portrayals, and as most Britons will never experience at first hand the Scottish drug-based subculture portrayed in *Trainspotting* (1996: D. Boyle), if they have watched the film, most of them will trust Boyle's representation of it and believe that to be what it is 'like'. 'Realistic' drama on radio will also be trusted by its listeners insofar as its portrayals do not conflict with their own experiences or those prior assumptions they have, on which they are not prepared to negotiate. Sometimes, though, it will ask listeners to suspend disbelief – as did Welles – and collude in the bending of common notions of 'reality' in order to accept the occurrence of the strange and the unexpected. One can argue that this lies at the heart of good storytelling, and as one important purpose of drama is to entertain (see Chapter 1) there is considerable justification for adopting such a position. However, there may be adverse consequences to irresponsible or lazy representations that routinely distort through **stereotyping** or through denying certain sections of society the recognition they deserve for their achievements and potential.

Therefore, analyses of dramatic texts should consider whether stereotyping has been used, and if so, why. Given the limitations of the momentarily blind listener's ability to perceive the pictures the radio producer wishes to create (see Chapter 1), there can be good reasons for the use of stereotypes: where time is limited and plots are complicated, a stereotype may be a useful shorthand expression for an otherwise elaborate idea. Vladimir Propp identified a number of common characteristics in Russian folktales (1968) that relate to both characterization (such as hero, heroine, villain, donor, receiver, helper) and plot (including seeking, finding, receiving and rescuing). His analysis bears comparison with most radio drama.

Just as such series as *The Whistler* suggested a sub-genre of 'radio noir' bearing similarities to 'film noir', other sub-genres exist within the wider field of radio drama. Even with its 90-minute duration, Dirk

Maggs's 'Hollywood blockbuster' radio play *The Gemini Apes* (BBC Radio Four, 1998) has an intricate plot with flashbacks woven into it and a large number of different locations to convey in a clear enough manner for listeners to remain engaged to the end. The characters need to be immediately conceivable by the audience, and so the elderly scientist sounds Russian, the villain sounds like a white, wealthy male representative of corporate America, the hero is instantly recognizable as a white American teenage boy and the operatives in Mission Control sound just like most people's own concept of how Mission Control operatives always sound. Few listeners in the United Kingdom, though, had met people in all these demographic and professional groups – their referencing will have been to other stereotypes seen or heard in other media texts. The synergy between the radio play and previously given images worked well in this instance, in effectively transplanting pictures from television and the cinema into a different narrative in a different medium. A stereotype, however undesirable from a representational perspective, can connote a meaning more powerfully and more quickly than one which has to be constructed afresh. For example, the talking, swipe-card operated security door does not sound like a surfer on Bondi Beach, because if it did, further explanation and contextualization would be necessary to complete the image.

The Gemini Apes does challenge its own stereotyping, in that another strong character is the daughter of the Russian scientist – although young, she too is a scientist, carrying on her father's work, and soon also battling against corporate greed and human cruelty to animals. Inevitably this narrative is rife with ideological positioning, and the moral questions raised by such a play that, through labelling itself a 'blockbuster' and drawing upon generic characteristics of Hollywood cinema, presents itself as an entertainment. As well as a fast-paced narrative, rich in sound effects and incidental music, this can be read as an ideological treatise: initially almost a rant against capitalist inhumanity and the negative influence of money. It is, of course – in the Hollywood tradition – restrained in its attack: the closed narrative structure (see above) allows a 'good' to prevail over the 'evil' in a resolution that accommodates a modified *status quo* with its reassurance that, after all, capitalism can be 'good'. **Ideology**, where it is apparent, will inevitably display different levels of sophistication, depending on the depth of passion and intransigence with which it is felt by its proponent. A more fervent rewriting of the plot could have been more damning of the 'common sense' values and beliefs that – in some territories – are shared so widely that they effectively underpin capitalism as the dominant ideology, although concern for endangered apes is not a characteristic of many competing belief systems. Only rarely can the discourse presented in radio drama be ideologically neutral, even if the situation it portrays is only reaffirming a *status quo* through **naturalization**. Blue's study of wartime and post-war American radio drama identified ideological struggles in many texts between racism and anti-racism, socialism and fascism, and anti-Semitism and religious tolerance (2002).

The raw materials used to **encode** meaning through radio drama are, of course, voice, sound and silence, each of which assumes some **semiotic** value for listeners to decode. Scriptwriting is the first inter-pretational act in the process because the writer conceives an idea, and then from it creates a written text. Secondly, this script allows others – in turn – to create the arrangement of sounds and silence that will enable an audience to hear it. The third interpretation is the listeners' own (McWhinnie, 1959, 35), so there is plenty of scope for confusion of the original concept as it progresses through such an elaborate process. Depending on the latitude allowed them, by **anchorage** of meanings through contextualization and description in the script and the production, individual listeners' readings of a drama may differ greatly from its origins. Each will bring a different set of experiences and prior assumptions to his or her reading, and actively interpret the drama accordingly.

The interpretive process may not end here, because listeners may tell others about the drama they have heard, encoding their own recol-lections and impressions of the broadcast text, for their own 'listeners' to decode, and possibly pass on to others. A very engaging radio play could, in theory, develop a life of its own far beyond the 'control' of its writer and producer, just as a funny joke may travel on *ad infinitum* being told and retold, evolving as it reaches new audiences. Much of the scriptwriting and production activity in making radio drama is usually focused on seeking incontrovertibility: trying to prescribe preferred readings by removing ambiguity wherever possible. Studying a radio drama text can usefully involve examining the semiotic value of the words and other sounds used, to determine how they might operate, both individually and in relation to one another.

For the relatively undertheorized field of radio studies, much has been written about the use of sounds in drama – notably by Crisell (1994, 146–9), Shingler and Wieringa (1998) and Crook (1999), and earlier sections in this chapter consider sound effects from production perspectives. A drama without the contextualization provided by words (that is, comprising sound effects only) presents particular challenges in both production and analysis, and Andrew Sachs's play *The Revenge* (1978) was met with considerable acclaim. The use of words as transcodifiers was discussed by Crisell (1994, 146), who also wondered whether effects alone could convey sufficient meaning without them. Certainly, drama can conceivably exist without sound effects without straying into the storytelling or book reading genres, but conversation without incidental sound could seem less 'real' because humans rarely remain completely still while awake. Language can be rich in meaning, because beyond the consensual understanding of a word among those who might use it as part of their *lingua franca* there are issues around who said it, how, and under what circumstances. Accent, tone, pitch, pace and context may all add meaning even to an utterance which superficially refers to a single, apparently incontrovertible object, such as an aardvark. Words that relate only to concepts can be still more ambiguous. Language also usually juxtaposes a *number* of words according to shared interpretations of syntax, so 'Are you going now?' may easily be widely read as less insistent than 'Now are you going?' although both can be said in such a way as to connote menace, depending on the delivery and the circumstance. For example, the speaker might also be understood to be holding a knife.

Some of the competing **models** of **audience theory** (see Chapter 1) are relevant here. The potential for different readings among audiences suggests that passive responses are unlikely, and that more active interpretations may be appropriate. **Uses and gratifications** theory is easily accommodated within most ways of listening to radio drama (see Chapter 6), particularly as listeners' needs may include distraction and escapism as well as for information and affirmation of values and impressions (Blumler and Katz, 1974). Soap opera can provide a particularly effective distraction to those who are preoccupied with life's worries or who wish to escape temporarily from their own situations, because their radio's regular visits to familiar locations and the characters that inhabit them reinforce the impression that they actually exist – and that even after the broadcast finishes they are carrying on with their lives. *The Archers* cast dress in character and attend Archers events for the enjoyment of paying fans who want to enjoy being with them and seeing the village of Ambridge for themselves, even though the location is entirely fictional and substitutes are used by the organizers in order not to disappoint.

Documentaries

Documentaries in context

The documentary **genre** is one with which listeners very often declare themselves familiar, as involving detailed, factual reporting. Those who listen exclusively to music radio will undoubtedly have been exposed at some stage to television documentary, even if the arrival of the multi-channel age has spread the concept of the generic channel from radio to its younger rival. Now, as has long been the case with radio, it is possible to watch channels that continuously stream generically similar output, such as cartoons or music videos, and some viewers will consider the documentary to be for others who actively seek it out by tuning to the Discovery Channel.

Just as television documentary makers tailor their output to attract and serve different audiences, so radio producers can choose between a variety of **conventions** and **styles** in order to make documentaries which suit different **contexts** and **target audiences**. In the United States, the kind of lightweight, yet sensational reporting that produces such popular television series as *When Animals Attack* exploits different skills and approaches than are generally to be found on the PBS network of public service channels. Similar televisual comparisons are possible between *Police, Camera, Action* (ITV1) and the output of BBC2 or BBC4. Choosing the most appropriate approach for the context and audience is, therefore, as important a part of the initial **proposal** stage of documentary making, as is the choice of subject and content.

The radio documentary has much in common with the shorter speech **package** (see Chapter 2) beyond the obvious quantitative differences in the **duration**, the number of contributors and the production time required. By contrast, a 'feature' programme is normally less journalistic and more creative and expressionistic (see Chapter 2). The extent of the **research** needed to underpin the documentary is likely to be much greater, too. Essentially though, like the package, the documentary is a means of communicating a story – factually correct, of course, as opposed to fictional – but one to which the producer expects an audience to be receptive. The greater duration allows the documentary producer more flexibility in setting the parameters within which the content will be situated, and this may be reflected either in greater breadth or in greater depth – or in a mixture of the two. While the package is inevitably a more superficial **product** than the documentary, it is just as important to decide early on in the **process** on a clear and compelling **angle** (see Chapter 2) from which the subject matter is to be considered.

Documentary forms

Documentary series offer the producer even more scope. The series of, for example, six programmes allows a relatively large subject to be considered from a number of different angles. Alternatively, the series may – in whole or in part – be structured chronologically, beginning with the origins of the subject matter and tracing its development over time. Choosing either option requires the early episodes of the series to create sufficient interest and impact for viable numbers of listeners to want actively to tune in to hear subsequent programmes, and this often precludes the chronological approach because the resultant history may be lacking in compulsion, spectacle or intrigue. For this reason, a chronology may be better accommodated within a single programme during the course of the series, rather than influencing the **structure** of the series as a whole. However the series is structured, there must be a clear and logical rationale behind it – otherwise it will lose coherence and probably listeners.

The same principles apply to the single documentary and to each individual episode of a series. The programme must be structured in a clear and logical manner which is both appetizing to those listeners who hear the beginning, and inclusive towards those who tune in after the start. As a common duration is 28 minutes, especially where speech predominates, the potential for indirection and hence alienation is

Figure 9.1

	£ (GROSS)
Presenters	1,000
Cast	150
Contributors, consultants etc	166.67
Executive Producer/Senior Producer	440
Producer	2,080
Broadcast Assistant	192
Studios	55
Studio Managers	35
Post-production	1,800
Location & travel	900
Other production facilities	250
Accommodation, IT, Telephony	100
Other overheads	566.87
Production fee	933.58
TOTAL COST OF PRODUCTION	8,669.12

Budget for a typical 28-minute feature documentary on BBC Radio Four.
Note that, depending on the nature of different productions, they are likely to be costed differently – and they may include other cost headings, such as for use of copyright music or for additional production personnel.

huge. Listeners need a constant sense of the direction in which the programme is going – or at least, to feel confident that they are not being left behind by it. New listeners tuning in after the beginning need to be able to rapidly orientate themselves in this new and probably quite complicated environment, otherwise they will soon decide that what they are hearing is intended for someone else and they will switch off again or tune away. This is also an argument for clear **sign-posting** (see pages 209–10).

Structure and style

The structure of the documentary bears comparison with that of the drama. Although always factually based, the **narrative** may quickly establish some element of disruption – an issue raised, an unexplained phenomenon described or a development produced from a previous equilibrium. As in drama, the sooner the arrival of the controversy, the more compelling the development of the plot will be. It is usually appropriate for the documentary to end with some kind of resolution, and if this is not necessarily as contrived as the dénouement of a whodunit, it may yet settle an argument, answer a worrying question or provide some other kind of release for the listener. Most single documentaries will have a **closed narrative structure**, although all but the final episode of a series may be regarded as **open** – and therefore inviting the listener to return for more. The producer's preferred conclusion to any programme in the genre may justifiably represent an enigma, because an issue remains unsettled or a controversy is expected to continue to polarize opinion.

Depending on its duration, the radio documentary often lends itself well to division into sections, each centring on a different theme that is closely related to the subject and the angle. At the proposal stage, the themes may already be apparent, or they may emerge as the subsequent research progresses. Knowing in advance which broad areas are to be included can help to focus the research, although flexibility later towards early and possibly ill-informed decisions can prove to be essential. Each change of section provides an opportunity for the signposting identified earlier as essential to programme coherence. The aural signpost briefly restates the **purpose** and direction of the narrative, draws some interim conclusions from what has just been heard, then indicates the next section of the journey to be begun. Scripting the signpost presents particular difficulties, not least because the paraphrasing above is too functional and clumsy to actually be repeated four or five times in a programme – needing contextualization, not generalization.

There remain important questions of style, and decisions have to be made as to which of a range of conventional approaches to follow. There is potential to innovate in documentary production, so the approaches listed here are not exhaustive, although they do relate to the most common examples of professionally broadcast work, and newcomers to the genre should be prepared to account reasonably for significant departures from them. Audiences can react adversely to the unfamiliar, and similarly the inappropriate cannot always be easily rationalized as being avant-garde. As audiences are implicated in the creation of conventions, they share with producers an investment in them.

A very common approach positions a single reporter in a central role of narrator, investigator or translator, guiding listeners through a body of relevant evidence which includes interview material, **actuality** and music. The reporter presents a core narrative that is illustrated and extended by the informed opinions and eyewitness accounts provided by a range of interviewees. In linking all the other elements of the documentary together, the reporter seems to have selected the material and the presentation of 'fact' is overtly personal. This may be more or less flavoured with personality, depending on how much the script allows it to be apparent. Complicated or unfamiliar concepts or detail may be interpreted by the reporter, who may paraphrase and explain ideas to assist listeners in their own **reading** of the **discourse** that the programme represents. Signposting at appropriate points seems a natural part of the reporter's role. In some programmes, interview material will always be included without any of the original questions – the scriptwriting techniques for introducing such clips are explained in Chapter 2. In other programmes, at times the reporter's questioning of an interviewee may be heard, when there is some special interest in how the one responded to the other – if, for example the interviewee was evasive, or became emotional. Generally, though, this style permits a more analytical approach, and interviewees who are heard once, may be heard again on further occasions when their responses to other questions can be contrasted with the opinions of others.

A more ponderous approach is one in which the reporter's questions are always heard, and the narrative assumes the character of a personal odyssey. Because the reporter is on a journey to find answers – even to establish a 'truth' about an issue – interviewees tend to be heard for longer on each occasion, but less frequently than in the first **model**. The reporter's own personality may be allowed more exposure, and **links** may affect 'real time' qualities, even being recorded *in situ* as, for example, he or she walks up to the interviewee's office and knocks loudly on the door, while commenting on the action. This approach lends itself well to the consumer-driven or investigative documentary, as exemplified by both *Face the Facts* and *File on Four* (BBC Radio Four), because the reporter's journey is one undertaken to find some resolution to listeners' problems with a rogue trader, a confidence trickster or a recalcitrant official or organization.

By contrast, some documentaries can be effective with little or no intervention from a reporter. Interviewees may introduce themselves, by simply announcing who they are and their credentials (see Chapter 2) before launching into their 'own', apparently unedited, discourse. Few real interviewees will have such refined communication skills as are needed to locate themselves comfortably within the stylistic conventions of this approach, though. Usually, therefore, various verbal prompts are needed to encourage them to 'perform', and these are actually **edited** out before transmission. Examples include 'Please speak into the **microphone** and say who you are, and what your role is' and 'Now please explain what your opinion is of euthanasia.' Using this approach presents two obvious difficulties. Firstly, returning to interviewees a number of times in a programme is rendered more problematic because there is no reporter to remind us of their identities – which may be forgotten by continuing listeners and will be unknown to those listeners tuning in later (see Chapter 2). Secondly, if an interviewee's apparent monologue is allowed to run for an extended period, it can begin to seem unnatural rather than spontaneous, and it may evoke the eccentric ramblings of the bewildered or confused – not an obvious endorsement of the interviewee's contribution. Certainly, any direct responses to missing questions should also be removed, otherwise a monologue which includes such sudden interjections as 'No, no, I wouldn't say that!' will sound very odd indeed. The most successful applications of this model use carefully applied **ambient sound** or music as punctuation within longer monologues, and to separate different contributions from each other.

Using the above approach may produce a documentary that appears to be more of a montage of sound and speech than would meet most listeners' expectations of the genre. A classic example of this was the BBC's *The Oil Rig*, which was broadcast in the 1970s to illustrate the possibilities of binaural stereo, with which some producers were experimenting at the time. The technique involves using two microphones positioned within a dummy 'head' to mimic as closely as possible the perspective of the average pair of human ears. When played back through headphones, blindfolded listeners can perceive the sounds thus recorded as if they are all around them, coming from discernible directions, so in this case it seemed as if they were actually visiting an oil rig and hearing both ambient noise and comments from the workers in real time. Because little radio listening is done through headphones, though, the technique is used less in practice than the quality of the output deserves.

As the range of alternative approaches to documentary style proceeds along this continuum, ever farther away from the clear – if rather unsubtle – **anchoring** role of the reporter at one extreme, at the other it reaches the soundscape. This discrete genre was the focus of the World Soundscape Project, which explored the impact of technology on naturally-occurring ambient sound, and it seeks more commonly to describe the aural landscape than to explain ideas and issues (Ferrington, 1998). In such programmes as *Soundwalking* (Vancouver Co-Operative Radio) and *One Visitor's Portrait of Banff* (Radio Rethink) Hildegard Westerkamp experimented with different techniques for the capturing of naturally produced **audio**, using at different times both roving and stationary microphones (1994, 87–94). Soundscape production accommodates the actual production of sound by, for example, scraping or scratching objects in order to convey aspects of their texture, although the action involved may not be apparent to the listener.

Sound artists also stretch notions of '**realism**' by close-micing objects and living creatures to such an extent that the recording includes elements that would otherwise be too quiet to be apparent to the human ear. Even without such producer intervention, most soundscapes are inevitably less a naturalistic portrayal of a single landscape, however broad or narrow, than an artificially produced montage of selected and perhaps **mixed** sounds – raising as many **representational** issues as any other documentary form. This is because pairs of human ears are much better equipped to distinguish between sounds produced simultaneously and from different directions when assisted by visual clues, than any combination of microphone and recording device. Exercises in solitary listening (Copeland, 1997), wherever the chosen location may be, have little in common with most audiences' usage of their radio receivers.

While it is, therefore, uncommon for soundscapes to be broadcast very often on mainstream radio, in the United Kingdom BBC Radio Four is among the most likely outlets for the genre. On 11 September 2002 the mid-afternoon drama slot was given over to a 'sound memorial' to the victims of the World Trade Center in New York, destroyed a year before. In *The Twin Towers: A Memorial in Sound*, Nikki Silva and Davia Nelson explained how for their ambitious project they had collected contributions from the many people who responded to their appeal for audio previously recorded from the buildings. Known as the Kitchen Sisters, the two had sorted, mixed and edited hours of different sounds into a 45-minute montage to represent the life of the buildings before their destruction.

Beginning with newsreel soundtrack from the opening of the Centre, the soundscape included a structural engineer's recording of one building's natural swaying in the wind, a tour guide's description of stepping out of the lift at the top and a commentary on a tightrope walk between the two towers. Mixed with it was the Latino music of the many South American workers in the buildings, a song that had been performed live in the Centre's concert venue and other tracks that were simply chosen for the melancholic mood they created. Only in the final 12 minutes did the soundscape progress to the terrorist attacks, and the aftermath of the disaster, yet the whole production can be read as a moving tribute to the people and the human activity that once existed there.

As co-producers with the BBC current affairs department, and because it was intended for a mainstream audience, Silva and Nelson had to ensure that the programme would be listenable, and not disorientate and alienate its audience – particularly given its extended duration. As well as their own limited commentary, which set the production within the context of their audio project, most of the material was firmly anchored in the narrative by description from the contributors, explaining its origin or the reasons why they wanted it included. Many of these descriptions were actuality taken from an answering machine, and preceded by the machine's own 'voice' noting the day and time the message was received. This brief passage shows that, given enough information by way of **anchorage**, audiences may be relied upon to draw conclusions that drive a narrative forward:

Answerphone:	"Received September eleventh at 8.59am." (beep)
Male caller:	"Hey Beverly this is Sean, in case you get er, get this message, er there's been an explosion in World Trade One, er it's the other building. It looks like a plane struck it, erm it's on fire at about the ninetieth floor and it's, it's, it's horrible. Bye." (sustained beep)
Answerphone:	"Received September eleventh at 9.02am." (beep)
Male caller:	"Hi this is Sean again. Erm looks like we'll be in this tower for a while erm it's (tannoy speaks in background) it's er secure here (tannoy again) I'll talk to you later bye." (beep)

```
Commentator(fades up):   "Oh my God, the next building just
                          blew up . . ."
```

Without the necessary contextualization exemplified by the answer-phone above, listeners would have been set adrift in a sea of sounds and voices, allowed too much latitude to make erroneous readings of the material being presented. How would they have reconciled the tightrope walk commentary with their own prior understanding of the events of 9/11, for instance, and how would they have conceptualized the sound recordist's structural motion audio? Inherently disorienting and confusing, the production would then have been unlikely to be sustainable for such an extended duration in daytime. Although advertised as a soundscape, because it had departed so extensively from so many of the stylistic conventions of the genre, the programme had more in common with a montage **feature** or a documentary.

In the same year, the BBC also broadcast a series of 13-minute programmes entitled *The Soundhunter*, which made an 'epic quest around the globe in search of disappearing sounds' (BBC, 2002, 129). Although widely promoted as a series of soundscapes, these programmes also relied heavily on spoken contextualization, and they positioned the presenter with much more prominence than the 'musical sand dune' and the other phenomena she 'discovered' on her journey. If soundscapes are meant to be analogous with landscapes, these examples were like oil paintings with detailed captions – and the corruption of the genre this would imply demonstrates popular broadcasters' real difficulties in programming soundscapes of even moderate durations if they are to retain their audiences.

Soundscapes do have an important role to play in the wider fields of audio production and theory, though, and in radio they can influence both documentary and drama production (see Chapter 8) by encouraging producers to think creatively about how ambient sound may be used to illustrate a more deliberately articulated narrative. As a production exercise during training, the discipline imposed on the producer by the requirement to assemble a sound picture without narration can foster a greater awareness of the descriptive potential of sound. A brief montage, although raising some real **ethical** questions about the presentation of 'reality' (see Chapter 2), can also add considerable interest and variety to an otherwise dry documentary. Furthermore, the care required to record individual or naturally mixed sounds can represent a worthwhile use of time in refining some of the basic techniques of audio capture (see Chapter 1).

Exercise 9.1

Continue the table below, adding more examples of documentaries on a range of different radio stations. Discuss your answers in class, explaining reasons for different approaches found.

Context and target audience	Duration	Content	Style
Scott's Perfect Christmas Song, BBC Radio One: Monday 9 pm – 15–24 year olds	58 mins	Investigated what it takes to create a catchy Christmas hit song	Upbeat, fast-paced presentation by Mills, constant electronic music beds and short bursts of hit recordings, interview clips very short with writers, experts and others
China's New Iron Rice Bowl, BBC Radio Four: Sunday, 5 pm – average age 53	38 mins	Explained how China is trying to improve welfare for its citizens	Medium pace; reporter presented a range of facts on poverty and need among the poorer citizens of China, and attempts to improve welfare, with comment from financial advisors
BBC Radio Five Live: 12.05 pm Sunday; *Five Live Reports: The Fishwife's Tale*	25 mins	Examined risk to Scottish fishing industry, from perspective of fisherman's wife	Medium pace; reporter followed the fisherman's wife to London to take part in protest about fishing quotas

Using music

Another important consideration in determining the style of a documentary is the use of music. On stations that schedule occasional or off-peak documentaries to complement their majority output of music sequences, this departure from their normal programming needs more careful integration with the programming around it. Speech stations that broadcast programmes from a range of genres, such as BBC Radio Four, may switch abruptly from a quiz to a panel discussion, to a documentary, with only brief continuity announcements between them.

Music stations, though, tend to recognize the importance of music to their audiences' listening habits, and to abandon their **music policy** for the relatively protracted period which a documentary commonly represents could be damaging to their audience **ratings**. So, while their documentary output needn't necessarily be *about* music, it is likely to feature a large amount of music, either incidentally to punctuate the spoken discourse and in the form of beds under the speech, or in an illustrative role. How this music is used impacts upon the total duration of the programme: if a number of individual tracks are to be played whole, for the documentary to have much depth, a longer duration of, for instance, an hour may seem more appropriate than a half-hour. If, by contrast, songs will only be heard as brief extracts and under speech, the half-hour **format** may be preferred.

The use of music in a speech-based environment, such as a documentary, should never be indiscriminate. This rule precludes the crude **segueing** together of a number of tracks in a non-stop **bed** that, on each occasion, changes from one track to another without regard to the spoken discourse over it. Even if the balance between the music and the speech is correctly maintained – so that the music never drowns the speech or renders it less distinct than it needs to be for listeners to understand it – it should not be used without thought and careful attention to the conventions of applying music to speech. Over decades, film and television have developed what is commonly referred to as the 'language of shots', whereby, for example, directors routinely use an establishing shot to identify a location and situate the characters and action within it, and then cut to a tighter framing, such as a close up (Orlebar, 2002, 266–7). Similarly, in radio there is a syntax (or grammar) that orders the various constituent parts of a narrative and organizes the elaborate relationships between them. Languages are, of course, rarely static – and just as new words become accepted as part of a vocabulary because their usage becomes more widespread, so does syntax change in response to a range of influences. In terms of television and radio, one of those influences can be innovation, but in order to affect production practices, innovation must be widely accepted as both effective and appealing.

One very robust rule is that music for incidental use should normally only be used if its title is unrecognizable and any lyrics don't compete with the spoken narrative playing over it. The main exception to this is where the title or a line of the song is clearly recognizable, it is of obvious relevance to the discourse – even to listeners who don't know the song well – and it can be played, briefly, *between* passages of speech to reinforce or illustrate a substantive point. Otherwise, known lyrics or melodies under the speech will inevitably compete with it and listeners may sing or hum along with it, while becoming distracted from the more important spoken narrative. **Library music** can be particularly useful in documentary making, because many of the pieces – although evocative – will be unrecognizable to listeners.

Secondly, in mixing and editing a documentary, producers should carefully consider where to place the in and out points of the music, and whether it should fade up or alternatively, begin decisively at full volume. Generally a bed needs only three or four seconds to establish itself, before it can be faded under the start of a section of speech. (If it has a particularly striking melody that takes a little longer than this to play out, an exception may be made, but speech-based programming which has long passages of music begins to sound as though it has been padded out because of a lack of original material.) This technique works well at the beginning of a programme, and where the narrative needs punctuation in order to enhance its clarity, to reinforce an important point or to accommodate the signposting that is necessary to regularly reinforce the direction and purpose of the discourse. Sometimes producers will want to fade music up at the end of a section of speech, and let it play for a few seconds up to its natural end. This can provide a neat ending to a section, or to the whole programme, because the final notes of the music add an element of finality to the narrative. It can also **signify** a pause – for example, before a commercial break.

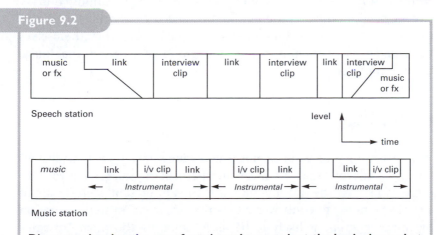

Figure 9.2

Speech station

Music station

Diagrams showing the use of music under speech at the beginning and at the end of a section. On a music station, the bed is more likely to continue under the speech, while on a speech station it would probably fade soon after the speech has become established.

Other sounds

The use of actuality requires similar care and attention. Where **atmosphere** has been recorded with the speech, only fairly sophisticated **processing** will be able to remove it. Where sounds are to be added to the narrative, though, like music they cannot be inserted indiscriminately. They can punctuate very effectively, but the main reason for using them should be to illustrate relevant points raised in the discourse. As discussed in Chapter 8, both music and effects can evoke places and eras in listeners' minds, and reduce the need for spoken description. Of course, this only works where the image sought is commonly associated with the audio, and associations that are vague or ambiguous are unlikely to inspire similar readings across whole audiences.

As with music, added sounds can require just a few seconds to be assimilated by listeners, before they can be faded under speech. It is also easy to over-use them. Listeners to BBC Radio Four often write to the comments programme *Feedback*, complaining of heavy-handed use of sound effects in documentaries and packages. One student punctuated a **vox pop** about the public's opinions on compulsory military service with machine gun fire between each comment: it created a rather surreal effect because the 'realism' of the pavement setting for their views was juxtaposed with actual, if brief, scenes of armed conflict. Some listeners imagined two contrasting locations, quickly cutting between them as the producer intended – but others perceived the gunfire to be in the same street as the public, as if they themselves were under fire, and for this second group of listeners the image became confused.

Ethical issues

Whether using a narrator or not, the documentary is such a substantial piece of work that producers are particularly vulnerable to criticisms of bias. As the documentary attempts to present a 'truth' about a subject – however controversial – any evidence of misrepresentation by the programme is likely to be seized upon by those who disagree with the 'reality' it portrays. This can include statements made by the reporter, if there is one, or even unfair selection of contributors and the material included (see the section on ethical standards in Chapter 2).

In tightly regulated environments, such as the United Kingdom, **codes of practice** or licensing agreements may bind broadcasters to high standards of conduct regarding balance and **impartiality** in matters of political controversy (BBC, 2013; Ofcom, 2011), but other aspects of representation may be left to the producer's own sense of honesty and fairness. To knowingly misrepresent an issue or a story is an act of deception, and one for which broadcasters can be rightly criticized. Someone who develops a reputation for courting controversy in this way may become less easily employable, because stations do not want the bad reputation to become attached to them. Dishonest reporting is, in fact, very rare – or at least, it is unusual for dishonest radio producers to be found out – and most documentary production is widely considered to be fair. Sometimes it is a matter of emphasis that attracts a complaint, and in July 2001 one was upheld against *Face the Facts* (BBC Radio Four) by the then Broadcasting Standards Commission (BSC, 2002). By contrast, a number of television documentaries have been found to have 'faked' content, and in 1996 Carlton Television was fined £2 million by its regulator, the ITC (Day, 2002).

Ensuring a programme is 'balanced' can be difficult, especially as not all controversies divide equally into binary opposites. There can be a range of different positions held by interested parties, and it may be difficult to reflect all of them with the prominence they deserve. Listeners often react according to their own established perspectives, too, and they may not begin listening to a programme without some already acquired knowledge – however correct – or some pre-conceived opinions. 'Realist' notions of programme making require the producer or the reporter to make reasonable efforts to make objective decisions about all available facts, and to try to represent them fairly, giving due prominence to each element of the resultant discourse. It would be easy to load a programme in favour of one viewpoint, by including more contributors who are sympathetic to it, or by giving them more airtime. The opposing view could be represented by a deliberately unimpressive range of supporters, or the less convincing parts of their argument could deliberately be used instead of their better contributions. However, responsible producers respect their audiences enough to resist such temptations and this aptitude for self-censorship is a requirement of the job.

It is normally reasonable, though, for a reporter to come to some reasonable conclusions about an issue at the end of a programme, having considered the evidence fairly presented in it. This sounds less incongruous where the approach has tended towards the personal odyssey. However reasonable the conclusions may seem, though, there is no immunity from criticism. An important exception to the rules on balance within a programme lies in the specific case of **advocacy journalism**, where the programme is presented from the clearly articulated perspective of someone with a partial perspective, who is seeking to legitimize it (Fink, 1988, 18). Such an opinionated programme may be presented as the views of a public figure, or a member of the public, who is not necessarily a broadcaster or a journalist. Usually, balance over a limited period of time would be maintained by allowing a reply in the form of a suitably resourced programme from someone of equal standing who could present an opposing case in the same slot the next day or a week later.

Exercise 9.2

Plan and write a proposal for a single documentary for the context and target audience of your choice. Identify the subject, angle, duration and style of the programme, as well as researching a list of strong interview prospects to cover the topic ethically. Explain your decisions in class.

Libel

Another important constraint on all broadcasters is **libel**. The consequences for seriously and unfairly damaging someone's reputation can be very high, and English law calls this **defamation**. Libel law tries to strike a balance between freedom of speech and the need to protect reputations. The dead are not protected, except where malicious falsehood can be proved to have damaged the property of the deceased's estate (Ezard, 2002). Although most libel actions are civil claims, in which a person or an organization sues for damages, there are certain circumstances where criminal prosecutions may be brought. Most successful libel actions result in large sums of damages being awarded by the jury, and it may be the employee who has to pay them – or this could even be someone on a **freelance contract**. The threat of an impending libel action and the length of any legal proceedings can be a cause of worry for several years, and because legal fees can be very expensive such situations are usually best avoided. Generally, radio stations are far more cautious than newspapers over risking libel actions being initiated against them, because they usually do not have the spare cash to comfortably pay up if they lose. Being cautious means not taking risks with other people's reputations, and only broadcasting allegations that might damage people's perceptions of them as honest, upstanding members of the community if you have very solid evidence which will be admissible in court and which seems very likely to convince a typical jury that your claims are correct.

Damage to someone's reputation may consist of wrongly saying he or she is dishonest, cheats on a spouse or partner, is of a different sexual orientation, is HIV-positive, is violent, acts inappropriately with children or has committed any kind of criminal offence, from theft to murder. A company's reputation could be damaged by claims it has acted wrongly or unlawfully, cheated a customer, or defaulted on an obligation. English law presumes people and organizations to be automatically worthy of a decent reputation, unless proved otherwise. Of course, it may be possible to prove a claim decisively in court, but most broadcasters would be expected to discuss their intention to take such a risk 'on air' with the editor or programme controller, first. The most senior people in the radio station may reasonably take legal advice before allowing a claim to be broadcast. One of the most frequently consulted reference **sources** on this issue in newsrooms and production offices is *McNae's Essential Law for Journalists* (Hanna and Dodd, 2012).

There are a number of defences under English law, which reduce the risk of being successfully sued for libel. Firstly, convicted murderers can't bring successful libel actions against broadcasters who call them murderers, because they have already been proven as such before a criminal court. Similarly, a foreign head of state who has waged an unprovoked war on a neighbouring country would be unlikely to win a case in an English court over being called a warmonger. Such claims would be considered justified. Other remarks may be considered to be fair comment: a creative work or a performance, such as a film or the way a football team played in a match, would be considered as a reasonable object for public comment. However, there is a crucial difference between saying 'on air' that an actress's performance in a play didn't seem very appropriate for the part, and alleging that she was drunk and so couldn't remember her lines. The second claim could damage her reputation as a professional who can be relied upon to work well and conscientiously in her job. Reporting what is said during court proceedings and in parliamentary debates is covered by 'qualified privilege', because the participants are themselves protected by 'absolute privilege', and the public has a right to know much of what is said there (see pages 222–4). The defence of innocent libel may apply where an allegation was broadcast without the consent of the broad-caster – for example, in a live interview – when immediate steps have been taken to disassociate the programme and the station from it and to apologize 'on air' for any offence caused. This obviously can't apply to a pre-recorded documentary.

Some of the biggest libel awards made by juries in the United Kingdom were in the 1980s, although more recently big awards have tended to be reduced on appeal (Tench, 2002). Often, though, libel actions are settled before they get to court, because one side or the other lacks the confidence in their case to hold out for a verdict that benefits them. Relatively recently, judges have been given the right to reduce the amount of damages awarded by juries if they consider them to be excessive, and in 2002 the politician and author Jeffery Archer returned £500,000 to the *Daily Star* after he was convicted of perjury in his previous libel trial against it (Hall, 2002). Unusually, also in 2002, the television journalist Donal MacIntyre chose to bring libel proceed-ings against Kent police making himself the plaintiff – and they were left with a £750,000 bill for damages and legal fees over allegations they had made about him (Wells, 2002b).

Reporting restrictions

Many countries place restrictions on the reporting of criminal proceed-ings, in order to protect the accused's right to a fair trial. In the United Kingdom, the historical context to this dates back to 1957, when Dr Bodkin Adams was being tried for the murder by euthanasia of a patient and 1966, when the moors murderers Myra Hindley and Ian Brady were accused of a number of child murders. In both cases, before the trials began, extensive and sensational media reporting had connected the accused so decisively with the murders, that there were real concerns that jury members would have read and heard so much that they would individually have already reached decisions over guilt and innocence. The Criminal Justice Act 1967 introduced tight restric-tions in order to prevent any future 'trial by jury'. Subsequent legisla-tion has extended and modified the rules. In this way, the law tries to balance the legitimate right of the public and the media to see that justice is being done in the courts, with the rights of the accused and the need to prevent guilty people escaping justice because they can claim to have been denied a fair trial. Under English law, once some-one has been charged with a criminal offence or if he or she is still being sought but a summons has been issued for him or her to appear before a magistrates' court, the case becomes 'live' and broadcasters must take great care over what they say about the matter.

The penalties for infringement can be high, and the individual reporter or producer can be found to be in contempt of court, for which judges may impose fines or even a prison sentence. Journalists have usually had a thorough training in reporting restrictions, but many still refer regularly to Hanna and Dodd (2012) to remind themselves of the detail. Generally, the following key points apply to English law:

▸ Minors must not be identified at all – even by association – if they are involved in criminal prosecutions and some civil matters such as divorce and custody proceedings.

▸ Special rules apply to victims of sexual offences, whose identities must be protected, although the accused can normally be identified as such, once charged.

▸ Reporting of trials should be contemporaneous and a 'fair' representation of what was said in court, except when a crown court jury is ordered to withdraw from the chamber or when the bench places extra reporting restrictions on the media.

▸ Certain matters may be 'confidential', to protect patents, trade secrets, national security and the victims of blackmail.

▸ Bail hearings, 'plea and direction' hearings and some other routine appearances in court that occur prior to an actual trial taking place are subject to specific restrictions which prevent all but the most basic of information being reported.

▸ It is wise to make clear in reports that what was said was *alleged*, rather than proven – because reporting is done under the qualified (or restricted) privilege allowed to the media, but which does not give total immunity from future libel actions which anyone involved in the case may decide to pursue.

A criminal case ceases to be 'live' when the jury (or the magistrates in less serious cases) reaches its verdict, even if the bench is not yet ready to pass sentence on someone who has been found guilty. There are sometimes grounds for appeal, but as appeals aren't heard by juries they are not subject to the same restrictions. Once reporting restrictions are lifted, programmes may again discuss such issues as the background to the case, the detail of allegations made in court, and why the accused was charged and tried for the offence. Now if the accused has any previous convictions they can be discussed for the first time, as can any implications they may have for a wider understanding of the case and the kind of sentence appropriate for someone found guilty. The observations on pages 220–2 about libel apply here, too – even in the case of a guilty verdict – because witnesses, relatives and associates of the accused probably still have valid reasons to protect their own reputations. Any unsubstantiated suggestion that the family of a murderer are probably also of bad character could result in a successful libel action by them.

The impact of reporting restrictions on documentary producers is clear: the nature and length of a documentary preclude its being considered suitable for broadcast during a criminal trial, if it is about the case or the accused. However, the great length of time taken by most important criminal cases to get to court means there is often time to produce a programme for transmission immediately after the verdict, just as in the United Kingdom, spectacular trials such as those of Rosemary West (1995) and the killers of James Bulger (1993) were followed by detailed retrospectives examining the crimes, the investigations and the trials. As the trial unfolds, further detail can be added of new information that was allowed in court, and alternative versions may be prepared – each one for a different verdict – providing that great care is taken to ensure the correct version is broadcast when the verdict is known.

Other legal issues

Programmes are also bound by other legislation covering such other issues as **copyright**, race relations, official secrets, and election periods. Copyright for the use of someone else's music will probably be covered in the station's normal licensing agreement – although in the case of an all-speech station there may not be one (see Chapter 4). Other material, such as sound effects and actuality from sound archives or on videos, DVDs and web sites is also very likely to be protected, and where no licence to broadcast applies, permission from the copyright owner may be necessary. Getting this can be time-consuming, so leaving it until the end of the production process is not normally an option.

Many countries have laws relating to the way ethnic minorities are treated, which might include such concepts as incitement to racial hatred, prohibited in the United Kingdom by the Public Order Acts of 1936 and 1976. Enlightened standards of behaviour towards others dictate anyway that broadcasters should not indulge in discrimination on the basis of ethnicity.

Different countries respond differently to what they perceive as threats to their national security, and responses can range from arrest and possible prosecution to violence and even torture, depending on how liberal or authoritarian the regime is. The Official Secrets Acts of 1911 and 1989 prohibit a range of activities in the United Kingdom which could be interpreted by the criminal courts as risking national security, but the treatment of a group of British plane-spotters visiting a Greek airshow in 2001 (Smith, 2002) demonstrates the need for caution when working near military bases and a certain wariness about obtaining official information by clandestine means, especially when abroad. The British media also agree with the security services from time to time that they will not cover particular matters that are then deemed by both sides to be covered by a D-Notice.

Normal considerations of political balance may be tightened by legislation during election periods, and in the United Kingdom various

Figure 9.3

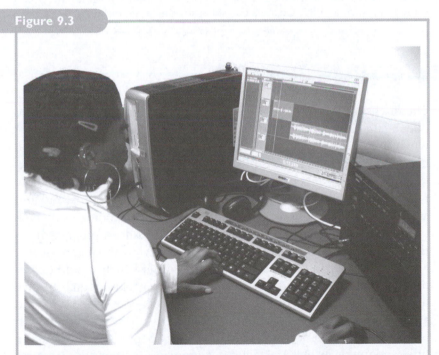

Post-production work on a documentary, using Adobe Audition to combine a variety of speech, music and actuality in a clear structure that respects conventional rules of syntax in presenting an effective discourse.

Representation of the People Acts tightly control the amount of airtime that may be given to candidates in general, local, regional and by-elections. Changes brought about by the Political Parties, Elections and Referendums Act 2000 have relaxed the rules on getting the consent of all candidates in a constituency before any one of them may appear, but individual politicians may anyway be interviewed more generally about an election providing they don't discuss in detail any issues that are particular to their own constituencies. On election day, though, no discussion of election issues is allowed, until the polling stations close. Some countries, such as France, have banned opinion polls in the last few days before the poll.

Exercise 9.3

Carry out detailed research for your documentary, arranging and recording a range of interviews. Plan the structure of the programme, developing a script around the most appropriate interview material and any music and/or actuality that will enhance your programme. Record any presenter links needed, and assemble the programme in a studio or on a hard-disk medium, such as a PC. Create a cue sheet for the programme.

Analysing documentaries

The discussion on pages 206–18 of different styles and approaches to documentary production, suggests that there is much to consider when analysing examples of the genre. The range of different and complementary conventions of style that can be used without subverting the genre so much as to make it unrecognizable by reasonably radio literate audiences, means the potential for comparing and contrasting different examples is vast. Useful methodologies include noting the occurrence of different events in a broadcast programme as they occur (such as links, sound effects, interview material and music), and then formalizing these into a **running order** which should resemble that used by the producer. Timing each event adds a quantitative dimension that may reveal more evidence about the style and approach used, as well as content issues such as those concerned with representation, balance and **ideology** (see Chapter 2). Transcribing links and interview material facilitates a range of methods of **discourse analysis** which examine the use of language from syntactical and lexical perspectives: which words were chosen by contributors and the scriptwriter, how were they put together in sentences and why? This may depend solely on the broadcast context, the target audience and the subject matter, or it may be that some ideological influence becomes evident in the process.

Ownership may be significant in the ideological positioning of a text. Public service broadcasters, if they are robustly financed and so protected from external influences, may be better placed than commercial stations to exercise the kind of independence of thought and expression on which documentary makers should thrive. In the United Kingdom, the BBC's funding arrangements (in which a licence fee based on television use provides a reliable income) and its constitution under a Royal Charter have insulated it reasonably well from successive governments since 1927. This independence has in some respects been illusory because the Corporation is reliant on regular increases in the licence fee, in order for its income to keep pace with inflation, and the Charter is subject to regular renewal by Parliament – itself normally dominated by the ruling political party. The provision of new services is often subject to government approval, and the BBC's plans for the digital television service BBC Three were subject to considerable interference by the Department for Culture, Media and Sport, which was itself under pressure from the commercial television sector over what it described as unfair competition (Deans, 2002). Now the controlling Executive Board is overseen by the BBC Trust, which includes political appointees, and although the tradition is to represent a cross-section of mainstream political opinion, regular controversies arise in the British media whenever key vacancies need filling (Bell, 2002).

Furthermore, the creation of the single **regulator** for all the communications industries, Ofcom, in 2003, was preceded by an anxious debate over the extent of the power it would exercise over the BBC, bringing as it did for the first time the responsibility for standards and complaints management under the same umbrella as that for the licensing of commercial operators (Bragg, 2002). It is difficult to imagine that when crucial decisions are being made in government, the BBC naively assumes that it can operate with impunity, although an alternative interpretation may be that by regularly asserting its independence it preserves it.

In theory, producers are insulated from any pressures felt higher up in the Corporation by the existence of the *Editorial Guidelines* (2013), which set clear standards of conduct for programme makers, and provided they work within them they can have confidence in their own day-to-day editorial decisions. The established procedure of referring upwards the more controversial issues of policy may compromise this, and the existence of such statutory and consensual controls as the Official Secrets Acts and D-Notices may act as a reminder that even in the public sector editorial freedom can never be complete.

Until 2014, the BBC World Service is funded separately by a grant from the Foreign and Commonwealth Office – an arrangement which further undermines notions of total independence, although its programmes are received with worldwide acclaim and it is rare for criticisms to be levelled against it of undue influence being exercised by the British government in the same way that during the cold war (1945–90) stations such as Radio Moscow were considered to be part of the Soviet propaganda 'machine'. Other international broadcasters today transmit very partisan perspectives on current affairs, with the intention of influencing public opinion in other countries run by what they perceive to be hostile regimes, but as the word 'propaganda' originates from seventeenth-century Catholicism, it is clear that it does not refer exclusively to party political or state ideology. Any reinforcement of entrenched views on an issue is likely to be perceived by those in an opposing camp to be propaganda of some sort, and **naturalization** of, for example, western capitalism, in a documentary which comfortably meets all the BBC's *Editorial Guidelines* might easily be considered by some followers of Islam, for example, to be unacceptable.

Audience readings of documentaries can vary widely, just as in the case of the shorter productions in that closely related genre, the speech package (see Chapter 2). Active **models** of audience behaviour suggest that because individual listeners may subconsciously bring their own positioning to bear on their reading of texts, their perceptions of balance and bias, for instance, are not likely to be uniform. Often, broadcasters claim that listener complaints of bias coming in from both sides in a dispute confirm their own impartiality and professionalism, because *both* sides feel the need to complain (Schlesinger, 1987, 171). In his ethnographic study of BBC employees, Burns found that it was the responses to their work of other colleagues that mattered most to them (1977, 137), rather than **audience responses** – and some of the Glasgow University Media Group's conclusions about self-perpetuating 'attitudes, expectations, truisms and commonplaces' among television journalists in the Corporation also suggest that some readings of their work were more important to them than others (1977, 203). Indeed, the Group's close **textual analysis** of television coverage of industrial strife was itself dismissed by the British right-wing press as 'mere' left-wing propaganda (McNair, 1994, 34).

While broadcasters rarely encourage audiences to consider the ideo-logical positioning, preconceptions and other factors that might have influenced them in production, listeners are expected to read the vari-ous **semiotic** elements within a documentary that uses actuality and other sounds to enhance its discourse. Producers normally have a **preferred reading**, which is the interpretation they would most like listeners to make (Hall, 1973). Realism is easily undermined by ambi-guity, and in journalism uncertainty can be dangerous – especially where the subject matter can easily inflame already difficult situations, such as over race, religion or politics. So notions of creativity or the avant-garde are uncommon in documentary making, and the use of montage or soundscape approaches normally tends to be conservative. A good test of the use of sound to create images is to isolate it from any contextualizing link or interview material which surrounds it, and to play it to people who have not already heard the programme, asking them to write down what, if anything, they think the sounds depict. If the responses vary widely, a second playing *including* the surrounding speech might prove to anchor meanings more firmly and produce a more robust consensus around the producer's preferred reading. If not, it would be interesting to consider possible explanations for this. **Alternative readings** and, in turn, rogue readings, are not always undesirable, but they may well surprise producers who think that their work is clear and unambiguous.

Some of the **codes** that operate in radio drama (see Chapter 8) may also operate in documentaries, and the differences between these two very broad genres become even more blurred in the hybrid case of drama-documentary. Where documentary strays into areas that are outside the personal experience of the producer and all the contribu-tors – such as all but relatively recent history – someone's imagination begins to take over, and 'actuality' begins to lose its authenticity. Some documentaries try too hard to illustrate the spoken discourse, and at the mere mention of drink, for instance, we hear corks popping and liquid pouring, even though the image remains in the background and we are never left alone in the unfolding scene, or allowed to hear the perspective of its participants.

Using non-**diegetic** sound for illustration also raises ethical issues about how far audiences should be fed representations that are at best false, and at worst, misleading. The 'reconstruction' is easily signposted by a simple caption on television, without any interruption to its discourse, but as with the financial disclaimer on a radio commercial (see Chapter 6), on radio time must be taken up by any such honesty and often producers are loath to be so transparent. Without being told the sounds are substitutes, few listeners will question their authenticity and the deception will be complete – although, with a shrug of the shoulder, this point is routinely dismissed by producers. Convention, of course, is the mother of self-confidence and a further affirmation of professionalism.

Appendix:
Finding work in radio

There are a number of useful strategies for gaining employment in the radio industry, once you have mastered a range of relevant skills in planning and production. They include the following:

▸ Take advantage of any opportunity to spend extra time in the studio or using editing and scheduling software, in order to become more familiar with their operation and to develop your ability.

▸ Volunteer for your local student, community or hospital radio station – perhaps working off air at first, but setting yourself clear goals for increasing your involvement in production, presentation and even management roles.

▸ Remember that radio is no longer just radio – learn how to use interactive media including social networking, how to post to a blog and how to put video and audio content online, as well as clearly written and correctly spelt text.

▸ Listen critically to the output of a range of radio stations and compare their output with your own work in class and in your own time.

▸ Record your own live work, including links and live features, and listen back to it critically, trying where possible to improve on subsequent attempts.

▸ Find work experience at a 'professional' radio station, by offering to help on such programmes as the Saturday afternoon sports sequence, in the newsroom or in creative production. An unpaid 'foot in the door' can lead to much better opportunities in the same station or somewhere else.

▸ Build up a database of contacts you make at different radio stations, either through doing work experience or through introducing yourself at public appearances and roadshows.

▸ Produce a **demo** of the very best of your work – no longer than two or three minutes in total – and/or burn it onto an audio CD. It is a good idea to record links in the style of the station you are sending it to, so they can more easily imagine you working for them.

- ▸ Create clear, literate and attractive letters of application, and a c.v. to match, then send them with your demo to possible employers. Telephone the station's switchboard first, and ask for the exact name and title of the person who listens to demo tapes – it may be the programme controller, a group programme controller working from a different address or the editor of a particular programme. Remember that if they are even half interested in giving you a chance, they may well search for you online – make sure you haven't posted anything on social media that they will find off-putting. If you have, take it down.

- ▸ Don't be put off by rejection, but, where possible, call back and ask politely for any constructive advice you could take into account in future. Many successful broadcasters had to cope with frequent rejection before achieving their first real career breakthrough.

- ▸ Set high personal standards of professionalism in your work and your attitude to others, but seek advice from people you trust if you feel you are being exploited or treated unfairly in some other way.

# Glossary

The first time a word defined below appears in any chapter, it is written in **bold** in the text.

A capella: jingle sung 'dry' without instrumental backing.

Acoustics: the reflective characteristics of different locations, insofar as they cause sound waves picked up by microphones to include some which have been reflected by walls, ceilings, etc.

Actuality: *realia* incorporated into radio programming either to establish a scene or to reinforce or illustrate the discourse. For example, ambient sound, archive recordings or the noise made by an object being described.

Advocacy journalism: does not attempt to provide a 'balanced' account of events or ideas, but is unashamedly partial in promoting a particular perspective (see also: impartiality).

Airchecks: 'off air' recordings of, for example, a presenter's links (see also: demo).

ALC: see automatic level control.

Alternative reading: a meaning listeners may derive from a piece of audio, that varies from that intended by the producer (see also: preferred reading).

Ambient sound: sound that exists, either naturally or due to human or animal intervention, in a given location.

Anchor: to fix an otherwise ambiguous item or concept to a particular meaning by associating it with a further, positioning statement. For example, a caption may anchor the meaning of a photograph to a particular interpretation, just as a voice-over may anchor a sound to a particular location or motion.

Anchorage: the way in which meaning is anchored in a text (see also: textual analysis).

Angle: an approach to a particular topic or subject.

Atmosphere, atmospheric effects: ambient sound, (for example, birdsong or waves lapping).

Audience research: the gathering of data relating to the size and nature of audiences, normally for programming and commercial purposes (see also: ratings).

Audience response: the behaviour of listeners, which can be attributed to what they have heard on the radio or experienced through other mass media.

Audience theory: relates to identified models of audience response (see also: model).

Audio: concerning sound.

Automatic level control (ALC): circuitry designed to prevent distortion of audio through over-modulation (levels being too high). Will raise low levels, too (see also: level, limiter).

Automation: pre-determined sequences of programming events broadcast 'on air' without real-time human intervention, often overnight.

Auxilliary output: second output from a mixing desk, configurable to supply a different mix of channels to another studio or a remote location.

Back announcement, back anno: a scripted or unscripted statement 'on air', relating to the previous item.

Back timing: beginning a song or an instrumental in time for it to end decisively before the news or another programme event, while not necessarily fading it up until nearer the end.

Bed: an instrumental music track used under a talkover.

Billboard: a relatively long speech package (see also: package, wrap).

Brainstorming: a sometimes chaotic, sometimes systematic process used to originate and develop ideas (see also: mind mapping).

Brand: the combined identity of a product, including its name, image and wider connotations.

Branding: the application of a brand to a product (for example, to a radio station).

Breakout box: connectable interface between a workstation, such as SADiE, and other equipment, such as a MiniDisc recorder or a mixer.

Bulletin: a news, travel or financial summary, typically of between one and ten minutes' duration.

Campaign: cohesive set of different, but related, advertisements for products or services. *Also* the time period over which one or more adverts are broadcast.

Cart machines: playback equipment used for carts.

Cartridge, cart: plastic casing containing a continuous loop of audio tape, used widely (until the growth of playout software) to put short items instantly to air.

Catch, catchline: one- or two-word code name for an item in a bulletin or a radio magazine programme.

Channel: a route through a mixer for a single sound source. May be either stereo or mono. *Also* the output from any stereo equipment, such as a mixer, is divided into two channels: left and right.

Characterization: the establishment and development of characters and their individual traits in radio drama.

Chinagraph pencil: a soft-centred pencil for marking edit points on an audio tape before cutting it.

Clean feed: a separate audio output from a mixer, which excludes one or more channels that have been faded up into the main output.

Clock: graphical representation of an hour of a programme, showing individual items, with their durations, arranged around a central point (see also: programming wheel, running order). *Also* a linear running order template, used by Selector.

Closed: narrative structure involving an act of closure.

Closed questions: are formulated in ways that encourage simple 'yes' or 'no' answers, rather than the detailed and often personal answers which are the more likely responses to *open* questions. For example, 'Did you cover up the robbery?'

Closure: the act of ending a programme or an item, in such a way as to make clear that it is finished.

Code: a way of conveying meaning to listeners without necessarily using words. For example, in a radio drama a fade down followed by a fade up is widely understood by producers and listeners to mean a scene change.

Codec: coder/decoder used at each end of ISDN lines.

Code of practice: set of rules, either consensual or regulatory, relating to conduct.

Compressor: circuitry designed to raise low levels and lower high ones in order to produce a more consistent sound.

Connote: to suggest, in the sense of Roland Barthes's second order of signification. For example, the word 'red' may suggest debt, anger, communism, socialism or danger, depending on the context within which it is used, and the perspective of the listener (see also: denote).

Context: the environment in which something is situated. For example, the general output of a particular radio station may be the context for a proposed new programme, and it will influence the nature of the proposal because they must complement each other.

Convention: an accepted way of doing something. For example, ending a commercial break with a jingle to identify the radio station, is generally accepted to be a good idea, so it is common practice.

Copy: scripted material for use in news, programming or advertising. For example, news copy, advertising copy.

Copyright: ownership of a work. Legislation protects the originators of artistic and intellectual work from those others who would use it without permission or payment of a fee.

Copyright returns: declarations to copyright licensing bodies.

Copywriter: someone who writes copy, most commonly for advertising purposes.

Cue: a signal to begin or end something (see also: out-cue). *Also* a written piece of copy to be read before an item. *Also* to line up an item ready for playback.

Cue sheet: a single-sided piece of post-production paperwork that includes key information about a recorded programme or item: catchline, introduction or continuity announcement, in-cue, out-cue, duration, back announcement, technical information.

DAB: see Digital Audio Broadcasting.

DAT: see Digital Audio Tape.

Daypart: a pre-defined segment of the broadcasting day or night, for example, breakfast, mid-morning, afternoon drive, overnight, etc.

Decode, **decoding**: the process of deriving meanings from a set of words, sounds and/or silence (see also: encoding).

Deconstruct: to analyse a text by considering each of its constituent parts in isolation and in relation to other parts.

Defamation: legal term relating to libel law and involving the unfair damaging of a person or an organization's reputation in the minds of 'right-thinking' people.

Demographic: relating to descriptors of social groupings (see also: target audience).

Demo: demonstration, normally a tightly edited and attractively presented sample of the work of an individual or an organization, for example, a presenter seeking employment (see also: airchecks) or a production house offering to make advertisements.

Denote: to indicate, in the sense of Roland Barthes's first order of signification. For example, the word 'red' denotes a colour most listeners can visualize (see also: connote).

Diegesis: set of known elements within a context. For example the internal diegesis of *The Archers* is centred on Ambridge and the characters who inhabit it, while the external diegesis includes the British agricultural industry and the challenges it faces.

Diegetic sound: heard in a situation, being inherent to a diegesis.

Digital Audio Broadcasting, DAB: the system of digital transmission of radio signals, adopted by the United Kingdom. Digital compression allows very efficient use of available frequencies (see also: DRM).

Digital Audio Tape, DAT: portable or studio-based recording technology that uses magnetic means to store large amounts of digitally encoded audio on cassettes that are smaller in size than domestic analogue cassettes. *Also* the removable storage medium used in a DAT machine.

Digital platform: conduit for the transmission and reception of digital programming (for example, in the United Kingdom, DAB, Sky and Freeview).

Digital Radio Mondiale, DRM: an alternative system (to DAB) of digital radio transmission.

Discourse: a series of statements or an argument articulated through written or broadcast texts (see also: textual analysis).

Discourse analysis: developing academic tradition providing perspectives on the nature and content of discourse in a range of human contexts.

Dramatization: creating drama from other contexts, such as in reconstruction or converting a reading into a play.

DRM: see Digital Radio Mondiale.

Drop-in: comedy insert between songs in a sequence programme.

Dub: to copy audio from one source (for example, tape or MiniDisc) to another (for example, a computer or a solid-state recorder). *Also* the result of the dubbing process.

Dubbing: the process involved in creating a dub.

Ducking: lowering the level of one channel, in order to allow another to be heard over it. (For example, for a talkover.)

Duration: how long an audio item lasts.

Edit: to remove unwanted sections of a recording or to rearrange others. *Also* the result of editing.

Edit decision list, EDL: a literal description of 'in' and 'out' points, mixes, fades and processing, as used by some computer applications, such as SADiE, for audio production. *Also* a running order for a recorded programme or item.

Effects microphone: used to capture audience reactions or atmosphere from a location.

Encode, encoding: using words, sounds and/or silence to convey a given meaning to an audience (see also: decoding).

Equalization, eq: (the use of) circuitry for processing audio in order to alter its tonal qualities, by boosting or reducing particular sound frequency ranges (for example, treble, bass and middle frequencies).

Era: time period used to classify songs from, for example, the 1960s, the 1970s, etc.

Ethical: concerning what is generally considered right and proper in terms of actions that affect others. For example, ethical issues include truthfulness, privacy, representation and balance.

Evaluate: to make a reasoned and detailed judgement about the value of something, assessing its strengths and weaknesses.

Fader: fine gain control on a mixer channel, allowing precise fading in and out of a sound source to the required level.

Feature: a term that is loosely applicable within a number of different genres, including the speech package, the drama-documentary, speech items in a live sequence and the extended variety programme.

Feedback: a noise caused by output being fed back into the input, either electronically or by a microphone picking up its own output from a loudspeaker (see also: howlround). *Also* information on audience or client responses to a radio programme or item, or work in progress.

Flashback: narrative device used to present past events out of sequence with the present.

Format: the agreed programming policy of a radio station, in terms of the type of music it plays according to musical genre and era, as well as the relationship between music and speech. *Also* the formula to which an individual programme adheres (for example, the structure and concept behind a panel game or a quiz show). *Also* a type of computer file, such as .wav and .mp3.

Franchise application: made to a regulator in a bid to be licensed to provide a certain service in a particular area. For example, as in early ILR.

Freelance contracts: legally binding agreements between radio stations and individuals who work for them as suppliers, rather than employees (see also: staff contracts).

Frequency spectrum: the full range of frequencies within which electromagnetic signals can be transmitted, for radio, television, data, mobile phone and all other means of wireless communication.

Gain: a coarse level control. Normally situated on an individual mixer channel, and used in pre-fading in order to set levels correctly (see also: PFL, fader).

Genre: the collective noun for a type of radio programme or item, individual examples of which share characteristics of style, approach or purpose. For example, each of Chapters 2–9 features radio products that are broadly related according to generic characteristics, such as sequence programmes, speech packages, etc. (see also: subgenre).

Handling noise: unwanted noise caused electronically when a microphone lead or its body is disturbed, most commonly when hand-held (see also: mic rattle).

Hook: the catchiest, most recognizable and commercially appealing part of a song.

Howlround: a high-pitched noise caused by output being fed back into the input, when a microphone picks up its own output from a loudspeaker (see also: feedback).

Hypodermic needle: a model of passive audience response which considers media products to be capable of injecting information and ideas into audiences' consciousness, which then provoke broadly similar reactions (see also: uses and gratifications).

Icon: a primary-level agent in the encoding and decoding of meaning (see also: index, symbol). For example, a siren may be iconic of a police car, simply because that is a sound they sometimes make.

Ident: station or programme identification (see also: stab, sting).

Ideology: systems of beliefs and values by which people make political, social, ethical and lifestyle choices.

ILR: see Independent Local Radio.

Imaging: the application of a station's brand to its output, including idents.

Impartiality: attempt to 'balance' competing perspectives on events or issues while being 'fair' to all (see also: advocacy journalism).

In-cue: how an audio item begins: either speech, music or effects. *Also* introductory copy to be read before an item.

Independent Local Radio (ILR): the first commercial radio stations to be licensed to broadcast from the United Kingdom mainland, beginning with LBC in 1973 and developing into a network of large and small local stations.

Index: a secondary-level agent in the encoding and decoding of meaning (see also: icon, symbol). For example, a siren may be indexical of police officers, not because officers sound like sirens, but because the siren can indicate they are present.

Institutions: the public and privately owned bodies involved in the production and regulation of radio programming (for example, the BBC, Clear Channel, Ofcom).

Intertextuality: the relationships between programme or item content which exists in more than one text (see also: textual analysis).

Intro: introduction to a song, often used in a presenter talkover or under a sweeper.

Investigative: narrative structure associated with an encyclopaedia or an interactive Internet radio station.

ISDN (Integrated Services Digital Network): high quality transmission of digitally encoded audio between different locations, each of which must be equipped with a codec ('coder/decoder').

Jingle: sung or musical ident for a station, or in an advertisement.

Jingle package: cohesive set of jingles used by a station.

Jump cut: an inappropriate edit which is too obvious a 'jump' from one piece of audio to another.

Landlines: dedicated wire connections between different locations, providing a music-quality signal. For example, between a studio and a commentary box at a sports ground.

Level: the amount of audio from a single sound source passing through audio equipment.

Libel: defamation of a person or an organization (unfair damage to reputation), disseminated over a relatively large population, for example through broadcasting or publication (see also: slander).

Library music: composed for use in radio, television and other audible media, allowing relatively cheap and easy copyright licensing, compared with commercial recordings.

Limiter: circuitry (see also: ALC) that prevents distortion of audio through over-modulation (levels being too high).

Link: programme material inserted between songs in a sequence programme or between interview clips in a package or a documentary. Normally consists mainly of speech, which enables an easy transition from the first item to the next.

Logistics: the organizational arrangements needed to get physical and human resources in the right place at the right time.

Logo: a symbol used to identify a radio station or another corporate entity on its publicity material, vehicles and stationery.

MD: see MiniDisc. *Also* Managing Director.

Menu: detailed tease of items to come in a programme.

Metadata: data which describe a saved file, usually embedded within it. For example, an exact duration or a description of a programme for use in an electronic programme guide (EPG) or a printed listings magazine.

Microphone, mic: a sensitive item of equipment used for converting sound waves into electronic signals which may then be mixed, recorded, processed and/or broadcast.

Microphone rattle, mic rattle: unwanted noise caused electronically when a microphone lead or its body is disturbed, most commonly when hand-held (see also: handling noise).

Microphone type: a group of different microphones that share common characteristics of design and sensitivity to audio (for example, directionality).

Mind mapping: a sometimes chaotic, sometimes systematic process used to originate and develop ideas (see also: brainstorming).

MiniDisc (MD): portable or studio-based recording and playback technology that uses a combination of optical and magnetic processes to store digitally encoded audio. *Also* the removable storage medium used in an MD recorder/player.

Mix: to combine audio from different sources (for example PC, CD, microphone).

Mixer, mixing desk: electronic device for controlling the audio from a range of different sound sources. For example, mixing, processing, fading down and up one or more sources at a time.

Mode of address: how someone is spoken to (for example, formally, informally, casually).

Model: typically occurring process. For example, academics have identified a number of different models of audience response to media products.

Multi-skilling: being able to perform a range of different job functions, as opposed to specializing in one or a very small number of discrete roles.

Multi-strand: the narrative structure characteristic of soap-opera, in which several storylines run in parallel across a number of episodes.

Music lines: see landlines.

Music policy: set of rules governing the rotation of current songs and any non-playlist material on a music station.

Music sweep: non-stop sequence of continuous music without presenter links between songs (see also: segue).

Myth: an explanation of often-contradictory phenomena as part of an attempt to portray 'reality'.

Narrative: an arrangement of words, sounds and/or silence into a sequence in order to convey meaning.

Narrative structure: the way in which key elements in a narrative are organized.

Naturalization: a process by which a 'reality' is constructed through repetition, often incorrectly.

Newstalk: programming based on detailed and often wide-ranging discussion of current news events, including phoned-in listener opinions.

Non-linear: generic term for relatively recently developed editing techniques which use digital (including PC-based) equipment and processes, rather than cutting and splicing tape.

OB: see outside broadcast.

Obituary procedure: predetermined 'on air' response to the death of a significant public figure.

Off mic: producing sound from outside the principal pick-up area of a microphone.

Omnidirectional: all-round microphone sensitivity (see also: unidirectional).

Open: narrative structure that excludes an act of closure, leaving an enigma or suggesting a continuation of the narrative at some future time.

Opener: strong song with immediate impact, preferably recognizable, with which to return to music after a news bulletin at the top of the hour.

Open questions: are formulated in ways which encourage detailed and often personal responses, rather than simple 'yes' or 'no' answers (see also: closed questions). For example, who, what, when, where, why, how.

Out-cue: how an item ends: either speech, music or effects.

Outside broadcast (OB): a radio programme originated from a location other than the studio.

Over-modulation: when an electronic audio signal is too high for the circuit.

Ownership: possession and, by implication, control of a commercial radio company (see also: regulator).

PA: public address system, used to provide audio to a live audience at an OB.

Package: a complete report for use in a bulletin or a magazine programme, including interview material and, where appropriate, actuality and vox pops (see also: jingle package).

Pan: to position a particular audio channel to the left or right of the centre of the stereo image.

Peak programme meter (PPM): a meter for measuring the volume of a piece of audio by indicating its high points, or peaks (see also: volume unit meter).

PFL: see pre-fade listening

Phone-in: radio programming involving listeners calling in.

Playlist: the definitive list of songs currently included in the regular output of a music station.

Playout software: can automate a station's output entirely, or operate in 'live assist' mode with limited human intervention in, for example, live links.

Polysemy: the ability to convey more than one meaning at a time.

Popping: distortion of microphone output, caused by air hitting its sensitive end during speech. Most commonly caused by the plosive 'p' sound (see also: windshield).

Population: a defined sub-group of the human race, which is being served or surveyed. For example, the TSA of a radio station is inhabited by its population, while the population surveyed through a question-naire may consist of all 18-year-olds in the same area.

Post-production: the work involved in preparing recorded audio for transmission. For example, editing, processing, re-mixing, preparing a cue sheet, labelling and paperwork.

Pot point: predetermined point in a pre-recorded item, such as a speech package, where it may be cut short without sounding odd.

PPM: see peak programme meter.

Pre-fade listening (PFL): a second audio circuit in a mixer, used for listening to a sound source *before* it is faded up. Uses include lining up audio to begin at a particular point, setting levels before playback and listening to the content.

Pre-fading: using PFL.

Preferred reading: the meaning a producer may wish listeners to derive from a piece of audio (see also: alternative reading).

Pre-production: the preparatory work involved in the early stages of the production process. For example, research, booking equipment, casting, etc.

Primary sources: research sources that are consulted first-hand, such as face-to-face or telephone interviews with eyewitnesses (see also: secondary sources).

Process: to alter the characteristics of audio. For example, adding reverb or a time-delay in order to create special effects. *Also* the sequence of events involved in pre-production, production and/or post-production.

Processing: see process.

Production methods: techniques used in the making of a radio programme or a single item.

Production schedule: a detailed plan for carrying out the specifics of pre-production, production and post-production.

Production values: notional term relating qualitative assessments of programme quality to processes and budgets.

Products: individual productions, either long or short.

Profanity delay: circuitry that postpones live broadcasting for, typically, ten seconds, enabling any unwanted material to be dumped before it goes to air. For example, cutting out bad language or potentially libellous claims made by a phone-in caller.

Programming wheel: graphical representation of an hour of a programme, showing individual items, with their durations, arranged around a central hub (see also: clock, running order).

Promo: promotional item, such as for an event or a competition run by a station.

Proposal: an outline idea for a new programme or an item (see also: treatment).

Public service announcement (PSA): live or recorded item broadcast in the public interest to convey information or change attitudes (for example, towards drinking and driving).

Purpose: the reason *why* radio products are created or broadcast.

Qualitative research: concerns findings other than numerical data, including descriptions of events, processes and emotions.

Quantitative research: concerns numerical data.

Radio car: vehicle equipped for remote broadcasting by presenters or reporters.

Radiogenic: aurally well suited to radio, in the way that a person's physical appearance can be photogenic in print media.

Rate card: price list for the sale of airtime to advertisers.

Ratings: data produced by quantitative audience research, often ranking stations.

Razor blade: used for editing tape. Has one very sharp edge to allow precise cutting of both audiotape and the splicing tape used to join it back together.

Reading: the interpretation of a radio text, as performed by an individual listener or academic (see also: textual analysis).

Realism: the presentation of a view of events that purports to be a faithful reproduction of what they are really 'like' (see also: surrealism).

Realist paradigm: a tradition of presenting through the mass media a version of 'reality' as perceived by the originator. Few representations of 'reality' explicitly remind their audiences of the selective nature of the production processes behind them.

Reflexivity: the unintentional, yet corrupting, influencing of research data by the presence and/or actions of the researcher.

Regulator: an official body (such as Ofcom in the United Kingdom and the FCC in the United States) set up by government to exercise statutory control over broadcasting organizations, according to relevant legislation. For example, restricting concentration of ownership, setting standards of taste and decency, etc.

Representation: the version of 'reality' created by a media product. For example, a health documentary with no female voices in it might wrongly suggest all doctors are male.

Research: finding out facts, including quantitative data that count things, and qualitative data concerning how people feel about something.

Respondents: participants in a survey.

Restricted Service Licence (RSL): granted in the United Kingdom to temporary or part-time radio stations, operating with low power to cover special events, run trial services or provide opportunities for education and training.

Reverb: similar to echo, in that sound is affected by the persistent effect of reflection from hard surfaces or electronic manipulation (see also: acoustics).

Risk assessment: detailed consideration of potential hazards in a particular location.

Rotation: the frequency with which a song may recur in a music policy.

Round table: discussion programme or item, featuring a small number of participants, possibly seated at a round table.

RSL: see Restricted Service Licence.

Running order: linear arrangement of the various elements in a programme, showing individual items, with their durations, in descending order down the page (see also: clock, programming wheel).

Scenario: set of events and characters organized into an outline narrative.

Secondary sources: research sources other than those people who can be consulted first-hand (see also: primary sources). For example, books, videos, newspapers, web sites, directories, etc.

Segue: transition between two pieces of music which are played without presenter interruption, often involving a brief period of simultaneous play.

Semiology, semiotics: the study of aural and visual signs, as they are used to make meaning in individual texts (see also: textual analysis).

Shout: ident consisting of a collection of voices shouting in unison.

Signature tune: see theme tune.

Signified: a meaning created by a signifier. *Also* an object of signification.

Signifier: signifies meaning (see also: signified).

Signposting: aurally indicating to listeners at appropriate points in programme material what is coming next.

Situation comedy, sitcom: a sub-genre of comedy drama series in which characters and situations remain constant, while responding in each individual programme to temporary and superficial changes in their circumstances.

Slander: defamation of a person or an organization (unfair damage to reputation), disseminated over a relatively small population, for example through word of mouth or letter-writing (see also: libel).

Solid-state recorder: a portable or studio-based recording device that uses internal circuitry to store and play back audio on demand.

Sources: places or people from whom facts are derived. *Also,* in a studio, each microphone, CD player, MiniDisc player, tape recorder, PC, etc. is a sound source.

Splice: to edit two sections of audiotape together with splicing tape. Such an edit point is *also* called a splice.

Splicing block: a convenient holder for use when cutting and splicing audio tape together.

Spoof: humorous satire of a narrative or the characteristics of a genre.

Spot effects: sound effects which are added to a scene to signify action (see also atmosphere).

Stab: short ident used to punctuate programming or a news bulletin (see also sting).

Staff contracts: contracts of employment between radio stations and individuals who derive from them certain benefits of being employees (see also: freelance contracts). May be full or part time.

Station sound: notional term for the general 'feel' of a station, its output and its 'on air' imaging.

Stereo image: arrangement of individual components of a radio broadcast along a continuum between the left and right loudspeakers, allowing a listener facing the centre to perceive spatial relationships between them.

Stereotype: simplistic, often inaccurate and misleading portrayal of a particular social grouping. Often based on assumptions and prejudices about particular 'types' of people, and a denial of differing characteristics and attitudes in people from similar backgrounds.

Stimulus-response: passive model of audience behaviour that suggests similar responses across audiences to like programme events.

Sting: short station or programme identification (see also ident, stab).

Strap line: positioning statement following a primary statement, such as the station name.

Stringer: remote contributor, possibly retained on a freelance basis.

Structure: how a radio programme or an individual item is constructed, in terms of the way its various elements are organized over the duration.

Style: the way an audio product is presented, in terms of pace, mode of address, and the inclusion of any additional material, such as music and speech. For example, upbeat, downbeat, serious, humorous.

Style sheet: set of rules and instructions issued to on-air personnel in order to achieve consistency of style and approach across a station.

Sub-genre: a subdivision of a genre. For example, the soap opera, sitcom and single play are all sub-genres of radio drama.

Surrealism: the antithesis of realism, presenting objects and/or events in ways that conflict with common understanding of their nature.

Sweeper: voiced ident, often listing locations within the station's TSA.

Symbol: a tertiary-level agent in the encoding and decoding of meaning (see also: icon, index). For example, a siren may be symbolic of crime, not because crime itself sounds like a siren, but because police sirens are generally associated with criminal activity.

Talkback: an intercom system connecting key production areas, such as studios, news booths, commentary points.

Talkover: presenter link spoken over music, either at the beginning or the end of a song, or over a bed.

Target audience: the group of people at whom a radio programme or a particular item is aimed, as defined by a range of geographic, demographic and other descriptors (for example, age, ethnicity, region, class, gender, lifestyle, interests).

Taste and decency: contentious area concerning the boundaries of public acceptability of salacious material or 'bad' language.

Tease: to promote ahead an upcoming item.

Telephone balancing unit (TBU): the electronic interface between the ordinary telephone line and the studio mixing desk.

Textual analysis: a mode of academic study of the media, which considers a programme or an item to be a 'text', albeit audio, as opposed to printed material (see also: deconstruct).

Theme tune, **theme**: music played at the beginning and/or end of a regular programme, inevitably becoming closely identified with it (see also: signature tune).

Total Survey Area (TSA): the editorial area of a station for the purposes of audience research.

Traffic: the scheduling and billing operation behind the playout of advertisements.

Trail: live or recorded item promoting a future programme.

Transcodifier: qualifies or alters the meaning encoded into a semiotic element.

Treatment: a detailed working-through of an initial proposal, often produced in response to positive feedback over the proposal.

Two-way: 'on air' conversation between a presenter in the studio and a reporter on location.

Unidirectional: microphone sensitivity in a single direction (see also omnidirectional).

Uses and gratifications: an active model of audience response which considers audiences to react to media products in ways that individually relate to their own particular needs and desires.

Voice-over: speech over music or other sound, such as actuality or effects.

Voice-over artist: specialist in providing voice-overs, normally for advertisements.

Voicetrack: pre-record links for later transmission through scheduling and playout software, such as Selector.

VoIP: Voice over Internet Protocol, the generic term for a range of Internet solutions for sending audio from point to point over the web, such as Skype. Some offer greatly enhanced audio quality for broadcasters.

Volume unit meter, **v/u meter**: a meter for measuring the volume of a piece of audio (see also: PPM).

Vox populi, **vox pops**: in its full form, literally Latin for the 'voice of the people'. Typically a short sequence of contrasting and complementary comments from a number of unnamed individuals chosen to represent the range of views within a given population.

Wild track: an extra recording made on location, of the ambient sound. This can be useful in production and post-production, to place within interview material or to mix with other audio.

Windshield: foam cover placed over the sensitive end of a micro-phone, in order to minimize popping and, when outside, wind noise (see also: popping).

Wrap: a relatively short speech package (see also: billboard, package).

Bibliography and Further Reading

Books

Alkin, G. (1991) *Sound Recording and Reproduction,* London: Focal.

Alleyne, M. D. (1997) *News Revolution: Political and Economic Decisions about Global Information,* London: Macmillan.

Argyle, M. (1988) *Bodily Communication,* London: Methuen.

Ash, W. (1985) *The Way to Write Radio Drama,* London: Elm Tree.

Barnard, S. (1989) *On the Radio: Music Radio in Britain,* Milton Keynes: Open University Press.

Barnard, S. (2000) *Studying Radio,* London: Arnold.

Barsamian, D. (2001) *The Decline and Fall Of Public Broadcasting: Creating Alternatives to Corporate Media,* Cambridge: South End Press.

Barthes, R. (1973) *Mythologies,* London: Paladin.

Barthes, R. (1990) *S/Z,* translated by R. Miller, London: Blackwell.

BBC (1990) *Writing for the BBC,* London: BBC.

Beaman, J. (2000) *Interviewing for Radio,* London: Routledge.

Beck, A. (1997) *Radio Acting,* London: A & C Black.

Becker, G. (ed.) (1963) *Documents of Modern Literary Realism,* Princeton: Princeton University Press.

Bell, P. and van Leeuwen, T. (1994) *The Media Interview: Confession, Contest, Conversation,* Sydney: University of New South Wales Press.

Berger, A. (1997) *Narratives in Popular Culture, Media and Everyday Life,* London: Sage.

Berry, R. (2004) 'Speech radio in the digital age', in A. Crisell (ed.), *More than a Music Box: Radio Cultures and Communities in a Multi-Media World,* Oxford: Berghahn.

Blu, S. and Mullin, M. (1996) *Word of Mouth: A Guide to Commercial Voice-Over Excellence,* California: Pomegranate Press.

Blue, H. (2002) *Words at War: World War II Radio Drama and the Postwar Broadcasting Industry Blacklist,* Oxford: Scarecrow Press.

Blumler, J. and Katz, E. (1974) *The Uses of Mass Communication,* US: Sage.

Borwick, J. (1996) *Sound Recording Practice,* Oxford: Oxford University Press.

Boyd, A. (2000) *Broadcast Journalism,* London: Heinemann.

Braga, N. (2001) *Pirate Radio and Video*, London: Newnes.

Brand, G. and Scannell, P. (1991) 'Talk, identity and performance: the Tony Blackburn Show', in Scannell, P. (ed.), *Broadcast Talk*, London: Sage.

Brewster, B. and Broughton, F. (2000) *Last Night a DJ Saved My Life,* London: Headline.

Briggs, A. (1985) *The BBC: The First 50 Years,* Oxford: Oxford University Press.

Briggs, A. (1995) *The History of Broadcasting in the United Kingdom Vol 2: The Golden Age of Wireless,* Oxford: Oxford University Press.

Bromley, M. and Stephenson, H. (2001) *No News Is Bad News: Radio, Television and the Public,* London: Longman.

Brown, S. (2000) *Radio Secrets*, New York: Chick Springs Publishing.

Buchanan, D. and Huczynski, A. (1999) *Organisational Behaviour,* London: Prentice Hall.

Burns, T. (1977) *The BBC, Public Institution and Private World,* London: Macmillan.

Carter, A. (1996) *The Curious Room: Collected Dramatic Works*, London: Chatto & Windus.

Carter, M. (1998) *Independent Radio: the First 25 Years*, London: Radio Authority.

Chambers, C. (2001) *Radio (Behind Media)*, London: Heinemann Library.

Chantler, P. and Harris, S. (1992) *Local Radio Journalism*, London: Focal.

Chantler, P. and Stewart, P. (2003) *Basic Radio Journalism,* London: Focal.

Chignell, H. (2009) *Key Concepts in Radio Studies*, London: Sage.

Cox, J. (2001) *The Great Radio Audience Participation Shows*, Jefferson: McFarland.

Cox, J. (2002) *Say Goodnight Gracie*, Jefferson: McFarland.

Crisell, A. (1986) *Understanding Radio,* London: Methuen.

Crisell, A. (1994) *Understanding Radio,* London: Routledge.

Crisell, A. (1997) *An Introductory History of British Broadcasting*, London: Routledge.

Crisell, A. (2002) *An Introductory History of British Broadcasting* (rev. edn), London: Routledge.

Crisell, A. (ed) (2004) *More than a Music Box: Radio Cultures and Communities in a Multi-Media World*, Oxford: Berghahn.

Crisell, A. (2012) *Liveness and Recording in the Media*, Basingstoke: Palgrave Macmillan.

Crook, T. (1999) *Radio Drama*, London: Routledge.

Crook, T. (2002) *Radio Presentation: Theory and Practice*, London: Focal Press.

Crook, T. (2011) *The Sound Handbook*, London: Routledge.

Curran, J., Fenton, N. and Freedman, D. (2012) *Misunderstanding the Internet*, London: Routledge.

Dahlgren, P. (1995) *Television and the Public Sphere: Citizenship, Democracy and the Media*, London: Sage.

Daley, B. *et al.* (1996) *Star Wars – the Original Radio Drama: Return of the Jedi*, London: Titan Books.

Douglas, G. (2001) *The Early Days Of Radio Broadcasting*, Jefferson: McFarland.

Douglas, L. and Kinsey, M. (eds) (1998) *A Guide to Commercial Radio Journalism*, London: Focal Press.

Dunning, J. (1998) *On the Air: The Encyclopedia of Old-Time Radio*, Oxford: Oxford University Press.

Durozoi, G. and Anderson, A. (2002) *History of the Surrealist Movement*, Chicago: University of Chicago Press.

Duval, R. (1979) *Histoire de la radio en France*, Paris: Editions Alain Moreau.

Ely, M. P. (2001) *The Adventures of Amos and Andy: A Social History of an American Phenonemon*, Virginia: University Press of Virginia.

Elzbieta, E. (2002) *Challenges for International Broadcasting: Programming the Heart of International Radio*, Canada: Mosaic Press.

Fairchild, C. (2001) *Community Radio and Public Culture*, London, Hampton Press.

Fink, C. (1988) *Media Ethics*, New York: McGraw-Hill.

Finkelstein, N. (2000) *Sounds in the Air: The Golden Age of Radio*, New York: Backinprint.com.

Fleming, C. (2002) *The Radio Handbook*, London: Routledge.

Florance, J. (2002) *Getting Started In Radio: How To Become A Top Radio Broadcaster*, Taunton: Studymates.

Gage, L. (1999) *Guide to Independent Radio Journalism,* London: Duckworth.

Garfield, S. (1998) *The Nation's Favourite*, London: Faber & Faber.

Glasgow University Media Group (1976) *Bad News*, London: Routledge & Kegan Paul.

Glasgow University Media Group (1980) *More Bad News*, London: Routledge & Kegan Paul.

Glasgow University Media Group (1982) *Really Bad News*, Writers and Readers' Publishing Cooperative.

Glasgow University Media Group (1985) *War and Peace News*, Buckingham: Open University Press.

Glover, F. (2002) *Travels With My Radio*, London: Ebury Press.

Godfrey, W. and Herweg, A. P. (1997) *Radio's Niche Marketing Revolution*, Massachusetts: Butterworth-Heinemann.

Gordon, J. (2001) *The RSL, Ultra Local Radio*, Luton: Luton University Press.

Gowers, E. (1968) *Fowler's Modern English Usage*, Oxford: Oxford University Press.

Grams, M. (2000) *Radio Drama*, New York: Mc Farland.

Grant, D. (1970) *Realism*, London: Methuen.

Hall, S. (1973) *The Manufacture of News*, London: Constable.

Hall, S. (1982) 'The Rediscovery of "Ideology"' in M. Gurevitch *et al.* (eds), *Culture, Society and the Media*, London: Methuen.

Handy, C. B. (1993) *Understanding Organisations*, Oxford: Oxford University Press.

Hangen, T. J. (2002) *Redeeming the Dial: Radio, Religion and Popular Culture in America*, University of North Carolina Press.

Hanna, M. and Dodd, M. (2012) *McNae's Essential Law for Journalists*, Oxford: Oxford University Press.

Hart, D. (2002) *Monitor: The Last Great Radio Show*, Carlsbad: Writer's Club Press.

Harte, B. (2002) *When Radio Was The Cat's Whisker*, London: Roseberg.

Hendy, D. (2000) *Radio in the Global Age*, Cambridge: Polity.

Hendy, D. (2007) *Life On Air: A History of Radio Four*, Oxford: Oxford University Press.

Hicks, W. (1998) *English for Journalists*, London: Routledge.

Hill, J. (1996) *Radio! Radio!* Devon: Sunrise Press.

Hilmes, M. and Loviglio, J. (2001) *Radio Reader: Essays in the Cultural History of Radio*, London: Routledge.

Holsopple, C. (1988) *Skills for Radio Broadcasters*, London: Tab Books.

Horstmann, R. (1997) *Writing for Radio*, London: A & C Black.

Kaye, M. and Popperwell, A. (1992) *Making Radio, A Guide to Basic Radio Techniques*, London: Broadside Books.

Keith, M. (2000) *The Radio Station*, London: Focal Press.

Knightley, P. (2000) *The First Casualty: The War Correspondent as Hero and Myth-maker*, London: Prion.

Ladd, J. (1992) *Radio Waves: Life and Revolution on the FM Dial*, London: St. Martin's Press.

Leavis, F. R. and Thompson, D. (1933) *Culture and Environment: The Training of Critical Awareness*, reprinted 1977, London: Greenwood Press.

Luckhurst, T. (2001) *This Is "Today"*, London: Aurum Press.

MacGregor, S. (2003) *Woman Of Today: An Autobiography*, London: Headline.

MacLoughlin, S. (2001) *Writing for Radio*, London: How To Books.

MacNamara, J. (2000) *The Modern Presenters' Handbook*, London: Prentice Hall.

Maslow, A. (1954) *Motivation and Personality*, London: Harper & Row.

McCann, G. (2001) *Dad's Army*, London: Fourth Estate.

McCoy, Q. (1999) *No Static: A Guide to Creative Radio Programming*, New York: Backbeat Books.

McInerney, V. (2001) *Writing for Radio*, Manchester: Manchester University Press.

McLeish, R. (2005) *Radio Production*, London: Focal.

McNair, B. (1994) *News and Journalism in the UK: A Textbook,* London: Routledge.

McQuail, D. (ed.) (1972) *The Uses of Mass Communication*, London: Penguin.

McQuail, D., Blumler, J. and Brown, J. (1972) 'The television audience: a revised perspective', in D. McQuail (ed.), *Sociology of the Mass Media*, London: Penguin.

McWhinnie, D. (1959) *The Art of Radio*, London: Faber & Faber.

Michaels, K. & Mitchell, C. (2000) 'The last bastion: how women become music presenters in UK radio', in C. Mitchell (ed.) *Women and Radio*, London: Routledge.

Miller, E. (2002) *Emergency Broadcasting and 1930s American Radio*, Philadelphia: Temple University Press.

Mitchell, C. (ed.) (2001) *Women and Radio*, London: Routledge.

Mitchell, J. (2000) *Visually Speaking: Radio and the Renaissance of Preaching*, London: Westminster John Knox Press.

Montgomery, M. (1991) 'Our Tune: A Study of a Discourse Genre', in Scannell, P. (ed.), *Broadcast Talk*, London: Sage.

Myers, S. (1992) *Radio Documentary,* London: Focal.

Neer, R. (2001) *FM: The Rise and Fall of Rock Radio*, New York: Villard Books.

Newby, J. (ed.) (1997) *Inside Broadcasting*, London: Routledge.

Nietszche, F. (1887) *Genealogie der Moral,* trans. D. Smith as *On the Genealogy of Morals: A Polemic by Way of Clarification and Supplement to My Last Book 'Beyond Good and Evil'*, Oxford: Oxford Paperbacks, 1998.

Nisbett, A. (1994) *Sound Studio*, London: Focal.

Norris, C. (1982) *Deconstruction: Theory and Practice*, London: Methuen.

Oei, R. (2002a) *Borderless Bandwidth: DNA of Digital Radio*, London: Times Academic Press.

Oei, R. (2002b) *My Radio: Three Dimensional Radio Programming*, Singapore: Open University Press.

Orlebar, J. (2002) *Digital Television Production*, London: Arnold.

Oxlade, C. (2001a) *Communicating Today: Radio*, London: Heinemann Library.

Oxlade, C. (2001b) *In Touch: Radio*, London: Heinemann Library.

Pavlov, I. P. (2001) *I.P. Pavlov: Selected Works*, University Press of the Pacific.

Peirce, C. S. (1960) *Collected Papers*, vols I & II, ed. Hartshorne, C. and Weiss, P. Cambridge, Mass.: Harvard University Press.

Pine, R. (2002) *2RN & The Origins Of Irish Radio (Broadcasting & Irish Society)*, Dublin: Gill & Macmillan.

Pohlmann, C. (2000) *Principles of Digital Audio*, London: McGraw-Hill.

Pointon, G.E. (1983) *BBC Pronouncing Dictionary of British Names*, Oxford: Oxford University Press.

Popperwell, K. (1992) *Making Radio: A Guide to Basic Techniques*, London: Broadside.

Priestman, C. (2001) *Web Radio*, London: Focal Press.

Propp, V. (1968) *Morphology of the Folk Tale*, Texas: University of Texas Press.

Proudhon, P. (1840) *Qu'est-ce que la propriété?*, trans. as (1994) *Proudhon: What is Property?*, Cambridge: Cambridge University Press.

Purves, L. (2002) *Radio: A True Love Story*, London: Hodder & Stoughton.

RAB (2000) *The Radio Multiplier: Radio and TV*, London: Radio Advertising Bureau.

RAB (2002) *Commercial Radio Revenues*, London: Radio Advertising Bureau.

Radio Authority (2001) *Programme Codes of Practice*, London: Radio Authority.

Reese, D. and Gross, L. (2001) *Radio Production Worktext*, London: Focal Press.

Rosko, E. (1976) *Emperor Rosko's DJ Book*, London: Everest.

Rudin, R. and Ibbotson, T. (2002) *An Introduction to Journalism*, London: Focal Press.

Rudin, R. (2011) *Broadcasting in the 21st Century*, Basingstoke: Palgrave Macmillan.

Rumsey, F. and McCormick, T. (2002) *Sound & Recording*, London: Focal Press.

Rusling, D. (2001) *Who's Who in British Radio*, Hull: Broadcastdata Publications.

Sadow, C. and Sather, E. (1998) *On the Air: Listening to Radio Talk*, Cambridge: Cambridge University Press.

Saussure, F. de (1916) *Cours de Linguistique Générale*, trans. as *Course in General Linguistics*, London: Duckworth, 1983.

Sawyer, B. (2001) *Online Broadcasting Power*, London: Muska & Lipman Publishing.

Schlesinger, P. (1987) *Putting 'Reality' Together*, London: Methuen.

Selby, K. (2001) *The Classic Serial on Television and Radio*, Basingstoke: Palgrave.

Seymour, C. (1996) *The British Press and Broadcasting Since 1945*, Oxford: Blackwell.

Shaw, B. (2000) *Voice-overs*, London: A & C Black.

Shingler, M. and Wieringa, C. (1998) *On Air: Methods and Meanings of Radio*, London: Arnold.

Siegel, B. (1992) *Creative Radio Production*, London: Focal.

Smethurst, W. (2000) *The Archers: The History of Radio's Most Famous Programme*, London: Michael O'Mara.

Starkey, G. (2003a) 'Are Radio Audiences Choosing to Reject Greater Choice?', in S. Ralph, C. Lees and H. Manchester (eds), *Diversity or Anarchy?*, Luton: University of Luton Press.

Starkey, G. (2004) 'Radio Five Live: extending choice through "Radio Bloke"?' in A. Crisell (ed.) *More than a Music Box: Radio Cultures and Communities in a Multi-Media World*, Oxford: Berghahn.

Starkey, G. (2007) *Balance and Bias in Journalism: Representation, Regulation and Democracy*, Basingstoke: Palgrave Macmillan.

Starkey, G. (2011) *Local Radio, Going Global*, Basingstoke: Palgrave Macmillan.

Starkey, G. and Crisell, A. (2009) *Radio Journalism*, London: Sage.

Sterling, C.H. (2003) *Encyclopedia Of Radio*, London: Fitzroy Dearborn.

Stoller, T. (2010) *Sounds of Your Life: The History of Independent Radio in the UK*, New Barnet: John Libbey Publishing

Street, S. (2002) *A Concise History of British Radio*, Tiverton: Kelly Publications.

Utterback, A. (2000) *Broadcast Voice Handbook*, London: Bonus Books.

Wall, T. (2003) *Studying Popular Music Culture*, London: Hodder Arnold.

Washington-George, M. (2002) *Black Radio. . . Winner Takes All: America's First Black DJs*, London: X Libris.

Watson, J. and Hill, A. (2000) *Dictionary of Media and Communication Studies*, London: Arnold.

Weightman, G. (2003) *Signor Marconi's Magic Box: The Invention that Sparked the Radio Revolution*, London: Harper Collins.

Weiss, A. (ed.) (2001) *Experimental Sound and Radio*, London: MIT Press.

Wertheim, A.F. (1979) *Radio Comedy*, New York: Oxford University Press.

Westerkamp, H. (1994) 'The Soundscape on Radio', in D. Augaitis and D. Lander (eds), *Radio Rethink: Art, Sound and Transmission*, Frankfurt: LPG Distribution.

White, T. (2001) *Broadcast News Writing, Reporting, and Production*, London: Focal Press.

Wilby, P. and Conroy, A. (1994) *The Radio Handbook,* London: Routledge.

Woodyear, C. (ed.) *Radio Listener's Guide*, London: PDQ Publishing.

Yoder, A. (2002) *Pirate Radio Stations*, Maidenhead: McGraw-Hill Education Europe.

Articles in newspapers and other periodicals

Bantock, A. (2002) 'Technical talk: disco inferno!', *Radio Magazine* no. 552, 9 Nov.

Barnett, S. (2002) 'If you can find one, then switch on your radio to the digital revolution', *Observer,* 1 Dec.

BBC (2002) *Radio Times*, vol. 315, no. 4103, 26 Oct–1 Nov.

Bell, E. (2002) 'Get rid of the governors', *Guardian*, 9 Dec.

Boshoff, A. (1997) 'Rise and fall of Radio One's gaffe-prone presenter', *Daily Telegraph*, 17 Jan.

Bragg, M. (2002) 'The crunch', *Guardian*, 2 Dec.

BSC (2002) *Complaints Bulletin*, Broadcasting Standards Commission, no. 53, 25 Apr.

Calvert, J. (2002) 'Commercial production', *Radio Magazine*, no. 542, 31 Aug.

Cassy, J. (2002) 'Mackenzie tilts at ratings', *Guardian*, 18 Sept.

Cecil, N. (2009) 'Presenters' bumper wages send cost of BBC radio soaring', *Daily Mail*, 5 Feb.

Copeland, D. (1997) 'Ten questions for a listener', *Contact!* vol. 10, no. 2.

Day, J. (2002) 'Fake TV: a history', *Guardian*, 20 Mar.

Day, J. (2003) 'Ambridge anguish boosts Archers audience', *Guardian*, 30 Jan.

Deans, J. (2002) 'BBC3 decision delayed', *Guardian*, 22 July.

Ezard, J. (2002) 'Pop star's family loses fight to halt radio show', *Guardian*, 27 July.

Gibson, O. (2003a) 'Web piracy hits music sales', *Guardian*, 10 Feb.

Gibson, O. (2003b) 'Spin inquiry committee unveiled', *Guardian*, 11 Feb.

Guardian (2002) 'Virgin fine file: offences since 1993', *Guardian*, 19 Mar.

Hall, S. (2002) 'Archer pays back libel award in £1.5m settlement with Star', *Guardian*, 2 Oct.

Harmon, A. (2002) 'Internet: house passes bill on net radio', *New York Times*, 8 Oct.

Hill, A. (2002) 'Accents block business success, say bosses', *Observer*, 21 July.

Hodgson, J. (2002) 'DJ fired after royal death threat', *Guardian*, 12 Apr.

Juste, A. (2002) 'Beyond our Ken', Kettering: Radio Magazine, 19 October.

Kelso, P. (2002) 'Censure of Ali G outburst leads to BBC issuing tighter radio guidelines', *Guardian*, 25 Apr.

Milmo, D. and J. Day (2002) 'City gives thumbs-up to Capital', *Guardian*, 26 Sept.

Plunkett, J. and C. Cozens (2002) 'Liddle steps down from Today', *Guardian*, 30 Sept.

Radio Authority (2002) *Programming and Advertising Review*, London: no. 7, Jan.

Radio Magazine (2002a) 'Capital adopts Powergold', no. 536, 20 July.

Radio Magazine (2002b) 'Tarrant to rest but return for £5000 a day', no. 547, 5 Oct.

Reece, D. (2002) 'The great Branson sell-off', *Daily Telegraph*, 3 Mar.

Smith, H. (2002) 'Greek appeal court clears plane spotters of spying', *Guardian*, 7 Nov.

Starkey, G. (2003b) 'Radio audience research – challenging the "Gold Standard"' in *Cultural Trends*, London: Policy Studies Institute, no. 45.

Starkey, G. (2012) 'Radio Studies: The Sound and Vision of an Established Medium in the Digital Age', *Sociology Compass*, vol. 6.

Sweney, M. (2012) 'Global Radio reports pre-tax losses of £27.7m', *Guardian*, 7 Aug.

Tench, D. (2002) 'Defame game devalued', *Guardian*, 5 Aug.

Wells, M. (2002a) '"Ladette" Cox routed in breakfast battle', *Guardian*, 2 Aug.

Wells, M. (2002b) 'Police pay damages to BBC reporter', *Guardian*, 8 Oct.

Wilson, J. (2003) 'Radio station fined for game that left three with frostbite', *Guardian*, 25 Jan.

Other references

BBC (2013) *Editorial Guidelines*, London: BBC www.bbc.co.uk/ guidelines/editorialguidelines/ (updated regularly online)

Capital (2002) Press release, 'Preliminary results for the year ended September 2002', London: Capital Radio plc, 14 Nov.

Ferrington, G. (1998) *Take a Listening Walk and Learn to Listen*, www.interact.uoregon.edu/MediaLit/FC/readings/listenwalk.html

Ofcom (2011) The Ofcom Broadcasting Code, London: Office of Communications, http://stakeholders.ofcom.org.uk/broadcasting/ broadcast-codes/broadcast-code/

Starkey, G. (2001) *Balance and Bias in Radio Four's Today Programme, during the 1997 General Election Campaign*, Ph.D. thesis, University of London: Institute of Education.

Starkey, G. (2002) *An Extraordinary Pirate: The Voice of Peace 1973–1993*, paper given at the Visions conference, University of Central Lancashire, Preston, June.

Index

a capellas, 111, 112
ABC, 167
Absolute Radio, 66, 98, 108
accessibility, of programme material, 36, 122, 125, 127, 171–2
acoustics, 11–12, 45, 112, 158, 186–7, 195, 197, 199, 200–1
actuality, 34, 36, 46, 51, 56, 179, 210, 213, 218, 225, 226, 229
Adams, Douglas, 180
Adobe Audition, 22, 24, 47, 112, 158, 197, 225
Adventures of Sherlock Holmes, The, 181
Adventures of Superman, The, 183
advertisers, 2, 3, 4, 103, 115, 144–9, 158
advertising, 3, 27, 60, 67, 72, 77, 78, 82, 84, 87, 98, 102, 103, 123, 126, 135, 143–64, 180, 183, 229
  central copy clearance, 153, 160
  humour in, 150–1, 163
  income, 5–14, 115, 143, 146
  restrictions on, 153–4
advocacy journalism, 52, 220
Afternoon Play, The, 183, 185, 186
airchecks, 65
Airforce, 149
ALC *see* automatic level control
allegations, 223
Alfasound, 109
ambient sound, 9, 11, 12–14, 44, 45, 155, 158, 200, 211, 214
American Forces Network, 70
Anand, Anita, 84
anchorage, 48–9, 56, 128, 160, 204, 212, 213–14, 229
angles, 51, 207, 209
  finding an, 38–40
anthropomorphism, 101

Any Answers, 84
Any Questions, 6, 83, 84
Arbitron, 115, 116
Archers, The, 3, 182, 183, 196–7, 205
Askey, Arthur, 166
Aspel, Michael, 113
atmosphere, 12–14, 46, 134, 135, 179, 186–7, 192–5, 200, 204–5, 218, 226
audience behaviour *see* models of audience behaviour
audience research, 31–2, 108, 114–18, 146–7
  definitions, 116
  electronic measurement, 115–16, 118
  ratings, 5, 64, 65, 66, 69, 93, 103, 105, 107, 108, 115, 116–17, 118, 124, 134, 143, 145, 166, 169, 185, 216
  recall, 115–16, 118, 134
audience response, 29–30, 36, 51–2, 83, 87, 113, 138, 147, 163, 179, 185, 187, 191, 198, 201, 204, 207, 208, 210, 211, 228, 230
  see also models of audience behaviour
audio
  capture, 6–14, 112, 179, 212, 214
  manipulation, 6, 14–24, 172, 197, 226
Audiometer *see* Radiocontrol
automatic level control (ALC), 13, 20
automation, 58, 59, 63, 75, 98, 99–101, 102
AutoTrack Pro, 94
auxiliary output (aux), 18, 112

back announcements (back annos),
    50–1, 71, 131
back timing, 124
balance, 3, 5, 31, 40, 52, 53, 54, 82,
    87–8, 133–4, 138, 140–2, 218–20,
    225–6, 228
Ball, Zoë, 64, 80
bandwidth, 135
Bannister, Matthew, 64, 65, 78, 108,
    133
Barclay, Liz, 130
Barthes, Roland, 28, 201–2
Bates, Simon, 65, 66, 78
Bauer Media, 90
BBC, 1, 2, 5, 25, 60, 63, 64, 67, 73,
    94, 104, 115, 117, 118, 120, 123,
    138, 159, 165–6, 167–8, 169,
    171, 175, 177, 179, 181, 183,
    184, 191, 211, 213, 214, 227–8
  1 Extra, 108
  BBC 7, 168, 177
  Board of Governors, 5
  Charter, 1, 5, 227
  Executive Board, 227
  Five Live, 62, 84, 104, 117, 120,
      122, 139, 215
  Forces Programme, 166, 177
  GMR, 139
  Home Service, 166
  Light Programme, 67, 82, 166
  Local Radio, 81, 109, 117, 159,
      170, 182
  Maida Vale Studios, 6, 15
  Producers' Guidelines, 5, 41, 219,
      227, 228
  Pronunciation Unit, 155
  Radio Cymru, 80
  Radio Four, 27, 34, 35, 53, 83, 84,
      104, 108, 117, 119, 121, 122,
      123, 140, 160, 168, 170, 171,
      177, 180, 182, 183, 184, 185,
      191, 203, 210, 212, 215, 218,
      219
  Radio Kent, 170
  Radio Leicester, 109
  Radio Merseyside, 81, 109
  Radio One, 2, 34, 35, 59, 63, 64,
      65, 70, 71, 78, 79, 81, 82, 104,
      108, 109, 110, 116, 117, 132–3,
      183, 215
  Radio Theatre, 167
  Radio Three, 71, 104, 107, 117, 184
  Radio Two, 63, 67, 75, 77, 81, 82,
      104, 110, 117, 182
  television, 108, 167, 177, 180, 206,
      227
  Trust, 227
  World Service, 35, 139, 228
  Writersroom, 184
beds, 61, 82, 109, 111, 112, 114,
    136–7, 152–3, 155, 157, 160,
    215, 216–7
Bedsitter, 182
Bentine, Michael, 167
Beswick, Allan, 84
bias see balance
billboards, 33, 45
Billy Cotton Band Show, 166
binaural stereo, 211
Birch, Philip, 110
Blackburn, Tony, 81, 82
Block, Martin, 58
Bogosian, Eric, 85
Boyd, Tommy, 85
Boyle, James, 171
Brain of Britain, 171, 176
brainstorming, 36–7, 38
branding, 68, 72, 97, 103–13, 138
breakfast shows, 62, 72, 79, 100,
    116
breakout box, 197
British Forces Broadcasting Service
    (BFBS), 101, 160
BRMB, 73
broadcast assistants see production
    assistants
Broadcasting from the Barricades, 179
Bruce, Ken, 81
BSkyB, 101
budgets, 60, 63, 101, 109, 111, 123,
    126, 129, 144, 150–3, 156–7,
    159, 185, 186, 208
bulletins
  news, 27, 29, 33–4, 67, 80, 84, 91,

98, 102, 107, 109, 111, 113, 114, 119, 120–1, 125, 126, 135, 143, 179
  traffic and travel, 28–9, 60, 61, 67, 78, 102, 109, 114, 143, 179
Butler, Billy, 81

C-Taxi, 19
campaigns, 145–6, 149, 163
campus radio, 2, 109
Capital Radio, 66, 72, 104, 108, 113, 144, 182
card readers, 23
cart machines, 158–9
cartridges, carts, 101, 158–9
Casablanca, 181
casting, 173, 174, 185, 196
catch, catchlines, 50, 51
CBS, 200
Century Radio, 104, 143
Change, The, 182
channels, 15, 75, 112, 197, 199, 201
characterization, 30
chart shows, 63, 68, 89
  countdowns, 63
Check Up, 83
chinagraph pencils, 22
Clara, Lu, 'N Em, 182
Classic FM, 35, 66, 104, 117, 144, 151, 166
Classic Serial, 185
clean feed, 18, 112, 135
Clear Channel, 5
cliffhangers *see* enigma
Clitheroe Kid, The, 167, 176
clocks, 60, 61–2, 91–2, 93, 98, 99
  see also running orders
closure, 46, 114, 136, 181, 182, 188, 203, 217
codecs, 135
codes, 27, 28–9, 35–6, 56–7, 82, 113, 162, 175, 189, 229
codes of practice, 28, 41, 138, 153, 158, 161, 164, 219, 227
Collins, Norman, 138
comedy, 35, 150–1, 163, 165–70
commercial producers, 154–9

commercial production (com prod), 149–58
commercials *see* advertising
Communications Act 2003, 5
Community Radio Association, 2
Competition Commission, 5
competitions, 63, 67, 68, 71, 72–3, 78, 109, 115, 116, 125, 129, 136
compressors, 76
connotation, 56, 81, 109, 137, 140, 176, 189, 203
continuity announcements, 174, 195, 215
conventions, 27, 28–9, 35–6, 68, 91, 113, 123, 136, 138, 162, 175, 180, 189, 191, 195, 206, 209–10, 226, 230
Cool Edit Pro, 22
  see also Adobe Audition
copyright, 37–8, 47, 60, 64, 96, 102–3, 152, 156–7, 159, 160, 168, 185, 186
  returns, 93, 94, 157, 159
Copyright, Designs and Patents Act 1988, 156, 224
copywriters, 149–50
Cotton, Billy, 166
Country 1035, 105
County Sound, 94
Creation, 4
creative production *see* commercial production
Crisell, Andrew, 25, 26, 31, 204, 205
cue sheets, 50–1, 174, 195, 226
cues, 35, 46, 48, 50–1, 74, 78, 80, 130–1, 133, 135, 159, 174
Currie, Edwina, 132

D-Notices, 225
DAB *see* Digital Audio Broadcasting
Dad's Army, 167
Dales, The, 182
Danger, 181
DAT *see* Digital Audio Tape
DAVE 2000, 22, 100
Dave Glass Productions, 169, 183

dayparts, 62, 78, 92, 98, 102, 118, 122, 146–7, 185
de Manio, Jack, 62
de Saussure, Ferdinand, 29, 176
decoding, 28, 57, 137, 191, 192, 204–5
deconstruction, 27, 78, 175
Dee, Simon, 80
defamation *see* libel
demographics, 30, 54, 55, 80–1, 90, 104, 105, 107, 118, 138, 145, 146–7, 162, 168, 190, 196, 202
demos, 65, 121, 150
denotation, 50, 123, 192
dénouement, 188, 209
Department for Culture, Media and Sport (DCMS), 227
devil's advocacy, 87–8
Dick Barton – Special Agent, 181
diegesis, 128, 180
diegetic sound, 193, 229–30
Digital Audio Broadcasting (DAB), 2, 101, 177
Digital Audio Tape (DAT), 19, 23
    protecting recordings, 21
digital platforms, 2, 90
Digital Radio Mondiale, DRM, 2
disco, 89
discourse, 26, 27, 29–30, 54, 56, 68, 71, 77, 82, 83, 87–8, 122, 136, 139, 140–2, 179, 203–4, 210, 211, 216, 217, 218, 219, 225, 229
discourse analysis, 79, 140–2, 226
documentaries, 37, 54, 179, 206–230
'doorstepping', 40–1
Double your Money, 167
drama-documentary, 179, 229
drama production, 11, 18, 28, 30, 120, 151, 160, 162–3, 168, 173, 176, 178–205, 209
    forms of, 181, 202–3, 214, 229
dramatization, 179, 180, 184–5, 214
drop-ins, 167, 169, 176, 182
dub, dubbing, 23, 24, 47
ducking, 17

Economos, Dr Andrew, 94
editing, 13, 22–4, 34, 50, 64, 73–4,
123, 158, 173, 174, 200, 211, 217
edit decision lists (EDLs), 47
editorial meetings, 37, 60, 126
editors, 126, 129, 221
effects microphones, 135,
    see also microphones
EMAP, 90, 106
encoding, 28, 57, 137, 162, 204
England, Steve, 109–10
enigma, 136, 181, 182, 187, 188, 209
entertainment news, 66, 67, 82
equalization (eq), 16, 18, 112, 158, 197, 201
equilibrium, 142, 176, 188, 191, 209
ethical issues, 35, 37–8, 41–2, 51–6, 202, 214, 218–20, 229–30
evaluations, 26
Evans, Chris, 63, 64, 65, 79, 81, 105
Everett, Kenny, 63, 66, 80

Face the Facts, 210, 219
faders, 16–18, 71, 76, 79
Farming Today, 53, 137
Fast Edit, 22
features, 33, 45, 207, 214
feature items, 60, 63, 64, 68, 77, 98, 109, 113, 115, 116, 120, 127–9, 130–1
    timelessness and topicality in, 120, 122–3, 125, 128
Federal Communications Commission (FCC), 161
Feedback, 218
feedback, 20, 113, 134
File on Four, 210
Film Programme, The, 121, 137
Five Live Reports, 215
flashbacks, 189
formats, 58, 64, 89–93, 98, 105–9, 128, 146, 170–2, 216
franchise applications, 100
Frank's Factory Flooring, 151
Freed, Alan, 89
Freeman, Alan, 67, 82
freelance contracts, 5, 220
Freeview, 101

frequency response, 7
Friday Play, The, 182
Front Row, 121

gaffer tape, 170, 199
gain controls, 15–18, 200
Galaxy, 104, 107
garage, 89
Gaytalk, 139
Gemini Apes, The, 181, 202–3
generators, 134
genre, 27, 78, 82, 119, 120, 136, 137,
    206, 209–10, 226, 228, 229
glam rock, 89
Glasgow University Media Group,
    53
Global Radio, 4, 144
Glums, The, 167, 176
Gold, 146
Good Morning Vietnam, 69
Goon Show, The, 167, 177
Gosse, Edmund, 201
Greening, Kevin, 64
Greenwich Time Signal, 124
Grimshaw, Nick, 66
Guardian Media Group (GMG),
    107
GWR, 4, 59, 66, 106, 110, 149–50

Hancock's Half-Hour, 167
handling noise *see* microphone rattle
Head of Music, 90, 92, 93, 98
headphones, 18, 85
health and safety, 21
Heart, 155
Heath, Edward, 161
Hitchhiker's Guide to the Galaxy, 180
Home Truths, 160
hooks, 68
horoscopes, 61, 62, 82
hospital radio, 2, 81
house, 89
house styles, 67, 71–2, 107
howlround, 20
Humphrys, John, 140
hypodermic needle *see* models of
    audience behaviour

I'm Sorry, I Haven't a Clue, 167, 168,
    175
I'm Sorry, I'll Read that Again, 167
icons, 29
ideas, generating, 34, 36–40, 126, 127
idents, 28–9, 58, 61–2, 68–9, 82, 87,
    98, 107
ideology, 27, 30–1, 53–4, 55, 82,
    138–40, 161, 175, 203–4, 226–7,
    228–9
ILR *see* Independent Local Radio
imaging, 109
impartiality *see* balance
in-cues, *see* cues
Independent Broadcasting Authority
    (IBA) *see* regulators
Independent Local Radio (ILR), 2, 5,
    33, 67, 92, 99, 101, 102, 104,
    111, 115, 166, 182
Independent Radio News (IRN), 34,
    114
Independent Television (ITV), 182
index, 29, 81, 176
Instant Replay, 76, 159
Inside Health, 122
Internet radio, 2, 28, 103, 124, 136,
    153
intertextuality, 27
interviews, 6, 7, 9, 10, 11–14, 21, 34,
    39–42, 52–3, 55, 68, 69, 78, 115,
    120, 125, 128–9, 131, 138,
    140–2, 210–11, 215, 216–17, 226
    choice of interviewees, 73–5, 82,
    218–9
    interruption, 140–1
    live, 131–4, 221–2
    on location, 37, 45, 127, 134
    planning, 42–6, 127, 132
    question types, 42–4, 141–2
IRN *see* Independent Radio News
ISDN, 44, 100, 135, 154
It's that Man Again (ITMA), 167
Ivieson, Alan, 138

Jack, Wolfman, 70
James, Trevor, 170
Jazz FM, 105

JICRAR, 115
jingle packages, 109–10, 111, 113
jingles *see* idents
  in advertisements, 148, 152, 157
John Peel's Music, 160
Joyce, William, 3
'Julian and Sandy', 176
Julius Caesar, 181
jump cuts, 45
Just a Minute, 167–8, 170, 171
Juste, Adrian, 59, 183
JY Show, 75

Kerrang!, 90
Key 103, 110

landlines, 44
LBC, 2, 85
Leavis, F. R., 25
legal issues, 220–6, 227–8
levels, 13, 15, 18, 20, 23, 24, 47, 50,
  75, 112, 155, 158, 193, 200
libel, 47, 73, 85–6
Liberty, 105
library music, 123, 156–7, 217
licence fee, 5, 104, 227
Liddle, Rod, 140
Life, 101
light entertainment, 165–77
limiters, 76
Lincoln, Dave, 81
Linker, 98, 100
links, 46, 47, 48–9, 56, 59, 60, 65, 67,
  71, 129, 160, 210, 216–7, 226
Little Britain, 177
logistics, 64, 132, 134–6, 174, 186–7
logos, 106, 108, 109
London Greek Radio, 105
Lord of the Rings, The, 191

MacKenzie, Kelvin, 115
magazine programmes, 33, 53,
  119–42
Maggs, Dirk, 183, 202–3
Magic, 104,109
Make Believe Ballroom, 58
Maltese Falcon, The, 181

Marantz, 19, 20
Marcher Pub Quiz, The, 170
Marcher Sound, 170
Marconi, Guglielmo, 1
Mark and Lard, 64, 116
Mark Steel's in Town, 168
marketing, 103, 117, 134
Maschwitz, Eric, 165
Maslow's hierarchy of needs, 164
Master Control, 94, 100
McClue, Scottie, 84
McKenzie, Tony, 81
MDs *see* MiniDiscs
Mechanical Copyright Protection
  Society (MCPS), 103, 152, 156–7,
  159
media studies, 25
Medicine Now, 119, 121
Medium Wave, 140
Melody FM, 109
Men's Hour, 120
menus, 61, 124, 129–30
Mercury Theatre Company, 179
Merton, Paul, 170, 171
metadata, 174, 241
meters, 16, 20, 23, 76
  PPMs, 16–17
  v/u, 16
MFM, 155
microphones (mics), 6–14, 15, 16,
  20, 21, 37, 44–5, 71, 74, 75, 77,
  86, 112, 132, 133, 134, 135, 143,
  170, 172, 173–4, 197–9, 200,
  211, 212
close micing, 13, 200
effects mics, 7
position, 10, 13–14, 44–5, 157,
  173–4, 199, 211
radio mics, 10
ratio of foreground to background,
  13
microphone rattle (mic rattle),
  10–11, 24, 44–5, 112
microphone types, 7–10
omni-directional, 8, 9, 14
unidirectional, 9, 13–14, 199
Milligan, Spike, 167

Mills, Scott, 215
MiniDiscs (MDs), 14, 19, 20, 23, 76, 159, 169
  protecting recordings, 21
Mitchell, Bill, 111
mixers, mixing desks, 6, 14–19, 20, 23, 44, 47, 75, 76–7, 86, 112, 135, 155, 156–7, 158, 172, 197, 199, 200
mixing, 13, 22, 24, 34, 47, 50, 64, 111, 112, 123, 150, 155, 158, 173, 192–3, 212, 214, 216, 217
models, of audience behaviour, 27, 31, 57, 83, 113–4, 137, 163–4, 177, 205, 228
  organizational, 62–3, 79, 126, 172, 186, 210–11
modes of address, 56, 69, 82, 122, 200
Mojo, 101
monitoring, 18, 174
montage, 211, 212, 214, 229
Mount, Peggy, 182
Moyles, Chris, 63, 64, 65, 79
Mrs Dale's Diary, 182
multi-skilling, 5
Murf Media, 169
Murray, Jenni, 132
music halls, 165, 166
music lines, 135
music policies, 89, 90–1, 94–9, 107, 216
music scheduling, 89, 90–3
music sweeps, 67
Myers, John, 143–4
myth, 53, 201
Myriad Playout, 100
narrative structure, 27–8, 56, 82, 114, 120, 136, 163, 176, 180, 181–3, 188–9, 203, 209, 213
narratives, 34, 77, 120, 163, 178, 180, 181, 184–5, 187, 188–95, 196, 203, 209, 210, 214, 216–17, 218
narrators, 184, 189, 190, 200, 210, 218
National Public Radio (NPR), 27, 181
naturalization, 30, 53, 82, 161, 175, 204, 228

Navy Lark, The, 167
NBC, 165, 182
Nelson, Davia, 212, 213
new wave, 89
news agencies, 6
news diaries, 128
News Direct 97.3, 114
News Quiz, The, 167
Newsbeat, 35
newstalk, 58, 75, 83
Nietzsche, F., 53
Nightingale, Annie, 79
Nimmo, Derek, 171

96.4 The Eagle, 100
non-linear editing, 22, 23, 24, 47, 112
Norton, Graham, 170, 171
Now Show, The, 168

obituary procedures, 99
OBs see outside broadcasts
Oil Rig, The, 211
On the Town with the League of Gentlemen, 177
103.4 Sun FM, 110
107 Spark FM, 110
One Visitor's Portrait of Banff, 212
openers, 91, 98
Opus, 4
Our Tune, 65,78
out-cues see cues
Out this Week, 139
outside broadcasts (OBs), 10, 15, 21, 58, 127, 134–6, 170
Ovaltineys, The, 166
ownership, 4–5, 26, 54, 227

PA see public address
packages see jingle packages, speech packages
Pallisers, The, 185
PAMS, 109, 110
pan controls, panning, 17, 18, 174, 198–9
panel games, 7, 167–8, 169–77
paralinguistics, 140

Parsons, Nicholas, 170, 171
Pavlov, I., 110
payola, 90
PC workstations, 14, 22, 23, 24
PDQ Comedy Daily, 169
peak programme meters (PPMs), *see*
    meters
Peel, John, 80, 160
Peirce, C. S., 29, 81
Performing Right Society (PRS) (PRS
    for Music), 102–3, 156, 159
perspective, 194–5, 197–8, 199
PFL *see* pre-fade listening
phone-ins, 27, 58, 59, 72, 78, 79, 82,
    83–8, 125, 130, 133
PhoneBox, 85
Phonographic Performance Limited
    (PPL), 102–3, 156, 159
Piccadilly Radio, 84, 109
Pirate FM, 99
pirates
    landbased, 2, 4, 109
    offshore, 2, 63, 90, 161, 166
Planet Rock, 101
playlists, 90–3, 99, 107
playout software, 14, 22, 76, 94, 100,
    158
plot, 188, 190, 195, 202, 209
PM, 123
polysemy, 31, 52
popping, 10, 154
populations, 54, 117, 118
Portable People Meter *see* Arbitron
post-production, 111, 112, 174, 185,
    186, 197, 199, 200–1, 225
pot points, 131
Powell, Mike, 94, 99, 100
Powergold, 96
PPMs *see* meters
pre-fade listening (PFL), 16, 18, 76
preferred readings, 87
presenters, 7, 9, 10, 15, 34, 43, 50,
    58, 59, 60, 61, 62, 63–6, 67, 68,
    69–71, 72, 73–7, 78–83, 84–8, 89,
    90, 92–3, 94, 100, 101, 108, 109,
    113, 115, 116, 120, 124, 126–7,
    129, 131, 133, 135, 136, 137,

138, 160, 172, 173, 174, 175,
    182, 214, 220, 226
press releases, 129
primary sources *see* sources
Private Parts, 59
Pro-Tools, 22, 197
processing, 13, 22, 24, 158, 197,
    218
producers, 1, 6, 10, 26, 28, 29, 31,
    34, 36, 50, 63–4, 65, 67, 73, 89,
    90, 92, 94, 111, 112, 113, 116,
    123, 124, 126, 130, 131, 135,
    137, 138, 139, 172, 174, 185–6,
    195, 197, 200–1, 202, 204, 207,
    214, 217, 219, 223, 224, 226,
    229, 230
production assistants, 63, 64, 135,
    155, 170, 172
production values, 64, 68, 169
profanity delays, 85, 133
Programme Controllers, 90, 118,
    221
programming wheels, 60
promos, 109
pronunciation, 155
proposals, 60, 83, 119, 121, 128, 172,
    185, 206, 220
Propp, Vladimir, 202
Proudhon, P., 53
public address (PA), 9, 135
public service announcements
    (PSAs), 3, 72, 98, 147–8
public service broadcasting, 5, 85,
    104, 226
punk, 89

Quackers Pack, 169
quiz programmes, 167–8, 169–77,
    215

radio
    and blindness, 25–6, 180–1, 186,
        187, 188, 192, 202, 218
    and intimacy, 69, 85
    nature of listening, 116, 166,
        180–1, 187, 188
Radio Academy, 25

Radio Active, 167
Radio Advertising Bureau, RAB, 145, 150
Radio Aire, 84
Radio Beijing, 3
RadioCentre, 115, 153
Radio Caroline, 2
radio cars, 73, 109, 135
Radio City, 81
Radio City Music Hall, 165
Radio Clyde, 104–5
Radio Computing Services, RCS, 94–6, 159
Radio Corporation of America (RCA), 1, 165
Radio K, 3
Radio Luxembourg, 1, 63, 90, 145, 166, 167
Radio Magazine, 150
Radio Moscow, 3, 30, 228
'radio noir', 202
Radio Normandy, 1, 166
Radio Northsea International, 3
Radio Radio, 101
Radio Studies Network, 25
Radio Times, 108, 182
Radio West, 122
Radiocontrol, 116
Radioman, 100
RAJAR, 115, 116, 117
rate cards, 109
ratings *see* audience research
razor blades, 19, 22
readings, 29–31, 114, 179, 210, 211, 228–9
  alternative, 52, 187, 229
  preferred, 87, 187, 204, 229
  rogue, 229
Real Radio, 107
realism, 35–6, 38–40, 41–2, 51–3, 55–6, 178–9, 191, 194, 201–2, 205, 212, 214, 218–20, 229–30
recording studios, 6, 9, 15
Red Rose Radio, 84
reflexivity, 56
regulation, 26, 138, 161, 164, 173

regulators
  Broadcasting Standards Commission, 219
  Federal Communications Commission (FCC), 101
  Independent Broadcasting Authority (IBA), 5, 68, 104, 143–4
  Ofcom, 5, 28, 67, 100, 144, 153, 158, 161, 164, 227
  Radio Authority, 5, 67, 100–1, 105, 143
Reith, J.C., 1, 25, 165
reporters, 6, 7, 33, 34–6, 37, 40–2, 46, 52–3, 55, 56, 127, 128, 131, 210–11, 212, 215, 219, 223
reporting restrictions, 222–4
representation, 27, 30, 34, 38–40, 41–2, 51–6, 137–8, 139, 162, 176–7, 178, 202, 203, 218–20, 226, 229–30
research, 40, 111, 113, 121, 141, 172, 207, 209, 212, 226
researchers, 63, 127, 172
respondents, 55
Restricted Service Licences (RSLs), 2, 109
Revenge, The, 205
reverb, 11–12, 112, 195, 197, 201
Rhys Jones, Griff, 150
rhythm and blues, 89
risk assessments, 37, 134
rock and roll, 89
rolling news, 59
Rosko, Emperor, 70, 90
Ross, Les, 66
rotation, 91–3, 97
round tables, 9, 78, 120, 125, 132, 133, 215
Round the Horne, 167, 176
RSLs *see* Restricted Service Licences
running orders, 62, 97, 98, 124–6, 226

S2blue, 149
Sachs, Andrew, 205
SADiE, 22, 23, 24, 47, 197

Saga Radio, 66, 97, 107
sales executives, 146
SAM Broadcast, 100
Sarnoff, David, 1, 165
scenarios, 146, 184–5, 188–9, 192, 194
Schafer, Paul, 101
scheduling software, 93– 101
Scot FM, 107
scriptwriting, 36, 44, 46, 47–51, 71, 112, 129, 149–54, 168–9, 172, 183–95, 204, 209, 210, 226–7
Secombe, Harry, 167
Second Thoughts, 167, 180
secondary sources *see* sources
segues, 68, 97, 216
Selector, 94–9
Sellers, Peter, 167
semiology, semiotics, 27, 29, 56, 81–2, 113, 140, 162, 175–6, 204, 229
sequence programmes
    music-based, 3, 6, 33, 58–83, 89, 100, 113, 114, 115, 118, 122, 124, 136, 137, 166, 167, 182–3, 215
    other *see* magazine programmes *and* phone-ins
'shock jocks', 85
Short-cut, 22
shouts, 109, 112
Signal Radio, 84
signature tunes *see* theme tunes
signified, 176
signifiers, 175–6, 189–90
signposting, 46, 61, 67–8, 71, 74, 84, 113, 120, 124, 131, 176, 208, 209, 210, 217, 229
Silva, Nikki, 212, 213
situation comedy (sitcoms), 31, 167, 168, 176, 180
Six-O-Six, 84
sketch shows, 167, 168
Skinner, Frank, 66
Smash Hits, 90
'Smashie and Nicey', 64, 108, 110, 137

Smooth Radio, 66, 97
soap opera, 28, 31, 176, 181–2, 183, 184, 205
solid-state recorders, 19, 23
Sound Box, 100
Sound (Broadcasting) Act 1970, 143
Soundhunter, The, 214
soundscapes, 212–15, 229
Soundwalking, 212
sources
    primary research, 39, 42–3
    secondary research, 42–3, 128–9, 221
    sound, 10, 12, 14–19, 62, 75, 94, 158, 197
Spector, Phil, 17
speech packages, 29–30, 33–57, 60, 61, 73, 78, 120, 122, 125, 131, 136, 206–7, 228
splices, 22
splicing blocks, 22
splicing tape, 22
sponsor credits, 159–60
spoof, 35, 151, 155, 163, 167, 179, 191
Sport Breakfast, 84
spot effects, 179, 192–5, 200, 204–5, 218, 226, 229
staff contracts, 5
Stage Mother, Sequined Daughter, 184
Stannage, James, 84
Star Wars, 181
station sound, 60, 64, 67, 91–4, 97, 107, 108, 109
Steele, Alison, 79
Steptoe and Son, 167
stereo image, 17, 174, 198–9
stereotypes, 30, 162, 176–7, 202, 203
Stern, Howard, 85
Steve Wright in the Afternoon, 61, 183
stimulus-response *see* models of audience behaviour
stings *see* idents
Stone, Oliver, 85
strap lines, 110
stringers, 128

structure
  of packages, 44, 45–7, 48
  of programmes, 136, 172, 176,
    207–9, 210, 226
studio discipline, 77, 133–4, 173
style, 27, 34, 63–6, 71, 82, 84, 107,
    109, 120, 150–1, 156, 206,
    209–12, 215, 219–20, 226
style sheets *see* house styles
sub-plots, 188–9
Sunday Service, 122
Sunday Supplement, 122
Sunrise Radio, 162
surrealism, 179, 188, 218
sweepers 110, 113
symbols 29, 68
syntax, 216–17, 225, 226

Take Your Pick, 167
Talk Radio, 144, 166
Talk Radio, 85
talkback, 9, 18, 19, 77, 86, 197, 198
Talking Heads, 192
talkovers, 15, 18, 61, 71, 77, 79, 91,
    123
talkSPORT, 84, 85, 104, 115, 116,
    117, 144
target audiences, 34, 51, 78, 79, 81,
    90, 91, 93, 94, 109, 111, 119–21,
    122, 128, 129, 134, 137, 138,
    139, 146–7, 159, 168–9, 172,
    174, 183, 206, 215, 220, 226
Tarrant, Chris, 66, 72, 108
taste and decency, 24, 73, 85, 132,
    173, 227
teasing, 116
technical operators, studio managers,
    63, 64, 75–8, 100, 127, 132, 135,
    172, 185, 186, 195, 197
telephone balancing unit (TBU), 44,
    86
textual analysis, 27–32, 56, 78, 81–3,
    138, 140–2, 162, 179, 226–7,
    228–9
theme tunes, themes, 66–7, 123–4,
    136–7, 156
This Gun in my Left Hand is Loaded,
    187, 191

Thompson, D., 25
time checks, 62
titles, 122, 172, 195
To the Manor Born, 167
Today, 62, 75, 119, 122, 123, 125,
    126–7, 133, 138, 140
Top Forty, 89, 91
Top of the Pops, 91
Torrington, Graham, 66
Total Survey Area (TSA), 115, 139,
    170
traffic, 159
traffic and travel *see* bulletins
trails, 27, 61, 72, 109, 143,
    159–64
Trainspotting, 202
transcodifiers, 187–8
treatments, 60, 83, 121, 185
Twin Towers: A Memorial in Sound,
    212
2-TEN FM, 59
two-ways, 125, 127, 131

Uhers, 19
Ulysses, 188
unidirectional *see* microphones
uses and gratifications *see* models of
    audience behaviour
USP, 147–8

Virgin Radio, 73, 104, 105, 117, 144,
    166
Voice of America, 3, 35, 139
Voice of Peace, The, 80
Voice of the Angry Bastard, The,
    109
voice-over artists, 111, 150, 152,
    154–5, 159, 162
voice-overs, 25, 110, 111, 112, 154–5,
    157, 160, 162–3
voice work, 49, 56–7, 71, 154–5, 185,
    190, 196, 200–1, 205
voicetracking, 100
VoIP, 135
volume unit meters (v/u meters) *see*
    meters
vox populi (vox pops), 34, 45, 54,
    145, 218

Waggoners' Walk, 182
Waite, John, 130
War of the Worlds, 179, 201
weather forecasts, 82, 113, 114
Welles, Orson, 179, 202
Wells, H. G., 179
West, Timothy, 187, 191
Westerkamp, Hildegard, 212
Whale, James, 84
What's My Line?, 167
Whistler, The, 200, 202
White Coons' Concert Party, The,
    177
White, Peter, 140
wild track, 13
Williams, Kenneth, 171
Winamp, 100
windshields, 10
WINS, 89

Wireless Group, The, 115
WNEW-AM, 58, 79
Wogan, Terry, 81
Woman's Hour, 119–20, 132,
    138–9
Workers' Playtime, 166, 177
World at One, 171
World Soundscape Project, 212
wrap, 33–4, 45
Wright, Steve, 63, 65, 66, 183
Wuthering Heights, 185

XFM, 105
XLR plugs, 6

You and Yours, 53, 119, 121, 122,
    127, 128, 129–30, 139–40
Young, Jimmy, 67, 75

'zoo format', 63, 65, 78